Born in 1942 to an Irish father and Australian mother, Sallyanne Atkinson has had a long career in politics and business. A former Lord Mayor of Brisbane, former Senior Trade Commissioner to Paris and former Special Representative for Queensland in South East Asia, she has been a non-executive company director since 1991 and is chairman or board member of several organisations. The author of *Around Brisbane* (UQP, 1978) and *Sallyanne Atkinson's Brisbane*, she regularly appears on television and radio and contributes to newspapers. She is a mother and grandmother and lives in Brisbane.

SALLYANNE ATKINSON

NO JOB FOR A WOMAN

UQP

First published 2016 by University of Queensland Press
PO Box 6042, St Lucia, Queensland 4067 Australia
uqp.com.au
uqp@uqp.uq.edu.au

© Sallyanne Atkinson 2016

Cover design by Stan Lamond
Cover photograph by Justine Walpole
Author photograph by Justine Walpole
Typeset in 12.5/16 pt Bembo by Post Pre-press Group, Brisbane
Printed in Australia by McPherson's Printing Group, Melbourne

National Library of Australia cataloguing-in-publication data is available at
http://catalogue.nla.gov.au

ISBN
978 0 7022 5411 6 (pbk)
978 0 7022 5738 4 (pdf)
978 0 7022 5739 1 (epub)
978 0 7022 5740 7 (Kindle)

University of Queensland Press uses papers that are natural, renewable
and recyclable products made from wood grown in sustainable forests.
The logging and manufacturing processes conform to the environmental
regulations of the country of origin.

To the memory of Ruth and Terry Kerr, who created not only me and my sisters but were also directly responsible for 15 grandchildren and 14 great-grandchildren — a lot of lives.

TABLE OF CONTENTS

PROLOGUE

'THEY'LL NEVER GIVE *that* seat to a woman,' they said. 'That seat' was the ward of Indooroopilly in the Brisbane City Council. The largest council in Australia, its wards are the equivalent of state government electorates, each with an average of 28,000 voters. Indooroopilly was so safe for the conservatives that in the 1972 election, when Labor had won 20 of the 21 wards, Indooroopilly was the only one it didn't. Until then no woman on either side of politics had been given a safe seat to contest; it was a standing joke that women were usually given the safe seats of the political party *other* than the one they belonged to.

Yet I won in the Brisbane City Council elections in March 1979 and went on to be the Alderman for Indooroopilly for the next two terms. At the time I was elected there were no women in the national House of Representatives; only four women had ever been elected to that House. Three had been one-termers and the other was the widow of a former prime minister.

Six years later I campaigned to be Lord Mayor, and the naysayers were at it again. Even my mother said I couldn't win.

'Brisbane is a Labor town, dear.'

On 31 March, the day of the 1985 election, I visited polling booths across the 1200 square kilometres that was the City of Brisbane, criss-crossing from Sandgate in the east to Chermside in the north, west to Toowong and south to Mount Gravatt. When the polls closed at 6 pm I went home to shower and change. I was keen to get into City Hall as soon as I could. As Leader of the Opposition I had an office there and when I arrived it was full of campaign people. With the tally room downstairs and results filtering in almost as soon as they were being posted, the excitement was palpable.

By 7.30 pm I had won the mayoralty and Liberal candidates had won 16 of the 26 wards. We had taken City Hall, and I had become the first woman Lord Mayor of Brisbane, and the first Liberal. I was ushered down to the tally room amid a crowd of jubilant supporters, Liberal Party people and my children's friends, to be greeted with cheers and applause. Roy Harvey, the outgoing Lord Mayor, graciously came forward to congratulate me.

In the swarm of reporters and photographers, someone from the *Sunday Sun* showed me the billboard they had printed for the next morning. Above my smiling face the headline read: 'She's Our Lord Mayor'.

Suddenly I realised I was.

In my new role I would be in charge of a city of three-quarters of a million people, with a budget of half a billion dollars and a workforce of 8000. I would have to lead and manage 26 elected aldermen, only two of whom were women and many of whom had recently been referring to me behind my back as 'the little troublemaker from the western suburbs' and to my face as 'Tinkerbell'. I was painfully aware not only that politics is probably the only profession for which there is no real training, but that city government also involves management for which I had no training either.

I also knew that my life would never be the same again. I had had a taste of public office, I had been on television and in the newspapers, but this was different. From now on I would be vulnerable, right out in front, taking leadership responsibility and possibly exposing myself to failure and ridicule. No longer did I have the comfort of being part of the pack, of being able to bury myself in the team. As an alderman I had some experience of being a public figure who must incorporate several different personae; other people see you through the prism of their own needs and prejudices and react accordingly. Sometimes you are happy to play the various roles. But it is vital, and often difficult, to keep hold of the person who is the authentic you.

For all these reasons, I knew that my new job was going to present a challenge, and in some ways a contradictory one. I would have to learn how to compromise and how to be firm, when to stand up for my views and when to yield. I would also learn how well my previous life had prepared me for what lay ahead.

AN ITINERANT CHILDHOOD

I WAS BORN in the middle of a cold Sydney winter right in the middle of World War II. Two months earlier the battle of the Coral Sea had been fought off the coast of Queensland. Weeks earlier, Japanese submarines had been detected in Sydney Harbour. Two days before I was born the Japanese had landed in Papua to be eventually repulsed along the Kokoda Track. On the very day I was born US general Douglas MacArthur, supreme commander of the South-West Pacific, arrived in Brisbane, having relocated his headquarters from Melbourne to be closer to the action.

My parents had met in glamorous circumstances in the exotic city that was Colombo in the 1930s. My mother, Ruth, whose maiden name was Helmore, was a beautiful girl of 17, sophisticated beyond her years and making her first trip overseas from her home in Sydney. She had been sent to Colombo to stay with her aunt and uncle, possibly in the hope that she would marry an eligible bachelor. My father, Charles Terence (Terry) Kerr, was handsome, almost twice her age and divorced, an accountant with a Belfast company that made machinery for the tea industry of Ceylon. He had spent much of his youth in Colombo and cut a dash in the fast-moving expatriate community.

When he met the very pretty Ruth, he assumed that she was at least 25, 'or I wouldn't have looked at her'. Ruth returned to Sydney and they wrote to each other over the next two years. He proposed and they were married on April Fool's Day 1939: the groom was 37, the bride 19. The wedding took place at St Stephen's Presbyterian Church in Macquarie Street, Sydney. My mother's wedding dress was the most beautiful I have ever seen, in a silvery crepe material it was high-necked and long-sleeved, and fitted her like a sheath. My mother, and probably her mother, would have preferred St Mark's Anglican Church at Darling Point, the most fashionable church in Sydney, but the Church of England did not accept divorcees. My mother's only brother, Norman, was best man. The bridegroom had no supporters of his own.

After the wedding Mr and Mrs Terry Kerr set off on a round-the-world honeymoon. Photographs show them in Suva, Fiji and in Banff, Canada. They sent postcards from every port of call. Finally they arrived in Belfast, where Mum was to meet her new in-laws, and most importantly her seven-year-old step-daughter Jill.

Dad's first marriage had been something of an accident. In his twenties he had been engaged to a Miss Shimmons in Belfast, the city of his birth. Where they had actually met we don't know, but shortly before the wedding Miss Shimmons called it off. Dad took the next ship back to Colombo. Not long after-wards, Miss Shimmons' sister, Hylda, went out to Ceylon and married the cast-off groom.

It was not a happy marriage. Their daughter, Jill, was born in 1932 and it was while she was pregnant that Hylda fell properly in love. Or rather improperly – Jill later told me that her mother had been six months pregnant and at a dinner party when she looked across the table and fell in love with the man opposite, one of Terry's friends.

Because Hylda had left Dad and he was the wronged party, he had gained custody of Jill. Jill had gone to live with him in Colombo but soon after her seventh birthday, and a few months before Terry came to Sydney to marry again, she was despatched by ship, in the company of a woman she didn't know, to Dad's family in Belfast. At the end of her life Jill remembered her mother standing on the dock in Colombo screaming, 'Don't take my baby!'

All her life my mother was critical of my father for having taken Jill from her mother, and then abandoning her, despite the fact that Mum was partly the cause of it. However, it was standard practice at the time for young children from India and Ceylon to be sent 'home' to relatives or boarding school; the climate of the East was held to be detrimental to their health and development.

Jill went to Belfast and was subsequently sent to Penrhos, a boarding school in Colwyn Bay, Wales. During Easter 1940 she was on one of two ships that crossed from Holyhead to Belfast. One was torpedoed by the Germans and sunk with total loss of life, and Jill was on the other. Not surprisingly, she didn't return to school in Wales, and spent the rest of the war living with first her grandmother in Belfast and then with our father's sister, Eva, and her family in Sligo. She did not see her father again until the war was over.

Jill was a truly tragic victim of divorce. Her mother married and went to live in New Guinea, and Jill did not see her again until 1949 – and then only by accident, via a customer in the shop where she worked. Only then did Jill discover that her mother had written to her in Ireland, but our grandmother had kept the letters from her, leaving Jill to think she had been forgotten.

After their honeymoon my parents settled in Colombo. But then came war and Mum was evacuated on the last ship to leave before the fall of Singapore in February 1942. She was pregnant with me at the time; I discovered later that I was a replacement baby. A son, Michael, had been born in February 1941 but had died when he was three days old. He had been delivered by forceps and my mother always blamed Colombo medicine for negligence.

Michael's death was one of the reasons Mum decided to have her next baby in Sydney, and in the end she had no choice. She arrived unannounced on her parents' doorstep in the Sydney suburb of Neutral Bay after the vessel had dodged enemy fire all the way across the Indian Ocean. We were always told that she sat on that doorstep heavily pregnant, waiting for her mother to come home. Only when I was grown up did I realise that she had been only five months pregnant: not exactly heavily. Such are the myths of childhood.

My father enlisted with his friends and other left-behind husbands in the Ceylon Planters Rifle Corps, and he might or might not have spent the war marching up and down the Galle Face Green, that long park on Colombo's seafront, and drinking pink gins. Mum was always very dismissive of his war service, but years later when I was given the honour of the Freedom of the City of Colombo, the mayor announced, 'The highest regards of our nation to your late father for his dedicated service to save our country from the perils of World War Two.' Ceylon was indeed bombed by the Japanese.

Sydney during the war was an exciting place, a heady mix of tension and the frenzied atmosphere generated by American and Australian troops on leave from the war zone and determined to have a good time. After my birth, my mother, just 22 and very pretty, safely married and with ready-made babysitters, had, I think, a very good war. She never said that, and perhaps I am just drawing conclusions, but my favourite toy as a small child was a koala called Fritz after the American soldier who gave it to me.

One of the few regrets of my life is that I never asked either of my parents about their courtship and marriage. Two years is quite a long time in the life of a young woman and their only contact had been through letters. Had he changed? Had she? I would have expected that the young woman who met her fiancé on the wharf in Sydney in March 1939 might have been rather different from the one who waved him goodbye in Colombo Harbour back in 1937.

Through most of my childhood I felt that my mother was a disappointed woman whose life had never fulfilled its early promise. Because of the Depression she had had to leave her Sydney school, Ascham, at the age of 14, something about which she was very bitter, and the reason for her determination that her own daughters would have a full education. She coped well with the changed circumstances that had her settle for most of her married life in a small Australian town, a long way from the glamour she had signed up for. She didn't criticise my father, whose circumstances were beyond his control. But as a little girl I was sensitive to her small barbs. And my father, who had already lost one wife, would not risk losing another, so was never sharp in return. In her low moments as I was growing up, my mother would say that her mother had forced her into the marriage. But her father, my grandfather, told me they had tried to talk her out of it but she was 'madly in love'.

This is not to say it was an uncomfortable marriage for us children. There was lots of affection and endearments. But I for one somehow felt this was not how an ideal marriage should be.

I remember my father as a kind and happy man, but one who wasn't very influential in my early years. It was Mum who determined the pace and content of our daily lives. She made the rules and set the standards, and consequently was a stronger influence. I really only got to know my father in the last few years of his life. He was diagnosed with a congenital heart defect at the age of 72, had an aortic valve replacement, and died of cancer of the larynx at 78. In those years, having treatment in Brisbane, he stayed with me and my family at Indooroopilly and for the first time told me about his early life and first marriage. I remember being surprised, because he had never said so, that he was proud of what I had achieved. When I was campaigning for Council in semi-rural Brookfield and Moggill he would say to the old farmers, 'You really should vote for this girl, she's very clever.'

My father told me that one of his strongest childhood memories had been the building of the *Titanic* in Belfast shipyards and its subsequent sinking. He kept an interest in the *Titanic* all of his life. At his funeral we sang 'Nearer my God to Thee', the hymn the band was playing as the ship sank. And though Belfast was strongly sectarian in his Protestant youth, I never knew Dad to go to church except for special events, including my wedding. When I married in the Catholic church he said as we stood at the door: 'Did you feel the ground rumble? That's my ancestors turning in their graves.'

Those ancestors had been lowland Scots who had settled in Northern Ireland in the seventeenth century, taking with them the Scottish love of travel. Grandpa Charles Kerr with his wife, May, and their three children, did a lot of toing-and-froing between Colombo and Belfast. Grandpa Kerr went out to Ceylon as a young man and made a name for himself photographing local dignitaries. The eldest and youngest brothers in his family of 11 went to Japan. The youngest, John Henry, married a Japanese woman and had a daughter, Mariette. They tried to go back to Britain at the start of World War I but he died en route in India and his widow and daughter were subsequently interned there.

Dad spent much of his childhood in Belfast, where he sang in the cathedral choir and later played cricket for Ulster. Good with figures, he went to work in the office of Belfast engineering firm Davidson & Co., who sent him back to Colombo.

My mother's family originated from Devon on the English south coast. My grandfather used to tell us that their name, Helmore, had been invented when the daughter of the man at the helm of the boat had married the man on the oar. Or perhaps it was the other way around. The Helmores were travellers, too. As a young man my great-grandfather, Thomas, had gone to America to work on rebuilding Chicago after the great fire of 1871. Afterwards, work dried up and he went to San Francisco where he met Ella Spaulding. When he decided to try his luck in Australia, she followed him and they were married.

Great-grandfather Helmore worked in the building trade all his life, which ended tragically and early. He had gone guarantor in business for a Mason friend, who then disappeared leaving Thomas to face the bailiffs. The family folklore had him dying of pneumonia, brought on by a broken heart, but his death certificate states that he died from 'cyanide of potash, self-administered, on Manly Beach'. He was 49.

Ella, a lone American in New South Wales, was left with eight children, the youngest just six. The three eldest girls, aged 17, 16 and 15, went out to work, as did the eldest boy. My grandfather, Will, aged nine, was taken in and educated by the rector of Christ Church St Laurence in Sydney, which gave him a lifelong love of both learning and the church. Each of these children lived to a great age, and all settled in Sydney or on the New South Wales south coast and kept in touch with each other. Their father was buried in a Presbyterian church cemetery and suicide was never mentioned in the family.

Will married Nell Davidson in 1913. My grandmother's family had come to Australia from Stonehaven in Scotland, where her father had been a stonemason. He was obviously successful because they lived in a solid two-storey house in Sydney's Paddington, which had been a middle-class suburb at the turn of the twentieth century. When I was growing up in the 1950s, Paddington was a slum and my grandmother used to say, 'Don't ever tell anyone that your grandmother grew up in Paddington.'

I like to think that I have inherited resilience from my American great-grandmother and a degree of restlessness from the wandering Kerrs. My strongest memory of my grandmother is that she was great fun and a constant source of stories about her Sydney girlhood. She used to tell us tales of the Paddington streets, of the rag-and-bone man to whom she inadvertently sold her mother's silver teapot. She told us how she would come home from school to find her drunken mother sitting on the front steps and had to cope, a story hotly denied by her son, my mother's only brother, Norman. In one of my favourite stories, she was walking down Martin Place in Sydney when the elastic broke in her knickers, and she simply stepped out of them and left them there.

My grandmother was very much her own person. For one thing, she had changed her name by deed poll in her twenties because she didn't like her birth name, Nell. Henceforth she was to be known as Helen, far more modern, and when grandchildren came along she was to be called Helen and never Grandma. She never admitted she was six years older than her husband.

Often it's easier for children to communicate with a generation once removed. It was my grandmother who talked to me about sex. A school friend from the outback had explained to me the mating habits of sheep and cattle and I said, 'My parents would never do anything so disgusting!' Helen gave me a much better picture of the facts of life.

My paternal grandparents have no shape in my memory, but I have a very clear picture of Mum's parents – Helen was short and plump, Will was tall and thin. From him and my mother I have brown eyes in a family whose members' eyes are mainly blue. His theory was that sailors of the sixteenth-century Spanish Armada washed ashore in Devon, married the local girls and created a long line of dark-eyed descendants.

By 1944 fighting was concentrated in the Pacific and Mum and I were able to cross the Indian Ocean to rejoin Dad in Colombo. It was still a hazardous voyage and it was not easy to get passage on a ship from wartime Australia, although family reunions must have taken some priority. My father had not been on active war service, though potential invasion must have been stressful.

At 22 months of age I met my father for the first time. Has there ever been any research on the thousands of children of my generation who didn't know their fathers in their early

childhood? If those very early years are definitive in the forma-
tion of later character and personality, a whole generation has
suffered from paternal deprivation. One of my friends remembers her father coming home, a strange man in uniform, and
her screaming in terror every time she saw him. For the men
coming home from war, family life must have been an uncomfortable experience.

In Colombo, once the danger of invasion had passed, life
continued much as it had before. These were the dying days of
the British Raj in India, but most of the Europeans in Ceylon
were only vaguely aware of the rumblings of discontent. For
my mother, it was a return to the life she had first experienced
in 1937 – grand colonial bungalows, servants and a busy social
program to fill the leisure time that servants enabled. There were
clubs for Europeans only – the Garden Club, the Prince's Club,
the Colombo Swimming Club – race meetings and polo matches.

My very first memory as a child is of falling out of bed.
Freudians might make something of that. We were up-country,
staying on a tea estate. I fell out of bed in the dark, not onto
the floor but into the mosquito net tucked around the mattress.
I remember screaming with terror as I thrashed around in the
netting and my parents rushing into the room. My father took
me onto his knee, while my mother sorted out the bedding.

I didn't know at the time, but this tea estate holiday was two
months before the birth of my sister Louella. There had been no
talk of a baby coming, and I suppose parents didn't talk of such
things to children. I remember very clearly falling off a swing
in the garden in Colombo and running into the house crying,
'Mummy, Mummy!' only to be told that Mummy had gone to
the hospital 'to get you a new baby'. But I didn't want a new
baby, I wanted my mother.

When Dad took me to visit my new sister at the Fraser Nursing Home, my strongest memory is of a snake under my mother's bed. Throughout my life I wondered how I could have actually seen under the bed, and I thought perhaps I had imagined seeing that snake. A few years ago I went back to the hospital and my memory of 60 years before was crystal clear. I remembered instantly which room had been my mother's, the first to the left of the entrance, about a foot from the ground, so its floor would have been at eye level for an almost-three-year-old walking up the path.

Snakes were a recurring presence during my Ceylon childhood. When I was about three there was great excitement one day when one slithered through the open rafters of the front porch of our bungalow and all the servants gathered underneath with long sticks, broom handles and much shouting. Once, a few years later, I was playing in the garden near an old brick wall and I turned to see the glittering eyes of a snake looking at me through a hole in the wall. At every children's party, at the Garden Club or Prince's Club, the gully gully man would play his pipe and his cobra would hiss and sway out of the basket while we watched in awed fascination.

The birth of my sister Louella (named after the Hollywood gossip columnist Louella Parsons, as I had been named after the film star Sally Ann Howes) was difficult for me. I had spent two years and ten months as a spoiled and pampered only child, not only of my parents but also of my grandparents and uncle in Sydney. No one had prepared me for the shock of displacement. And the hurt didn't disappear with her actual arrival. My mother later told me that I had insisted on perching on the arm of her chair while she fed the baby, and I remember, to my great shame now, putting salt in Louella's orange juice. I am comforted by the fact that she wouldn't have known at the time, and would forgive me now. During our itinerant childhood we often had no other companions but each other and so were close, as we are to this day. The next baby was not to come along for another eight years.

The Pacific War ended in August 1945 and in February 1946 we took a ship for Britain to rescue Jill. It was hard to get passage, because every ship sailing from Colombo was full of troops returning from the East and the war against the Japanese. But with one other civilian family we did manage to get berths on the SS *Sontay*, which had become a troop carrier, and there were few signs of its former life as a passenger liner. Mum used to tie Louella's pram to the ship's rails when we were on deck.

I remember only two things from that voyage. One is going through the Red Sea and the Suez Canal, when it was very hot. The other is being in a cabin with a naked man and being given jellybeans. Neither is an unpleasant memory. But as I grew up I wondered whether they were real. The burning heat of the Red Sea was a documented reality, but I wondered whether the man in the cabin was a figment of my imagination.

When my mother was in a nursing home in her final years I told her about this childhood memory, wondering whether it could possibly be true. She said, 'Oh, yes, that was Lieutenant Simpson!'

I nearly fell off my chair, and asked: 'So what did you do about it?'

'Well, your father was extremely cross.'

'Cross!'

'What could we do? It had been hard to get passage on the ship, and we were only there under sufferance.'

I include this incident because I'm sure it was supposed to

have had an effect on me. But my memory is very short on details. I remember a man being naked and on a bed and I remember the jellybeans. I have no idea how or why I was there. In my forties, when I discovered the story was true, I had a series of feelings. The first was anger at my parents for letting this happen, I had apparently said, 'That man hurt my bottom.' And then I was angry at the Royal Navy for putting young children in the way of men who had been at war and away from their families for six years.

Over the years since, and especially now that so much has been revealed about sexual abuse, I've thought a lot about my experience; I have never remembered it with horror. Is this because it was a one-off and I didn't know the man involved? Perhaps much of the trauma of child abuse comes from a familiarity with the perpetrator. When my mother told me she had known about it, I was angry with her. But then I did understand her defence, that she couldn't have done anything about it, we were on a ship at sea and at the mercy of the British Navy. Perhaps I subconsciously wanted to let go of any anger, to move on from it.

We went to Strandhill, a small seaside town in County Sligo, Ireland. Sligo was almost on the border of Eire and Ulster and many men had gone to fight in the war, to the dismay and contempt of others. Stories were told of soldiers changing out of their British uniforms at the station of Enniskillen, the border town, before they boarded the train for home. This was where my grandfather lived. Dad's parents were now separated, although not divorced, as divorce was not permitted in Ireland.

Jill came to live with us in a guesthouse called 'Ocean View' and I played with the local children, friends of the son of the owner, Mrs Park. I remember Mrs Park's mother's funeral, which women in Ireland did not attend, and Mrs Park sitting sadly at the kitchen table. We children watched the procession down the street from behind lace curtains at a first-floor window. I remember being taken on a walk to Queen Maeve's grave, a huge stone cairn onto which you threw a stone. Jill was a Girl Guide and I went with her to a church hall to meet Lady Baden Powell, wife of the scouting founder. In the barn outside the guesthouse, where we children played, there was a great portrait of an old man with a white beard. 'That's God,' said Ian Park, aged five. And that's how I always thought of God, until, as Lord Mayor, I went to Brisbane's St Patrick's Day dinner at the Irish Club. There was the portrait, not of God but of St Patrick.

We spent the summer in Strandhill, an Irish summer far too cold for us to swim. Then we went to Belfast and had Christmas in Mrs Tait's boarding house. The winter of 1946 was the coldest for many years, perhaps the coldest on record. I saw snow for the first time and my first live theatre, the Christmas pantomime *Babes in the Wood*; my first thrill, never to leave me, was at the red velvet curtain before it rises. Belfast was a grim city still in the grip of wartime rationing. As an industrial city it had been badly bombed, and there were holes in the ground and bombed-out buildings. Everything seemed difficult. One day, Mum hung the washing on a fireguard in front of the gas fire, and it toppled over and all the clothes were burned. My mother's weeping seemed to symbolise the misery of war and its aftermath. I'm sure it was with enthusiasm that we departed for Liverpool and a ship to Colombo.

We sailed in February 1947 on the SS *Scythia*. The ship was packed to the gunnels with women and children returning to the East after the war and desperate to do so. These were families who had been sent 'home' ahead of the Japanese invasion to suffer the horror of the war in Britain with its unfamiliar cold, wet and bombing, away from their husbands and fathers.

Mum, Jill, Louella and I shared a cabin with about thirty others. Dad had already gone back to Colombo after his leave. We were squashed like sardines into bunks and there was little peace, with babies crying throughout the night and mothers trying to soothe them. There always seemed to be a baby crying in a long non-stop wail.

At night the women would tie red cellophane over the lights to dim them enough for children to sleep but to give enough light for the mothers to undress by. Some time on the voyage Mum got dengue fever and was put into the ship's hospital and 15-year-old Jill looked after us. There must have been some fun, too, for Jill won a box of Chinese chequers in a deck game.

When we arrived in Colombo we went straight to the Galle Face Hotel. However, rumblings about independence from British rule had grown louder in our absence. Hotel servants went on strike, including the kitchen staff. With the true British spirit that had carried them through the war the guests mucked in. Most of them had never had to do as much as make a cup of tea.

There were pockets of unrest all over the island. Louella and I were coming by train from up-country with our *ayah*, the nanny who looked after us. As the train got closer to Colombo it suddenly stopped and there was a great commotion, shouting and yelling from outside. We little girls were pushed under the seats and made to stay there until the train took off. Curious as we were, we never really knew what happened.

Ceylon became independent in February 1948 with much celebration. There were ceremonial flags and marching, up and down the Galle Face Green, and we enjoyed it all enormously.

THE COLONIAL EXPERIENCE

CEYLON, NOW CALLED Sri Lanka, was a British colony that had also been Dutch and Portuguese. The effects of all that colonising were still there, in attitudes, architecture and even the name 'burghers', a Dutch word that described people of mixed European and Singhalese or Tamil heritage.

Colombo was the commercial hub of the island, home to the offices of the big tea firms such as Brooke Bond and Liptons, and the banks that had made their money in the East, including the Hong Kong and Shanghai Bank. In many ways it was a garrison town, with the presence still of the Royal Navy. In the hills around Nuwara Eliya the tea estates were still mostly owned by individual planters. Nuwara Eliya itself, with its Hill Club, golf course and Grand Hotel, was where the white citizens of Colombo escaped the heat. The houses had names like 'Bonnie Doon' and 'Braeside', reminiscent of home. There was also the Hill School, a boarding preparatory school to which we yearned to go. Expatriate children were sent there as an alternative to being sent to school in

Britain or Australia – they often had to travel by ship, alone and unsupervised.

Poor Jill, at 15, was to be uprooted again. She was sent to Sydney to live with Mum's parents, people she had never met in a city where she had never been. Though she had a feisty personality, she never seemed to harbour a grudge about her upbringing. Once when I was seven and complaining that something wasn't fair, Jill said, 'Nothing in life is fair.' I understood. Even as a little girl I felt guilty knowing that her life had not been easy and thinking that somehow I was responsible.

Our early childhood in Colombo was lived in proper British colonial style, and our lives were as regimented as those of the royal family. Up early and into our little cotton playsuits, shorts with a pinafore bib, we were taken out for a walk by our *ayah* whom we called 'Nanny'. This was not a social occasion but a brisk constitutional, along the roads with their heavy scents of wet earth and lush foliage, carefully stepping over the red stains of betel nut on the footpaths. Then it was home for breakfast and getting ready for school, which finished at lunchtime. Afterwards, we rested for a couple of hours. When we were small we slept, and later it was a great time for reading. We didn't have to sleep, just lie quietly, which I still think is a very good habit.

Then it was up and off for another walk, but this time to a park where the *ayahs* would congregate while the children would play together. The *ayahs* would chat about their charges' families. When I was very small, if asked my name I would say 'C.T. Kerr's daughter' because that's how my *ayah* described me. In spite of the British snobbery, which meant my parents and their friends didn't mix socially with the native Ceylonese, among our park companions were the Senanayake children whose uncle was to become Sri Lanka's first prime minister, and we would visit their very large and palatial home. There was no class or race distinction in very young children, though a few years later I was to find that it developed.

We would come home to afternoon tea with our parents in the garden, the tea things set out on a small table with comfortable chairs around. Parents led grown-up lives. Dad went off to work each morning, driven by a chauffeur in the office car. Sometimes he would come home to lunch, sometimes it would be taken to him in a tiffin tin. Mum gave orders to the servants, played bridge, went shopping, talked to her friends and generally led a life of little purpose.

I'm sure as we got older we had some meals with our parents, or saw them at other times, but I only remember that on our *ayah's* day off our mother bathed us and dried us roughly, which was so much better than the gentle patting by nanny. And I have a memory of Mum getting her licence, and then losing it. Well, not so much losing as leaving it. She must have been a reluctant driver as well as a nervous one. I recall her panicking in the middle of the traffic one day and just getting out of the car. I can't remember how we got home, but I presume we caught a passing rickshaw, and I have no idea what happened to the car.

Our ordered existence came to an end the year I turned ten. All of our homes in Colombo had been rented ones, usually company bungalows whose occupants were on leave for six months. Between houses we camped at various hotels. That year we moved into the Mount Lavinia Hotel, a glorious wedding-cake pile which had once been a governor's beach house. Louella and I were considered old enough to dispense with our *ayah*, and I suppose there was no room for one in the hotel. We had a suite on the top floor and for a few months we ran wild. We collected hermit crabs on the beach and kept them in a big basin in our room until they got out and spread all over the hotel. One of our favourite tricks was to take the shoes that guests had left outside their doors and swap them for others, causing havoc each morning. But our best trick came after an electrician, using a manhole in our ceiling to get under the roof, left a ladder in place there. Up we got, under the roof and out onto a parapet overlooking the courtyard of the hotel. I can still see and hear the commotion below as two little white faces suddenly appeared hanging over the top. A few years ago I was back staying at Mount Lavinia, looked up to the roof and realised what shock and panic we must have created.

After Mount Lavinia, we moved into an apartment across the road from the Galle Face Hotel. We would often walk along Galle Road to the Colombo Swimming Club, which was at least a 15-minute walk along the busy main road. We would spend whole afternoons in the pools with no supervision. Our freedom is now a source of great wonder to me, as there never seemed to be any thought that little girls wandering about a busy city could be in danger – another question I wish I'd asked my mother. We hung about the Galle Face Hotel while Vivien Leigh was staying there to make the movie *Elephant Walk* with co-stars Peter Finch and Dana Andrews. There were dark whispers about Miss Leigh having a nervous breakdown or at least an affair with her co-star. The film was eventually recast with Elizabeth Taylor as the lead, at a cost of $3 million, which made it one of the most expensive movies of its time.

My schooldays began in Colombo when I was five and with them the exhilaration of learning to read. I can pinpoint very clearly the exact moment when I could read; the place, the book. Well, not actually the book but certainly the author. Mum, herself a great reader, used to read us a book by Mabel

Lucie Attwell and I knew it by heart. The moment came when I could suddenly match memory to the words on the page in the book on my lap, under a tree in the park. When I studied ancient history at school and read about the German professor who could suddenly decipher hieroglyphics, I could totally relate to his excitement. Years later, on my first grown-up visit to Colombo, I had a driver and asked him to take me to that park ... and there was the tree.

The first school I went to, and with enormous excitement, was what was called a dame school. It was indeed run by a dame, Miss Raffel, and it was held in a room in one of Mum's friends' bungalows with 12 small pupils, all children of friends. We must have learned the basics, but what I remember most is the smell of the Lakeland coloured pencils and an Easter activity when we wrote letters to the Easter Bunny (so we did learn to write, too) and left them for the postman in the bungalow's letterbox. I don't remember whether they got us results.

I made my first stage appearance in Miss Raffel's Christmas play, where I played Wee Willie Winkie, and was very jealous of my friend Jane who was Mary Mary with cockle shells. It was on the back terrace, the guests sitting in the garden, and I had to 'run through the town', which I did with my head down and eyes lowered in a paroxysm of shyness.

Mum decided to come back to Australia, bringing Louella and me to Sydney in early 1949 on the *Orion*. I have never really understood the reason for this decision, but perhaps my mother adopted the prevailing view that the tropics were considered unhealthy for European children. Those were the days when newspaper reporters would meet the big liners out in Sydney Harbour and get stories on, and pictures of, the passengers. There could have been no big stars or important people onboard, for we were photographed for the social pages. I think Mum must have had an instinct for publicity: in the picture Louella and I are wearing Breton-style hats trimmed with organdie and flowers, which would have caught the photographer's eye. We were made to wear them to Sunday School in Sydney and oh, the embarrassment.

We lived with our grandparents in Avenue Road, Mosman, where bread was still delivered by the baker's horse and cart and the iceman carried up the ice for the icebox. We were staying there to save money because of the high cost of living in Colombo. The four of us, for Jill was there too, slept in one bedroom. But no sooner had we departed than Dad moved first into the Galle Face Hotel, and then into a 'chummery' with two mates, where he lived very comfortably indeed and where I imagine the cost of his social life outweighed any savings our move might have made.

I started at Queenwood, a private girls' school overlooking Balmoral Beach and where the school song began 'Happy is our school around us', to the tune of the German national anthem, despite the recent war against Germany. I like to tell my children and grandchildren how, at six, I would catch the tram from Balmoral Beach up to busy Military Road at Mosman Junction, collect Louella from her kindergarten at the top of Avenue Road and the two of us would walk all the way home to our grandparents' house near the bottom. Parent pick-ups did not exist then, nor apparently did fear of child assaults.

Queenwood was where I had my very brief and longed-for ballet career. Through my first term I used to avidly watch my classmates' ballet lessons. When I finally convinced Mum to let me learn too, I already knew the feet and arm positions and was level with the other girls. That year I was given a proper role in the school concert in the Mosman Town Hall. But, alas, it was the end of my dance career. From then on, no schools I attended had ballet lessons until much later, when we couldn't afford them anyhow. I've always thought about what might have been …

The other 'performance' I enjoyed was an odd one: reading aloud from the *Sydney Morning Herald*. My grandparents' neighbours were a newly married couple who sailed every weekend in Mosman Bay and would bring their friends home for a drink afterwards. I don't know how it started but they would pop me up on the kitchen table, a very small six-year-old, and have me read great swathes of the very serious *Herald* to loud applause. I greatly enjoyed the attention. I'd come a long way from Wee Willie Winkie. I had no idea what caused the applause, because I took reading for granted. The first grown-up book I read was Nevil Shute's *A Town Like Alice* when I was eight.

Dad came out to Sydney in July 1950 on the six months' leave that Europeans in the tropics take every couple of years. By the time he arrived, two awful situations were in play. Sydney was having its wettest July ever and Louella and I had ringworm, one of the nasty childhood conditions of the time (the others were boils and impetigo). The cures were pretty nasty, too. We often got boils and our mother would apply hot poultices of antiphlogistine to the offending spot to draw out the pus. We would scream with the heat and the pain. Ringworm, apparently caused by contact with a cat, though we didn't have one of those or even know one, were circular red weals all over the skin. Louella had them all over her body, including on her scalp, and had to have her head shaved. The treatment was bathing in a mixture of Condy's crystals, which stung like mad. As ringworm was highly contagious we weren't allowed near any other children, so I didn't have a birthday party that July.

When I think of childhood medical complaints, screaming is very much part of the memory. In Colombo I had my six-year-old molars removed. I was sitting up in my parents' bed in our Bagatelle Road house and our doctor, Dr Thiagarajah, came in and perched on a chair. I started screaming then, and presumably stopped only when he held the jar of chloroform over my face and the dentist yanked out my teeth.

The rain and the ringworm meant that our father didn't want to spend his leave in Sydney. He had met a woman who had been on holiday to Surfers Paradise and Dad thought that any place with a name like that had to be okay. We never heard where he met this woman. Perhaps it was on the long flight from Colombo to Sydney, a flight that stopped overnight in Darwin where its passengers spent the night before climbing aboard next morning. But anyway, to Surfers Paradise we went.

It meant a long train journey from Sydney to South Brisbane, and then another train journey that ended at Southport. Brisbane was a terrible shock, its wooden houses with their rusting tin roofs a contrast to the red-brick suburbia I'd been used to in Sydney. Southport then was a country town, and the house that we had rented on the Esplanade was a typical old Queenslander, with enclosed side verandas and steps leading down to a large backyard. It was called 'Beach Villa' and Mum absolutely hated it. There was linoleum on the floor throughout and cockroaches scurrying everywhere. Paradise it certainly was not, and at some stage in our four-month stay we moved out and into a guesthouse called 'Ocean View', which wasn't luxurious but at least didn't need housework.

Years later Southport and Surfers Paradise became part of the Gold Coast, but in 1950 Southport was its own town where ordinary people lived, and the big houses belonged to the wealthy graziers from western Queensland who went there to escape the heat and take the sea air. Surfers Paradise was a hotel with a zoo attached where there was a talking horse and a six-legged cow. The horse didn't actually talk but tapped its foot in response to questions, and the cow's two extra legs were rather disgusting limbs hanging around its neck. The most interesting house was in Cavill Avenue, named for the builder of the hotel, a two-storeyed white wooden home with a board in front of it on which was written, in full, the Joyce Kilmer poem beginning, 'I think that I shall never see/ A poem lovely as a tree'.

We often swam in the Broadwater or walked across the Jubilee Bridge to Main Beach. The ringworm meant we weren't allowed to play with other children, and Louella wore little cotton caps to cover her shaved head when we went out in public. So it was a strange existence, though good for family bonding, and I do have happy memories of catching a boat to Stradbroke Island and the bus to Burleigh Heads to walk around the headland, hoping to see a koala.

It was probably about this time that our parents began to think about the future and our ultimate home. Dad's leave would be up in December and Mum had obviously started to think of our education, in spite of the fact that I was currently missing six months of my present one. Sitting on the shore of the Broadwater, that wide expanse of still water that leads to the mouth of the Nerang River, she watched nuns step fully clothed into the bathing boxes and come out the other side, lowering themselves discreetly into the water. She assumed they were Anglican nuns from St Hilda's. It was on that basis that St Hilda's was later chosen as our school. (It wasn't until years later that Mum discovered the nuns were actually Sisters of Mercy from the Star of the Sea convent; there were no nuns at St Hilda's.)

But for now, Dad's return to work took priority. In December 1950, aged eight, I embarked on my fifth ocean voyage. We set sail from Sydney on the *Orontes*. These three-week voyages were great adventures for children. There were sports competitions and fancy dress parties and in between we ran about the ship. We had Christmas at sea that year.

When we arrived in Colombo we moved straight into the Grand Oriental Hotel, known as the GOH. Bella Sidney Woolf, sister of Leonard, had observed in 1905, 'If you waited long enough in the hall of the GOH, as it is known throughout the world, you would meet everyone worth meeting.' The hotel looked over Colombo Harbour, then one of the busiest in the world, and was located in the middle of the Fort, the busiest business and shopping area of the city.

We went to school at Bishop's College, a Church of England girls' school run by the Sisters of St Margaret. Today there are Bishop's girls all over the world, including Australia. It was there I had some early uncomfortable lessons about exclusion, and not in the classroom. Most of my fellow pupils were Ceylonese and from wealthy families. There were only three European girls in my class and we were certainly made to feel different. We ate our lunches alone together and were never asked to the homes of our classmates. This was a time when there was intense snobbery and racial prejudice, and I felt it acutely. I understood, even as an eight-year-old, that I was not being ostracised personally but that these girls felt they came from a superior class. I have never forgotten the discomfort, and I think it was about that time I started stuttering.

Mum was friendly with the headmistress of another school in Colombo, the Royal Naval School for the children of the British service personnel still in Ceylon after the war, and so we left Bishop's and went there instead. It couldn't have been more different. The teachers were a mix of civilians and navy personnel. One of our subjects was mental arithmetic, taught by Lieutenant Fox in naval uniform of white shirt, shorts and long socks. He used to march between the desks rapping us with a ruler for wrong answers. I have blamed him ever since for my being bad at maths. Our school houses were named after English seafaring heroes, Mountbatten, Nelson, Rodney and Cunningham. We were in Mountbatten, whose colour was blue. The school was in a collection of military huts on the edge of the sea close by the Colombo Fort. The greatest treat was when naval ships were in port, they would have parties for children with a canvas slide that was actually the sling transporting sailors from one ship to another.

By 1953 my parents had finally reached a decision about our future schooling. Once again Mum, Louella and I set sail from Colombo on board the *Himalaya*. We didn't know it, but this was to be our last journey from Ceylon. We also didn't know that Mum was pregnant. I claim some credit for the pregnancy. The year before, when I had begun to tire of playing with dolls, I had started to nag Mum about having a baby and she did. This must have been a deliberate decision because she and Dad had moved into separate bedrooms when I was six. Holly Margaret was born in November, and I was rarely to feel such an outpouring of love as I did for this baby that I felt was mine. It also skewed my attitude to birth control later; I implicitly assumed that babies only came along after some intellectual decision and that you wouldn't get pregnant without having made such a decision.

When the *Himalaya* steamed into Sydney Harbour in April 1953, we again attracted the attention of media photographers.

Freezing in the early morning, we were huddled together in Mum's fur coat and so we appeared in the *Sydney Morning Herald*. But we were not staying in Sydney this time. Once more we made the journey to South Brisbane and took a train to Southport.

I don't think it was sentiment for those significant transits that made me, years later, nag Queensland Transport Minister Don Lane into preserving the old South Brisbane station when it was redeveloped. That station had been the gateway into Queensland from the south. At Southport we moved into a flat attached to the Bauer Street house of real estate agent Mr Harding Smith (whose daughter Holly was to give her name to our sister) and we made lifelong friends among the families in the street. At 11 I was the oldest child and I organised the games and the plays and allocated the parts. I think this was the start of my bossiness. We played games of imagination: Burke and Wills on the vast expanse of sand behind the houses on the river side of the street, and Robin Hood and Maid Marian in the trees that lined it. Sir Edmund Hillary climbed Mt Everest and I cried because I had wanted to do that. The Queen was crowned, but we could only see that at the movies because television had not yet come to Australia.

I started at St Hilda's, wearing a navy tunic and distinctive red beret. At first I was teased for my posh English accent and my habit of saying, 'I say!' But the teasing had no effect and soon stopped, as did the accent. I was used to being thought of as different – in Colombo I had got attention for my Australian accent, at Bishop's College I was white and at the Naval School I had a civilian father.

St Hilda's was to be where we would stay, as day girls and boarders, to finish our education. And Southport was now our home. We were Queenslanders.

NOT YET THE GOLD COAST

THE GOLD COAST was an idea whose time had yet to come. Southport, at the northern end of a long strip of seaside villages, was very much a typical country town where people lived and worked, where the professional folk socialised together. The doctors and the dentists, and there were only three of each in the 1950s, were friends. The bank managers and their families lived above the banks in Nerang Street, and I used to love going to their places to play after school.

Because it was by the sea, people visited for holidays. Families from the bush had big houses, mainly on the Esplanade facing the Broadwater. Brisbanites made the journey from the city; back then it took a couple of hours by train to get to Southport station, followed by a drive to Surfers Paradise. Surfers consisted of the Surfers Paradise Hotel built by Jim Cavill in the late 1930s, which had become a convalescent home for servicemen during World War II. This was long before the frenetic postwar development that continues today. Further south were the Currumbin Bird Sanctuary where multicoloured lorikeets were handfed by visitors, and Jack Evans' porpoise pool at Coolangatta.

There was a definite pattern to south coast holidays. Queenslanders came down in December and January to spend the Christmas holidays. From May through the winter months of June and July, visitors came up from the south, mainly from Melbourne. These were the people, amazed by the winter sun and the still-warm sea, who would invest in and ultimately create the Gold Coast. I have always thought it interesting that all the major investment from the 1950s onwards came from the south. Brisbane people somehow just took the south coast for granted. Bruce Small (later Sir Bruce), the first mayor to promote the area actively to the rest of Australia, began his working life with a small bicycle shop in Melbourne that became a national company. He retired to the coast, became a property developer, and gave his canal and island developments glamorous though inappropriate names such as Capri, Sorrento and Miami, creating the glitz that became the Gold Coast.

Sixty years on, the Gold Coast is a city of skyscrapers by the sea. To have no physical evidence of the place where you grew up is disconcerting, to say the least. I was in Surfers recently, staying on the thirty-first floor of a hotel on the site of the original two-storey Surfers Paradise Hotel, and from my balcony I looked at even higher buildings. At the bottom is a huge shopping centre that could have been in Singapore or Hong Kong. Almost the only buildings left from my child-hood are the bathing sheds on the Broadwater and at Main Beach, although it is still possible in the morning to gaze at the sun coming up over the glistening ocean, and there is still that wonderful strip of sand that stretches from Southport down to Burleigh Heads. When I swim at Main Beach, where I first swam in the Queensland sea, I walk over the sand, keeping my eyes firmly ahead as I plunge into the surf.

St Hilda's, my fifth school in a little over five years not including the six months when I went to no school at all, was essentially a country boarding school, and in 1953 there were 250 girls, of whom about 60 were day girls. Now St Hilda's is called St Hilda's Gold Coast rather than St Hilda's Southport, and its 1250 girls include only 250 boarders. (There was a brief time during the war when boys from Toowoomba Prep School were moved down to the coast while the girls were evacuated to Stanthorpe. Oddly, all girls' schools on the east coast were evacuated west, but little boys were presumably considered expendable.)

St Hilda's had wonderful grounds, acres of mainly bushland, which must have made the country girls feel right at home and made me feel truly Australian. There were six tennis courts, and as tennis was considered a compulsory accomplishment for country life we had to play every afternoon. I have always thought we were lucky to grow up in beautiful surroundings. Schools now seem to measure their standing in terms of bricks and mortar.

Like Queenwood in Sydney, it had been founded by one of those indomitable women who did so much for the education of girls in the early twentieth century. It was known as Miss Davenport's Private School until it was bought by the Archbishop and the Church of England in 1911. It was a Church of England school (Anglican had not yet become a brand name) and religion played a major part. We had assembly with prayers and hymns every morning (I still know most of those hymns by heart) and the dormitories were called after early English saints – St Cuthbert, St Wilfred, St Audrey, St Chad and St Bede. Every Sunday the boarders would walk to nearby St Peter's Church, two-by-two in a crocodile line, wearing white frocks.

Louella and I yearned to be boarders, imbued as we were with Enid Blyton's tales of boarding school at Malory Towers, and Angela Brazil's school stories. It was quite common then for small children of five or six to be sent to boarding school for various reasons. Two of my best friends in the early days were girls whose mothers had died. My chance came when I was twelve, when Mum had to go to Sydney for some specialised dental treatment, taking Louella and Holly with her. I was a boarder for a term and absolutely loved it.

The next year, we were boarders for the whole year when Mum and Holly went back to Colombo. We spent the school holidays in May and August with our grandparents in Sydney and flew from Coolangatta. The memory of those plane trips are still with me. The planes were the old DC3s and I vomited most of the flights. In fact, I would start to feel sick a few days before we were due to travel, so there was little pleasure in anticipating the journey.

Many years later the 1982 Commonwealth Games in Brisbane were to be the beginning of my passion for sport, though not then or ever as a participant. I was always very bad at sport at school. I was not actually very bad at running and swimming, but seriously awful at ball games. It was common practice in sport sessions for two girls, obviously stars, to be picked as captains and for them to pick their teams. So it was a case of, 'I'll have her' and, 'I'll have her', and as the pool of team members shrunk, I'd be standing there looking at my sandshoes and knowing that I would be the last to be chosen. No one wanted me on their team for tunnel ball or netball, perfectly ghastly games where I would drop the ball and be hissed at by everybody else.

When I later told this story to my doctor sister, Kim, who was good at sport and had actually been in the school hockey team, she was appalled and said that this rejection must have been damaging for my psyche. But I don't think it was. I just knew I was bad at ball games, and I concentrated on what I was good at. That has proved to be an important lesson throughout my life and one I share with young people – find what you are good at and know what you are not. And understand that not being good at something is not all that bad.

What I was good at, and enjoyed, was being on stage. My first starring role was in Christopher Fry's *The Boy with the Cart* in which I played 'The Boy'. At fourteen, skinny-legged and flat-chested, I looked right for the part. Dad had to come to a performance because Mum was in hospital. When I asked him afterwards what he thought, hoping for compliments on my acting talent, he said simply, 'Fancy being able to learn all those words by heart.'

Dad was never a great supporter of our drama and choir activities. He thought they interfered with schoolwork, but I think they are an important part of education. There's the brain-power needed to learn the lines and the discipline of having to turn up to rehearsals and take directions. Drama at St Hilda's cut across age lines. As I was a shy child and a stutterer, just being able to walk on a stage was a huge boost to my confidence. It's somehow easier to be playing a role because then you are not actually yourself.

My stutter was a huge burden to me, though interestingly none of my friends or family remember it. In class we would each read out a paragraph aloud and I would count ahead to see what I was getting. If my paragraph began with a consonant I knew I was in trouble. I developed coping techniques. If the word was, say, 'King', I would cough and say 'ing'. The odd thing was that on stage I didn't stutter.

As teenagers, we always had to have a boyfriend, an accessory as necessary as a handbag and an obligatory status symbol. During the Easter break, just before we turned 15 my friends Joan, Elizabeth and I realised we didn't know many boys and decided a good way to get to know some was to have a party. As we didn't know any to invite, we made lists of the sons of our mothers' friends. There was Tom the doctor's son and Eric the chemist's son, and John who lived over Elizabeth's back fence and his friend Earle, and Len, Joan's friend Kay's first cousin. The party, which turned out to be great, was in Elizabeth's backyard. We jived to Elvis Presley and Bill Haley and Elizabeth's father, George Ross, devised a game where the girls walked under the Hills Hoist hung with sheets and the boys had to guess whose legs they were. At the end of the party, I kissed Kay's cousin Len and was gauche enough to inform him that he was the first boy I'd ever kissed. I don't remember his reaction to this important piece of information.

In my second last year at school I played the princess in the school play, wearing a beautiful white dress of Mum's cut down. This produced a result that had nothing to do with theatre. Boys from The Southport School always came to the dress rehearsal to give us an audience. The captain of the First XV Rugby team was smitten with me and subsequently asked me out. We were to be an item for the rest of the year.

The best holidays of my childhood were in the Queensland outback, that mythical place we call the 'real Australia' even though we are one of the most urbanised nations on earth. In my sub-Junior year, I was invited by my best friend Jennie to spend the August holidays on her family's sheep station near Boulia in western Queensland. These were the days when Australia rode on the sheep's back, when wool was worth a pound per pound and the graziers who produced it were our aristocracy. We travelled up from Southport by train and were met at South Brisbane station by a man from Dalgety, the stock and station agent, who took us to our hotel then out to dinner and the movies that night. We stayed at the Canberra, a temperance hotel, alcohol-free and safe for young ladies. In fact, it was so safe that when we would stay there a few years later, to go to parties and dances in Brisbane, the doorman would not allow any young male to cross the threshold. The next day we were dropped at the airport and flew to Winton, where we were met by Jennie's father who drove us the 360 kilometres to Boulia. Before we set off he took us to lunch at the North Gregory Hotel, where the waitresses wore frilly aprons over their black dresses and frilly white caps: the hotel is still there, albeit without the fancy waitresses. Winton is where Australia's national song 'Waltzing Matilda' was first sung, and in that hotel are the sandblasted glass doors etched by the famous artist Daphne Mayo. In a nice twist of fate, I'm now on the board of the Waltzing Matilda Centre in Winton and I have been named an Ambassador for the North Gregory Hotel and always stay there.

Gordon Pooley, Jennie's father, had won Pathungra station in one of the land ballots of the 1950s. Since 1916 the Queensland government had raffled off crown land and would-be graziers could enter the ballot. But it was no easy win. Pathungra was more than 400 square kilometres, of which a large part was desert, and the Pooleys with their four young daughters started from scratch. Many of the ballot winners had no experience farming that kind of land. Gordon Pooley had been a citrus grower at Gayndah. But they worked hard, putting up fences and digging holes for the outdoor dunnies. It was shearing time that August, and Mrs Pooley spent her days baking scones and cooking meals for the workers. Mustering had to be done, and though I'd never ridden a horse I didn't want to be left at home. On the first day my horse threw me off about 15 kilometres out from the homestead and there was nothing for it but to get back on, which did earn me some kudos. My greatest fear was of rats, which I was told came in waves across the flat parched land, so that when I had to go to the lavatory in the night I ran down the backyard to it and just as quickly back again.

When I was 16 I went with my friend Joan to visit her relatives in north Queensland. We stayed with Joan's aunt, Betty Perkins, and her family in Townsville, and it was here that I had my first taste of alcohol – not with the family but at the local amateur races, a big social event and my first experience of the racetrack. Actually, it wasn't my first taste of alcohol because I would sip my father's whisky and my mother's shandy, but this was the first drink that belonged to me and it was champagne. I remember what I wore, a red dress with white trimmings that I had seen in a Simplicity pattern book and that was made for me by Joan's mother, Edie. It's funny how often a long-ago memory comes complete with fashion illustration. From Townsville we went west by train to Richmond, a 500 kilometre journey, with stops along the way at stations where the cafes served strong sweet tea.

Understanding the country is really important for city children, and the only way to do it in an authentic way is to live the life. Queensland is not only large but also diverse. Wandoan on the northern fringe of the Darling Downs, where I stayed with Helen Turner and her family on 'Glendoan', is very different from Winton and the Channel Country, while Kingaroy where Mary Lewis's family held an annual race meeting on their property, 'Burrandowan', is very far in every way from the Gold Coast. But it's all Queensland.

SWIMMING UPSTREAM

A CHILDHOOD IN retrospect is a collection of memories, happy and sad, all jumbled up. Teenage years are always turbulent, but for various reasons one particular year turned out to be especially traumatic.

In 1956 Dad had come out to Southport on leave, which turned out to be a bad career move; while he was in Australia he lost his job in Colombo. His job loss was part of the process of independence of Ceylon. The government of Ceylon under Prime Minister Bandaranaike (whose wife later became the world's first female prime minister), had embarked on a program of nationalisation. This made Sinhala the only official language and forced all businesses to employ a quota of Singhalese. So Dad, conveniently out of the country, was told not to come back.

For the first time in his life, Dad was out of work. He had spent his entire career at the same firm, a company that made tea-producing machinery, going from office boy in Belfast to chief accountant in Colombo. There was no tea-producing machinery in Southport and he had no business contacts. So, at the age of 55 and with a young family to support, he took to the streets selling insurance. We sold our lovely old Queenslander, which had been Mum's pride and joy and the first house we had owned. We moved to a smaller house in Labrador on the Pacific Highway, which had been called 'Rumah Puteh' by a previous owner from Malaya. This was a house with a flat underneath, which Mum and Dad planned to rent. But when they did, it turned out not to meet with Council approval.

At the time it all seemed very inconvenient and most disruptive. It was only years later that I felt enormous respect and admiration for my father for picking himself up after being sacked and starting life in a new country in a new business. In many ways it was great training for politics because he was an insurance man of the old-fashioned sort, who knocked on doors to make a sale and then cared for his clients when they had a claim. Many times the phone would ring late at night and Dad would go out to help a fisherman fill out the forms for a storm-damaged boat. Dad made me understand the importance of caring for people and their problems, and doing it personally.

In April 1957 my brother Charles was born, the first boy after we three girls and the son to replace Michael who had died many years before. But when he was 15 months old, two days after my sixteenth birthday, something terrible happened – an event I cannot think about, even now, without choking up.

My mother used to hang a toy on a string on the rails of Charles's cot, and his head got caught in it. That day Mum had kept me at home from school to look after her because she was sick, and I had gone out into the garden when I heard her scream. She had got up to have a bath and come back into the bedroom to find Charles choking and blue in the face. She picked him up and carried him across the busy highway, with me running beside her and holding up traffic, to the doctor around the corner. After the doctor had taken them inside, I sat on the wall beside the beach across the road and prayed, 'God, if you let Charles live I'll become a nun.' For years afterwards I felt guilty about that, surely God knew I would never have become a nun.

It was too late. Charles was dead. Louella and Holly were taken away by caring friends, and I was left alone with my anguished parents. There are so many pictures still in my head – our well-meaning rector saying it was God's will and Mum screaming at him; Dad sobbing, 'My son, my only son!'; Mum saying, 'No man can feel what it's like to lose a child.'

When it came to arranging the funeral, neither of my parents was able to do it. So I did, and that was when I began to grow up. I began to realise that even in marriage people can be terribly alone, for my parents were no support to each other. I remember nothing at all about the funeral in St Peter's Church, but I can still see Mum throwing herself on the grave as the little coffin was lowered.

Afterwards, I went back to school and to an inter-school sports day in Brisbane as though nothing had happened. There was no counselling support then. For Mum and Dad, I suppose, it was a case of just getting on with things. For me, apart from the grief and shock, there was a feeling of bewilderment that I had acted as an adult for those few days and was now being treated like a child again.

But the year was not unhappy as a whole, and it makes me realise how resilient is youth. It was my sub-Senior year, today's Year 11, with the important public exam to take place the following year. It was a time when it was possible to follow your interests in particular subjects, knowing that the year after was the one for hard work and focused attention. An extra layer of excitement was that many Southport School Senior boys had come back to school just to row in the school Eights and play Rugby. They were older and had cars, and because they didn't have to study they were available to us girls. We would spend our Sundays beside the pool at the newly built Chevron Hotel in Surfers where the manager encouraged us, presumably as a bit of indirect marketing. The pool was very fancy, with glass windows people could look through and see the swimmers underwater.

There was teenage angst too. A friend who lived around the corner took me on a double date with two Sydney boys, Sydney being a code word for sophistication. At sixteen I was still flat-chested so I shoved Kleenex tissues down the front of my dress to give me a bosom. There was never any danger that those tissues would be dislodged. The next Saturday was the school swimming carnival, and it had not long started when my friend said in excitement, 'The boys have come!' I was absolutely mortified. In my cotton-knit Speedos there was no hope of disguising my shape, or rather lack of it. I spent the whole afternoon with a towel around me.

Actually, cotton-knit Speedos were a factor in the demise of my swimming career. We would train in the afternoons after school, then hang up our swimsuits in the dressing sheds ready for training early the next morning. In the cold early morning they were still wet and slimy, and I'm afraid I just stopped training. I obviously didn't have the temperament of Kieren Perkins or Susie O'Neill.

Our senior year, 1959, was Queensland's centenary year. It was 100 years since Governor George Bowen had declared this state to be separate from New South Wales and installed his wife Lady Diamantina Roma in what is now Old Government House in George Street. I was charged with writing the editorial for the school magazine that year (Mrs Hunter, our English teacher, was the editor). Having mentioned the importance of the centenary I wrote:

> *St Hilda's School is Queensland in miniature. It would be hard to find a school that is more thoroughly representative of our great State. We have girls from the capital city of Brisbane; from Coolangatta on the NSW border to Cairns in the tropical North; from cattle stations and sheep properties; from cane farms and the wheat districts of the Darling Downs. There are very few aspects of Queensland life that are not represented among us.*

I was a boarder for that final term. Miss Horton, the headmistress, had thought that I would be able to study better at school than at home with the younger children and Mum about to give birth; she was pregnant again. Being a boarder at that stage was a little irksome. At home, even in the midst of the family and studying at the kitchen table, I had been able to set my own pace and could study until 10 pm. At school we had regulated prep time and lights out at 8.30 pm and as a result we sixth formers would take our books into the lavatories and sit there for a couple of hours. Goodness knows if the powers that be ever noticed that a group of senior girls might appear to have bowel and bladder problems. We were a dedicated lot, and the results showed. There were only 15 in our class, and of those, ten went on to higher education, six with Commonwealth scholarships to university.

The big event of my Senior year was the birth of my youngest sister Kim. She happened to be born on 26 October, the day of my first exam, the English paper. The next day I went to visit her and Mum at the Southport General hospital, conveniently located across the road from the school. A few weeks later Mum brought her up to school for me to show her off to the class. Needless to say I was the only girl in my year whose mother had given birth during our senior year. A few months earlier Louella and I, walking down the street after school to catch the bus home, had discussed the possibility that Mum might be pregnant ('She's knitting booties!') and how bizarre that might be.

It did mean that during the Christmas holidays I was sometimes on babysitting duty, but it hadn't made any difference to my exam results and I can say, modestly now, that I left school with a swag of prizes for English and history. I won the Barnes Cup for Languages and the Baker Cup for Citizenship.

SOMETHING TO FALL BACK ON

I WAS THE first in my family to go to university. At St Hilda's we had a wonderful English teacher whose Scottish brogue gave an extra musical dimension to her reading aloud of poetry. She said to my mother when I was 15, 'It will be a trrragedy if this child does not go to university.' My mother was happy to agree. She had always been absolutely determined that her daughters should have a proper education.

My father was not so enthusiastic about university. He thought we should do shorthand and typing and become secretaries: 'So you can help your husband in his business and if he dies have something to fall back on.' This, I should point out, was not an unusual view for the times, nor was his opinion that the university was a hotbed of sin and debauchery. Nor indeed was his advice not to be too intelligent, 'or men won't find you attractive'. But as his general parental philosophy was, 'Whatever your mother says', to university we all went – including Jill, who went on to do an Arts degree as a mature-aged student in Sydney.

Jill had left school after doing the Intermediate Certificate, and worked in a chemist shop, which was where she found out about her mother. After Jill went to join Hylda in Port Moresby, we heard very little from her for some years. She came back to Sydney after a broken engagement, got her Leaving Certificate and went to the University of Sydney, where she trained as a teacher and played cricket for the university. For the rest of her professional life she taught in and around Sydney, at schools as diverse as Frensham (a private girls' school) and Rooty Hill High.

I had won a Commonwealth Scholarship, as did anyone then who was half-bright, and in my case it came with a living allowance because of my father's low income and my three siblings still at home. I chose to do Arts with honours in French – I had won the French verse speaking competitions for schools run by the Alliance Francaise and the fearsome Miss Katie Campbell-Brown of the French department at the University of Queensland.

With six of my classmates I went to Women's College, which only a couple of years earlier had moved from an old house, Chislehurst at Kangaroo Point, to its new building at St Lucia. Another school friend only lasted there a week before she moved into Lennons Hotel, then Brisbane's smartest, where her country family kept a suite with their own bed linens.

College was one of my life's most exciting experiences. Life, admittedly, hadn't been very long but I can still remember and feel that sense of anticipation, of the whole world opening up to endless possibilities. Away from home and family regulations there were few rules and every evening of the first week I dropped my clothes on the floor of my room, the first to be mine alone, and no one told me to pick them up. There were also boys, a hitherto fairly unknown species en masse, and more of them than us, so girls, pretty or not, had a flatteringly good time. At the University of Queensland in 1960 there were 8700 students, of whom only 1900 were female.

By today's standards there were lots of regulations at college. You had to fill in 'The Book' when going out at night, and write down 'Where going', 'With whom' and 'What for' (which caused lots of witticisms). You had to be home by 10 pm with only two late nights per term. You were not allowed to hang your washing on the clothesline at weekends for fear of exciting the men playing Rugby on the nearby oval, and you were not allowed to wear shorts outside college. I got into great trouble one weekend for going from the front door to my parents' car, wearing shorts for a family picnic.

Our principal, Miss McIndoe, was in a constant nervous state. She had been headmistress of a girls' school in Sydney where a student had been murdered in a dormitory, and Miss M was fearful at every suggestion of danger. When the boys from St John's College stole the plugs from our bathrooms to prove they had actually got into Women's, she was in hysterics. When we first-year freshers were being dunked in the lake at the bottom of the drive, I can still see Miss McIndoe, her black gown flapping, hurtling down the driveway crying out, 'No, no. I have a bronchial fresher!' This was me, and so I was saved from the cold and slime. Miss McIndoe always wore her academic gown, as did we to dinner at night, as well as conservative dress to lectures and around the campus.

Now as president of the College Council I think how shocked Miss McIndoe would be at today's plunging necklines and short skirts. Male friends are allowed in the rooms, for sleepovers ... so long as you write their names in 'The Book', in case of fire.

I had a wonderful first term, in spite of the intellectual rigour of French honours with Miss Campbell-Brown. There were balls and parties, and lots of sitting around the refectory talking about the problems of the world. The refectory was in the GP hut, which was a Nissen hut left over from World War II, when General Sir Thomas Blamey had had his headquarters at St Lucia. GP meant 'general purpose' so we not only ate in the building but rehearsed our plays and revues on its stage. I threw myself with gusto into the College Players' production of Gilbert and Sullivan's *Iolanthe*, where I couldn't sing well but was appropriately small to fill the bill as a fairy in the chorus. We fairies had lights in our hair wired from batteries tucked down our bras. Engineering students were in charge of the batteries, so their proper placement involved much girlish giggling and boyish fumbling.

The college of the players was St John's, all male, and the producer was Bryan Nason, who would make an enormous mark on Queensland's theatrical life. Many years later, as Lord Mayor, I agreed to a small but thrilling part in his production of *Troilus and Cressida*, that of Helen of Troy. But when we got down to details, Bryan insisted that Helen be carried onstage wrapped in a carpet, naked. I had to decline, as much for vanity as for political reasons.

There were also the Kings College Women's Players; in a play about Ned Kelly I played Ned's sister, Kate. The next year, Bryan produced *The Importance of Being Earnest* for the Uni Dramatic Society and I played the ingénue role of Cecily, with Jennifer Maruff, the most beautiful girl at the university and the student president of Duchesne, the Catholic women's college, playing Gwendolen. I can still remember the names of the entire cast.

There was an extra dimension to university theatre productions. There was still the discipline of learning lines and turning up to rehearsals, the nervous tension of going onstage. I could still do my lines without stuttering, but now there was the unique camaraderie among theatre people, with fellow students as the producers and technicians.

My stutter, or perhaps stammer, hadn't got any better. It had only become worse, as my mother would often snap at me to stop and it caused me agonies talking to strangers that I would now meet. My stutter was cured in a way that now seems incredible: in the labour ward when I was 22, giving birth to my eldest daughter Nicola. Feeling immensely pleased with myself, when we passed a doctor who was the father of one of my journalist friends, I said, 'Hello, Dr Dique. I've just had a baby!'

'People usually do in the labour ward, my dear,' said he. I suddenly realised I'd said those two '*ds*' without stuttering. And I never stuttered again.

Like so much else in my life, I fell into journalism by accident. Midway through my first university year, it was beginning to dawn on me that I was neither an academic nor an intellectual, and long hours in the library were starting to pall. One of my friends Chrissie said that her cousin, a reporter on the Brisbane *Telegraph*, had asked her whether she knew anyone who might like to be a cadet journalist. Apparently a senior woman reporter had suddenly become seriously ill and they needed someone in a hurry. I had been interested in journalism as a schoolgirl but had dismissed the idea, especially after my grandfather described it as 'no job for a woman'. Besides, I was Going to University.

Now, I was beginning to realise that I had no ideas about a future career and I would soon need a job. I had considered the diplomatic service, but changed my mind when a man from Canberra came to college to talk to aspiring students. He didn't quite say it was no job for a woman, but he did tell me that it wasn't glamorous, that I would be sent to nasty mosquito-ridden places in the beginning, and if I married I would have to resign. Those were the days when every right-thinking girl and her mother saw marriage very much as a goal in itself, so despite my French honours studies I decided the diplomatic life was not for me.

I had always thought that to be a journalist you had to be a good writer, and I didn't think I was. I had been good at English essays at school, mainly by coming up with an original point of view, but I had never seen myself as a writer. I was to find out later that those cadets who had wanted to be writers soon became disillusioned and dropped out. Good writing was not among the criteria for employment at the *Courier-Mail* or the *Telegraph*.

It was a dilemma. To leave university meant giving up my Commonwealth Scholarship and my French honours degree. There was no one from whom to get solid advice. My mother just said, 'Whatever you think, dear', which I felt was most inadequate. (This was the first of only two times I was seriously upset with my mother. The other was years later when I rang to tell her that my daughter Nicola had got 985 for her school leaving exam score and Mum immediately said, 'Kim got 990', competing with me over our children.) Both the man from the Commonwealth Scholarship office and Miss Campbell-Brown told me I was making a big mistake. I was warned that I could not get my scholarship back if I gave it up.

While I was loving university life, I felt guilty about it. I realised I was not a genuine student and was not going to get long-term satisfaction out of my studies. I didn't enjoy sitting for long hours in the library to research assignments and the glow of intellectual curiosity of my last years at school was flickering and fading. I was restless for the world beyond St Lucia.

I also had the family to consider. I had been home for the mid-year holidays and was aware of how hard up they were and would continue to be for a long time yet. Louella had three years left at school, Holly was only six and Kim just seven months old.

So, still undecided, I asked Mrs Erica Parker, women's editor on the *Telegraph*, if I could come in for a day to see if I liked it. She must have been astonished but agreed. I cringed for years at the cheek of it, for what I didn't know then was that each year a few hundred school leavers applied for cadetships and only a handful got them. And here was I, a mere 17-year-old, making conditions. But I did spend a day there, and I did like it. I had to meet with the editor, the terrifying John Wakefield, who asked me why I wanted to be a journalist. When I brightly replied that I wanted to meet interesting people he snapped, 'You'll meet some bloody boring ones.' I had to have a check-up by Dr Phyllis Cilento, the *Courier-Mail*'s 'Medical Mother' columnist, presumably to make sure I didn't fall by the health wayside. Later, as Lady Cilento, she would give her name to the Children's Hospital.

My two and a half years on the Brisbane *Telegraph* were among the best years of my life. The *Telegraph* building was located in Queen Street. Nearly 30 years later I was able to preserve its facade as part of the city streetscape. I loved the excitement of an afternoon paper, with five changing editions a day and Mrs Parker barking out, 'We need two inches, down on the stone in ten minutes.' One of us would have to write something to fill the missing two inches and take it down to the composing room. This meant going down the round iron staircase, with all the comps looking up your skirt because we didn't wear trousers to the office in Women's News. I loved the thrill of feeling the presses roll because the whole building would rumble and shake. I loved the fact that at the end of the day, your job was done – the stories were written, the paper was out, and each new morning was a fresh beginning.

I enjoyed the camaraderie and the friendship not only of the other three girls in Women's News, but also with the men in General News. There were the doyens of the racetrack, people like Keith Noud, Bill Ahern and Bill Boyan who taught us shorthand (which I never mastered), and the top reporters such as Glyn May and Pat Lloyd, the Lovable Lad with the Lightning Left. Pat had been a policeman and his father a senior inspector in the Queensland Police Force so he had very good contacts and got all the best stories. In Women's News we reported on the social happenings in Brisbane, fashion and other stories that women might find interesting. Once a week we produced the Teen Page, of which I was the editor, and meant I had to find a story to write each week about an interesting teenager. These ranged from a medical student at St John's College named John Haines who took up knitting, considered newsworthy (he's now a retired anaesthetist) to tennis champion Robyn Ebbern (whose son is now married to my daughter's best friend) and Annette Allison, who was sent out by department store Weedmans to find out what other teenagers were wearing (she later became a nationally successful radio and television personality).

The closest we got to mixing with our male colleagues was on Saturday mornings and Tuesday nights. On Saturday, when only one of us was on duty, we went with a photographer to cover weddings and came back to the office to write variations on, 'The bride was a picture in tulle and lace …' We then helped out with the races. The Saturday afternoon edition was important for racing news and results, and it was a change of interest for us girls. Tuesday nights we had a photographer allocated to take social pictures of whatever we could find happening, but because the paper was on an economy drive he had to cover training for the sports pages. I got to go where I would otherwise never have been, to boxing halls and Rugby League training. The most interesting follow-up to the social pages was the phone call the morning after we had taken a photograph at one of Brisbane's few fine restaurants. 'Mr Smith' would call to ask us not to publish his picture because he wasn't actually dining with 'Mrs Smith'. But there were many others desperate to get their pictures in the paper, and I also had the interesting experience of having to refuse bribes.

One Saturday morning I was sent by chief-of-staff Frank (Wattie) Watkins to cover the traumatic funeral of some children murdered with an axe. On Monday Mrs P gave Wattie the rounds of the kitchen for having sent one of her girls on such an unsuitable assignment. 'Suitable' seemed to be important. After much pleading and nagging, I was sent to cover courts. On my first day I was sitting in the press box when the young man in the dock was asked a question. He hesitated and said, 'I can't answer that, Your Honour, because there's a young lady in the court.' The judge looked up and said testily, 'Young lady, go and find one of your male colleagues to come and take your place.' So I had to scuttle out and find Hec Holthouse, the *Telegraph*'s senior court reporter, who was not pleased. My court reporting career on the Brisbane *Telegraph* ended as soon as it had begun.

I had given up my university life, but not university altogether. As part of the cadetship scheme we had to take an evening course towards a Diploma of Journalism. This included prescribed subjects like political science and economics, as well as Journalism A and Journalism B which concerned ethics and the laws of libel. We went by bus out to the University of Queensland in St Lucia to attend evening lectures a couple of nights a week, where I usually fell asleep.

As a cadet I also had to learn shorthand, which I did in company with the cadets of the *Courier-Mail*. This was how I learned to have boys as friends. I became best friends with Hugh Lunn, who later wrote a book called *Head Over Heels* about being in love with me. Though I could tell he liked me, I was just pleased to have a very good friend who was a boy. And he never did ask me out, although he thought he did. In *Head Over Heels* he describes ringing me to ask me what I was doing at the weekend and me saying I was going to the coast to visit family. In the book he said, 'I'll be round about seven to see you', which to me sounded like a visit, not a date. When he arrived, I was in shorts and a shirt, not wanting to appear presumptuous but ready to change if I was asked out. Instead, Hugh sat talking to my father about cricket, and being charming to my mother and sisters. I kept thinking, 'Is he going to suggest going out?' But it got late, and there was still cricket talk, and then Hugh said he'd better be going. I walked him to the gate and didn't even see his beautiful car, which he had specially polished. I tell this story to show how simple we were back then.

Hugh was a good friend, and has continued to be over the years. In fact, many of my friends now have been journalists in the past. There's been nothing deliberate about this, but obviously you have something in common with people who have the same calling. Or do your traits that happen to be in common lead you to the same calling? I'm still in touch with 'the girls' from the Brisbane *Telegraph* – Helen Adam, Suzanne Blake and Judithann Guerassimof. I have stayed friends with Jillian Rice

SOMETHING TO FALL BACK ON

and Malcolm Dean from my days on the Sydney *Telegraph*. Malcolm was an English journalist and later returned to London and worked at the *Guardian* for the next 50 years; I stay with him and his wife, Clare, whenever I'm in London. Jeanne Pratt worked on the Sydney *Telegraph* just before me, Marina Craig was former women's editor of the Adelaide *Advertiser* and Maryanne Weston and Robyn Besley were Brisbane journalists – they are all friends to whom I feel very connected. One of my best friends is Robert Allan, who had been the City Hall reporter for the *Sun* newspaper, and became my press secretary and later chief-of-staff.

One of my theories in life is that we are all shaped by our first real job. I saw this particularly in politics where a person's first job – teacher, bank teller, farmer, nurse – seemed to inform his or her character and personality. For example, if someone had been a teacher, it was not hard to see their teacher persona inside their politician self. All of the skills I learned as a cadet reporter I have used in later roles. I had to overcome my shyness to interview strangers, to ask people questions and compile their answers into reports. When I became the Alderman for Indooroopilly and in Opposition, I would draw on this experience and ask questions about constituents' problems then put them together as a written submission to Council. It can apply to student jobs as well as chosen careers. Three of my daughters have been waitresses which taught them a lot about people as well as how to carry a lot of plates at once.

Early habits become habits of a lifetime. Every morning when we got to work at the *Telegraph* the cadets had to come up with three news topics for the day. All the way in the tram from West End to Queen Street, after crossing the river from St Lucia, I would be looking about me for newsworthy topics. If we got to the office without a news story of our own, we would 'suggest follow-up to the *Courier-Mail* story on such and such ...'. We were never allowed to sit idle. If it appeared we were, Mrs P would pop a piece of copy paper into our typewriters with 'Bubble, bubble!' scrawled on it. And bubble we did, thinking desperately for a story idea.

Our training was carried out on the job, in spite of going to university. We worked alongside senior reporters who gave us tips of the trade, and we started with menial jobs, such as reporting on the markets (food not finance) and posting the results of the Golden Casket, the state lottery. As the *Telegraph* published five issues a day, we also experienced the very real tension of meeting a deadline for each edition.

As a cadet I also learned the more cutthroat aspects of the newspaper business and got a taste of how competitive journalism could be. I had gone to Surfers Paradise to interview the manager of the newly upgraded Chevron Hotel. After our chat, the manager turned to a colleague and said, 'Shall I give her my daughter from behind the Iron Curtain?' And he did. His teenaged daughter had escaped from communist East Germany; her photograph and the story made the front page of the paper with my name on it. This was in the days when having your name on a story was very special. My excitement and pride were dashed a few days later when the editor, John Wakefield, passed me in the corridor and said, 'Good story, Miss Kerr ... that Mrs Parker wrote for you!'

I was too stunned to reply. But I learned the valuable lesson that generosity doesn't always come with success and sometimes insecurity does. This lesson would stand me in good stead later, when I found that credit isn't always given to the person to whom it's due and that a competitive streak lurks just below the surface in most human beings. It would be useful knowledge in the political sphere.

I learned, too, the lessons that come with failure – of not only getting up again but of benefiting from it. I failed my driving test five times, then I wrote a story about it for the *Telegraph*. I did pass a few years later. My future brother-in-law Tony Atkinson gave me lessons and my future mother-in-law came with me to the test. She sat in the back seat, clutching an unopened bottle of champagne and chatting gaily to the policeman-examiner who was presumably quite happy to accept it when I passed.

I moved into a flat in New Farm with two school friends. It was a one-bedroom flat with a pull-down sofa in the living area and we had a rotating system where every third week you slept on the sofa, and the other two weeks in the bedroom. While I was living there I had my very own Queensland Police adventure. Studying late one night, I decided to go for a walk in nearby New Farm park, then considered one of Australia's top three rose gardens. I needed to clear my head, and was jumping over rose bushes when a cruising police car pulled up beside me. A policeman leaned out and said roughly, 'Get in.' So I did.

They started questioning me and asked what I was doing.

I said I was just going for a walk.

They asked: 'How old are you?'

I told them I was 18.

The policeman said: 'Don't give us that. You're not a day over 14.'

Until then I had been thinking it was all a lark, a bit of a giggle, but then I started to get worried. So I said, 'I'm a reporter on the *Telegraph* and I work with Pat Lloyd.'

This had an effect and after a bit more questioning they drove me home. I was hoping none of the neighbours were looking.

The next morning I went into the office full of outrage at being treated in such a way. But the police had already been in touch with Pat Lloyd, whose outrage certainly outclassed mine. He tore strips off me for being stupid and said, 'That's a very dangerous area at night. It's where the sailors go from the ships nearby.'

The real thrill in journalism came from the unexpected stories that you came upon by accident. I went one evening to an art show at the gallery at Finney Isles store (now David Jones), from which I was to buy my first painting. At the event I saw the artist Jon Molvig throwing a pie at Roy Churcher, for reasons that I've now forgotten, but which gave me a colourful news story.

Ever restless, after two and a half years with the *Telegraph* I decided it was time to move on. Those were the days when really successful young Australian writers, artists and journalists went to London. Those of us in Brisbane went to the 'big smoke' of Sydney or Melbourne. I had not finished my four-year cadetship, but wrote off to David McNicoll, editor-in-chief of Australian Consolidated Press, asking for an interview. Off I went to Sydney, and was offered a job as a D-grade reporter. It was the lowest rung of the ladder, but at least it was on the ladder. McNicoll was a big racing fan, and my mother's close friend's husband, Noel Richard, was secretary of the Australian Jockey Club. McNicoll later said he was impressed that I hadn't mentioned it at the interview.

Working on the *Daily Telegraph* in Sydney was very different from working in Brisbane. For one thing it was a morning paper – we started at 2 pm and finished at 11 pm. I lived with my grandparents in Cremorne and for the life of me I can't remember how I got home. It must have been by bus, for I remember walking up to Cremorne Junction to catch one into town. But coming home? The safety of young women was apparently not such an issue.

I was at last a real reporter. In Brisbane we had always gone out on assignments with a photographer who drove the car. In Sydney we had to find our own way from the *Telegraph* building on the corner of Park and Castlereagh streets. My first Sunday I was sent to cover a church service up at Kings Cross.

'How will I get there?' I asked the team in the newsroom.

'You walk up Palmer Street to the Cross,' they directed.

When I got back, the boys were waiting for me with big grins. 'How'd you go?'

'Oh, very well,' said I. 'All these nice men in cars kept stopping and asking me if I wanted a lift.' There was great mirth all round. What they hadn't told the little girl from the country was that Palmer Street was the prostitutes' beat.

The *Daily Telegraph* was not the world's greatest literary journal, it was rough-and-tumble journalism. Owned by Sir Frank Packer in the days when a proprietor really did own a newspaper and could fashion it to his whims, the sub-editors could, and did, yell with impunity at young reporters. Every evening all the blokes would rush in a horde to the King's Head pub for the six o'clock swill, which meant downing beers as fast as possible because the government tried to curb drinking by closing the public bar at 6 pm. Women were not allowed to drink in public bars so my friend Jillian and I, two of the four female journalists, would dream of a major story – the Town Hall up in flames, the Sydney Harbour Bridge falling down – for which we would get the scoop by being the only reporters in the office.

Sir Frank was very much a presence around the building. At that time he was attempting to win the America's Cup with his yacht *Gretel* and any stories involving sailing always got a good run. There were apocryphal rumours about him. Oft-repeated was the tale of the boy in the lift whose tie Sir Frank didn't like, or maybe it was a tune he was whistling. Sir Frank asked, 'How much do you earn, son?' When the boy told him, Sir Frank pulled out some cash and said, 'Take this and don't bother coming back to work.' The bemused boy had only been delivering a telegram.

There was another yarn about Sir Frank sacking a chap in the lift because he was carrying a six-pack of beer. This was Ced Culvert, the highly esteemed and valuable police roundsman. Chief-of-staff Jack Toohey told Culvert to hide for a week until Sir Frank had forgotten the incident.

There was a rumour that the reason the *Daily Telegraph* was pro-Prime Minister Bob Menzies and the Fairfax-owned *Sydney Morning Herald* was anti-Menzies was because the PM had had an affair with the wife of a member of the Fairfax family.

In those days there were four Sydney papers, the *Daily Telegraph* and *Sydney Morning Herald* in the morning and the *Sun Herald* and *Daily Mirror* in the afternoon, and there was great rivalry between them. When Pope John XXIII was dying in June 1963, the great question for us was: When would he die and which paper would get the scoop? Every evening that he lived past the *Daily Telegraph* deadline would take him onto the front page of the *Sun* and the *Daily Mirror*, and then he would hang on past their deadline. I actually can't remember who finally got the story of the death of this very popular pope.

In Sydney I had a particularly significant lesson about the importance of preparation, and of honesty. One Sunday afternoon I was told to go down to the Australia Hotel, then Sydney's poshest, to a news conference for the minister of finance from Singapore. Because it was Sunday and a quiet news day I thought there would be a lot of reporters there asking questions, so I didn't bother to look up the minister in the library or find out anything about Singapore. When I was shown up to the minister's suite I found, horror of horrors, no one else there. I had to confess to him that I knew very little about Singapore and absolutely nothing about finance. He was charming and I'm sure secretly pleased, because he was able to tell me exactly what he wanted and I got a satisfactory story. I learned never to go unprepared, and that if you don't know something, it's always best to admit it.

The biggest story of my time at the *Daily Telegraph* was the Bogle–Chandler murder case, still unsolved. Dr Gilbert Bogle, a CSIRO scientist, and Mrs Margaret Chandler, the wife of a colleague, were found dead on the banks of the Lane Cove River on New Year's Day 1963, cause of death not obvious. They had been at a party in Lane Cove. The story had all the elements of a scandal: murder, mystery and sex. It was further spiced up by the fact that all the people surrounding the deaths were 'clever' people, scientists and the like, at a time when Australians were deeply suspicious of too much intellect. The fact that Chandler and Bogle were married, though not to each other, further scandalised Sydney. The police bungled their investigations, as always seemed to happen with crimes at Christmas or New Year; evidence was tampered with. For example, Mrs Chandler's dress was pulled down 'for reasons of modesty'.

The media were in a fever of excitement and investigative reporting. Margaret Chandler's husband, Geoffrey, who later wrote a book called *So You Think I Did It*, belonged to a bohemian set known as 'The Push' who drank at a particular pub. I was despatched there to mingle and see what I could find out, but I had only been there five minutes when one of the other drinkers said, 'So, what paper are you from?'

Another day I was sent to the home of Mrs Bogle to get an interview with the grieving widow. I knocked on the door, and of course she didn't want to talk to me, so I just muttered my apologies and fled. A pushy reporter I was not. One Saturday a photographer and I spent the whole morning up a tree outside Geoffrey Chandler's house waiting for him to appear so we could get a picture. After a couple of hours the photographer said, 'I've had enough of this. I need a beer.' We shinned down the tree and went to the pub around the corner. When we got back Geoffrey Chandler's car had gone and so had he.

A scientist at the University of Queensland named Robert Endean had a theory that the couple had been poisoned by the venom of the box jellyfish, *Chironex fleckeri*, whose name I remember to this day. It was one of many and varied theories, including suicide, murder (Dr Bogle was working on a matter of national security), and accidental overdose of some mysterious unknown drug. But the case has never been solved, or the reason for their being on the banks of the river on New Year's Day, or the truth of their relationship.

One of the best things about newspapers then was the rivalry between them, which meant you had to get your facts straight, your spelling right, and make sure the other paper didn't get the story you hadn't. This kept reporters on their toes and made for healthy creative tension. I think it gave us a better media. It also meant that systems were devised. When I went up to Queen's Square to cover courts, I was told by the three other court reporters that 'the system' was that one of us sat in the court and took notes while the other three went to the pub. This person would then share their notes so that no one was 'scooped' or missed the story. The only problem for me was that I wasn't interested in going to the pub and really wanted to stay in the court. One night I was at the airport and left the reporters' room, where we pooled our information, to go to the bathroom. On my way back I recognised my hero, Sir Edmund Hillary, waiting for his plane. Of course, I rushed over to him and started talking. Fairly quickly the other reporters saw us and came over, and I was accused of trying to grab a story for myself.

Some journalistic practices were dodgy to say the least. If a Sunday afternoon was particularly quiet we would ring up the Minister for Works at his home (because we could), and say we had heard that the Opera House was such-and-such an amount over budget. He would say, or yell, that this was rubbish. The next day's story was, 'Minister denies Opera House blowout'. The Sydney Opera House, finally opened in 1973 and one of the wonders of the modern world, controversially cost over $100 million to build. It was well over budget.

It was a friendlier, more personal time. Not only could you ring ministers at home, but there was not the oppressive security around them there is today. Sent to Sydney airport to farewell the Queen and the Duke of Edinburgh in early 1963, I walked out across the tarmac to the plane with the prime minister and his party. It was raining and Sir Robert held his umbrella over this young girl reporter.

I had been part of the Royal Tour by accident. The two senior reporters covering the Northern Territory leg had got into a fight and I was sent up to replace one, probably as the reporter least likely to have a stoush. There was a roster of reporters to cover events and I got to cover an official royal lunch. The main point of my story was that the Queen powdered her nose at the table, something that would have horrified my mother.

After a year in Sydney I was missing Brisbane, and returned home to the *Courier-Mail* newsroom. I moved into a flat in Clayfield with friends, a step up in sophistication from the student flats I had shared before. We had parties with candles stuck in chianti bottles and one night I brought home half the cast from *Fidelio*, the opera playing at Her Majesty's Theatre.

I also came back to pursue my rather short television career. *Meet the Press* was a popular Sunday evening program, the forerunner of many current affairs shows. It was hosted by Reg Leonard, the overall boss of the *Courier-Mail* and the *Telegraph*, and later to be knighted, like so many of his contemporaries. Each week a guest would be grilled by a panel of journalists and Reg would sum up the discussion at the end. One evening, the chief-of-staff wandered through the newsroom and told me I would be on the program the following Sunday night because they wanted a female journalist. The show was broadcast live, which would have been daunting if I had not been even more scared by the fact that the one regular panellist was John Wakefield, former editor of the *Telegraph*.

It must have turned out alright, as I went on to join an afternoon panel show, *Beauty and the Beast*, with four women as the 'beauties' and Eric Baume as the 'beast'. People (mainly women) would write in with their problems which would then be discussed by the beauties, whose answers were loudly scorned by the beast. Well-known women, such as Maggie Tabberer, Pat Firman, Noeline Brown and Hazel Phillips were on the show.

Eric Baume was succeeded by Stuart Wagstaff, John Laws and Rex Mossop among others. The show, which began in 1963, was produced in Sydney but once a month would be filmed in Brisbane's Channel Seven studio on Mt Coot-tha. A couple of the Sydney 'beauties' would come up, and very worldly they seemed. The Brisbane panellists included the glamorous Karen Brady and Shirley Bushelle. I was the youngest panellist, newly married at the time and I also seemed to be permanently pregnant, which provided a good talking point, as most of the Sydney beauties were divorced. I actually went into early labour during a recording and Channel Seven's publicity department put out a release saying I had called the baby Eric, which caused some family hysteria. (He was actually Damien, and he didn't get a name for three weeks.)

All the while I continued studying externally at the University of Queensland. On the Brisbane *Telegraph* one of my cadetship subjects had been political science. I had absolutely no knowledge or understanding of politics and my parents and grandparents had always voted for Robert Menzies, who had been prime minister for almost my entire life. It was some sort of omen that political science was the subject I found most fascinating, although I never would have guessed what a big part it would play in my future.

THE SWINGING SIXTIES

THE SO-CALLED SWINGING sixties was an era all of its own. It was the time of the Beatles, fashion icon Mary Quant, of John F. Kennedy in the White House, Neil Armstrong on the moon and Sean Connery in the first Bond film. The Beatles did come to Brisbane and Sean Connery married our own Diane Cilento, but apart from that Brisbane wasn't really swinging.

In our world sex before marriage was taboo; the risks enormous, the consequences great. My mother used to say she'd rather have a daughter in jail for murder than one who came home pregnant, which was a strong deterrent. Girls who 'fell' were an embarrassment to their families. There were shotgun weddings and large babies born 'prematurely', some after only seven months! Various churches set up homes for unmarried mothers, presumably those whose families had thrown them out. There was one at Toowong, not far from the university.

It's difficult for young people today to comprehend all this. They find it impossible to believe that we were virgins at our weddings, for instance. A year or so ago, in a speech at a Catholic girls' college, I said we went up the aisle as virgins and came down the aisle pregnant, a reference to the pressure on young Catholic wives to be 'in the family way' as soon as possible. There were giggles all round.

The contraceptive pill has been the single greatest agent for change in the lives of women of my generation. The pill removed the fear of pregnancy from new marriages. It meant that young couples could choose the timing of their families without the complications of clumsy contraception, which was often not properly understood. It gave educated young women a chance to use that education and for the first time to take control of their lives.

Brisbane was still a bastion of Australian conservatism and we were quite proud to regard ourselves as 'a big country town'. The only whiff of rebellion was against the Vietnam War, which Australia entered in 1962, with protest marches through the city. Fresh from the University of Queensland, I was against the war although I didn't even consider joining the protest rallies. For one thing, I could see that marching was not going to influence the government in any way.

Growing up, I had never expected to have a career, having always assumed I would marry a nice man, have nice children and settle down to a nice life. If I had done only that I wouldn't have had a career at all. Career opportunities were limited then anyway – most people thought that for a woman a job was only what you did before you got married. I had wanted to be a teacher, but in my last year at school I was a prefect and found no one respected my authority at all, so I didn't think I was cut out for it. I was lucky that I fell into journalism.

I think we all model ourselves, even subconsciously, on our parents and their marriages, editing them to decide what we like and what we don't, and what we want for ourselves. I always had a feeling that my mother was unhappy or disappointed about the way her life had turned out and that she somehow felt that my father was the cause. And he, after the experience of his first failed marriage, wanted to do what he could for her, and he knew that whatever he did was not enough. I knew I wanted to marry a man who was strong and successful.

Like many of my friends, I married at 21, which seems absurdly young today but didn't then; three others in my high school class married that same year. I first met Leigh Atkinson conventionally, at a party for his sister Elizabeth at their family home in East Brisbane. Elizabeth had been a friend from school holidays at Surfers Paradise where the Atkinsons had a holiday house. She and I had met through a mutual boyfriend who had crossed the great Catholic–Protestant divide. I hadn't known she had an older brother. Leigh, a medical student, was good-looking in a Clark Gable sort of way, and I found his older-brother bossiness attractive and masterful.

We met again about a year later at a friend's twenty-first birthday dance at 29 Murray Street, Brisbane's leading venue for dances and weddings, after which a group of us went back to the National Hotel, whose manager Max Roberts was married to another friend. I mention the National because it later became notorious for all kinds of goings-on including prostitution, but we young innocents knew none of that. I remember gaily climbing up the fire escape to the bedrooms above, which must have led to all kinds of unfulfilled expectations.

Leigh and I were interested in each other, but I already had a boyfriend and he probably had a girlfriend. It wasn't until the next year, when my romance had ended, that we started going out. I actually made the first move by asking him to the Physio

Ball in a group with my two flatmates who were physiotherapy students. He then asked me to the Med Ball with a pre-ball party at his parents' house, and then to dinner, and we soon became an item.

Our first real date was a trip with a group of friends to the beach at Surfers Paradise. We dropped in to visit my parents on the way through Southport. Some days later my mother had a letter from Leigh congratulating her on the good behaviour of her children, which he attributed to their upbringing. She was pleased and surprised, at the letter though not the compliment. Leigh was always a stickler for good manners. One of the things I found most attractive about him was his genuine interest in art and theatre, so very different from other medical students, and in fact from most of the boys I knew.

The pathway to our marriage was not straightforward. I almost missed his proposal. We were sitting late one night in Leigh's car outside my flat, talking about my going to Sydney to work on the *Daily Telegraph* when he said, 'You'll have to have the phone on your side of the bed.' It took me a few minutes to register what he meant. When I went inside I said to the girls, 'I think Leigh has just proposed to me!' (The bit about the phone was not really an accurate prediction for our married life. I'm such a heavy sleeper that if I had had it on my side of the bed I probably wouldn't have heard it. And in fact, when Leigh took a call from the hospital, got up, got dressed and drove off into the night, I often didn't even wake up.)

Back in 1962 I duly went to Sydney as planned. Leigh and I wrote to each other, and I missed him. I confided my news to my grandparents. Religion could be a problem, and ours was to be what was called a mixed marriage – he was Catholic, I was Anglican. My grandfather, who was a committed Mason, nonetheless urged me to consider adopting the Catholic faith. He would drive me to Coogee to have instruction with two priests of the Sacred Heart order that ran Downlands College in Toowoomba where Leigh had gone to school. Fathers Dixon and Dando were very impressive men, with intellectually challenging and stimulating views that they did not impose on me. And Leigh never asked that I should convert to Catholicism. I later continued the discussions with Father Guest at the order's parish in Camp Hill, Brisbane.

Becoming a Catholic was not a major problem for me. Our family were 'High Church' Anglicans in Sydney, where the Church was polarised between 'High' and 'Low'. In Queensland the Church of England was more akin to the Catholic Church than to the other Protestant denominations, which people assumed was partly because of the great friendship between the Catholic archbishop James Duhig and Reginald Halse, who unusually for an Anglican bishop was a bachelor.

We got engaged on 12 December 1963, which happened to be Leigh's birthday, and I went off to work as usual at the *Courier-Mail*. One of my daily assignments then was to go to the Mater Children's Hospital, photographer in tow, to write a story on a sad but attractive small child for the Children's Hospital Christmas Appeal. As we walked up to the front door of the hospital we saw, ranged on the steps, a large gathering of white-robed nuns. 'What's going on?' muttered the photographer.

Sister Mary St Gabriel, tall, elegant and imposing, stepped forward. 'We wanted to get a look at you, dear,' she said to me. 'We want to know how you got him. We like to reserve our doctors for our nurses.'

Our wedding on 1 May the following year was fraught with the usual tensions. Mum, Dad and my sisters had come up from

Southport to stay at the Camp Hill Hotel, more a drinkers' pub than a place to stay but close to the church. Louella hogged the bathroom as we were getting dressed and four-year-old Kim tore the flowers out of her hair. The ceremony took place on the Friday night of the May Day long weekend and the bar was full of drinkers who cheered us as we left. Halfway down the aisle my veil caught on one of the sprigs of ivy decorating the pews and I stopped; Dad thought I had changed my mind. Despite this, the service was wonderful, a most beautiful Gregorian mass sung by Brisbane's Polish choir, and even Leigh trying to push my wedding ring onto the wrong finger didn't mar it.

The reception was at Wanganui Gardens on the banks of the Brisbane River, now knocked down and rebuilt as a private house by Olympians Mark and Tracy Stockwell. There was lots of tension during the evening. I had asked my bridesmaids not to smoke but they did. One of them was flirting with the master of ceremonies, to which her boyfriend objected. The MC, a doctor friend of Leigh's, said he'd take the boyfriend outside and fight him, which I told him was not a good idea as the boyfriend was a state boxing champion. Another friend's fiancé was threatening to drown himself in the river because she was flirting with someone else, and yet another friend kept asking why she wasn't seated next to the man she liked. She didn't know he had asked not to sit next to her. Then there was the question of religion. The priest who had married us made a speech in which he spoke of Catholics and non-Catholics, which upset my mother. It was a Friday night and the Catholics had been given special dispensation to eat meat, which caused a bit of a stir.

It might sound as though the wedding was a disaster, but it wasn't – the tensions were the bases for jokes later. But I do remember being glad when the time came for me to change as convention dictated into my going-away outfit, a Jackie Kennedy–style ensemble of hat and coat in cream silk. We were only going a mere few kilometres away – as far as the Sunnybank Hotel.

Leigh and I went to Noumea for the first week of our honeymoon and then did a tour of the Snowy Mountains project in a car convoy. We spent a few days in Canberra where the artificial Lake Burley Griffin had only recently been filled. We had trouble getting accommodation in Canberra and one of my journalist mates found us a bed in the Hotel Kurrajong, a single one. Not long after we came home I started feeling sick in the afternoon. To my surprise (because Mum had seemed to make deliberate decisions about this) I found I was pregnant, thus fulfilling the prophecy of the *Courier-Mail* editor Ted Bray who had said when I got engaged, 'Well, you'll be pregnant soon.' Getting pregnant was what every young Catholic wife was supposed to do, and I've always credited the single bed in the Hotel Kurrajong.

I had gone back to work straight after the honeymoon, much to the chagrin of my new mother-in-law who said, 'People will think Leigh can't afford to keep you.' This was a typical attitude of the time. Her son was more supportive of my working, saying very sensibly, 'I don't want you saying when you are 40 that you never had the chance of a career.' But I was not to last long. Within a few months I was told it was time to leave. A photographer had complained of embarrassment at going out on assignment with a pregnant woman.

It was an experience repeated eight years later at the start of my fledgling career on the ABC's *This Day Tonight*. As the Queensland edition's first female reporter I was given 'appropriate' stories like the quality of knitting wool and the difficulties of adoption, and not many of those either. The producer, Derek White, told me they'd never had a pregnant reporter on the ABC. I remonstrated that at least half their viewers would know that babies didn't come from under cabbage bushes. Derek said, 'But it's your fifth! Who knows where it will all end?' So, despite the sympathy of colleagues Kerry O'Brien, Andrew Olle and Des Power, I had the unique distinction of being sacked from the ABC for being pregnant.

But back in 1965 I was quite happy to leave the *Courier-Mail* and throw myself into being a young wife and mother. With other young mothers, actual and potential, I gave dinner parties and went to morning and afternoon teas. The dinners were a bit of a strain, for those were the days when everybody expected the meal to include entrée, main and dessert, all using our wedding-present cutlery and crockery. I had never cooked, and spent days poring over recipe books and asking advice. Some days, a group of young mums would play tennis at Fancutts Tennis Academy at Lutwyche which then had a swimming pool as well, and we would all take turns watching our babies.

I have often wondered if the circumstances of birth have any effect on the way a child's nature is formed. Not the birth itself, because labour seemed remarkably similar each time, but the circumstances surrounding it. Nicola's birth was very much that of the First Child. Though I'd been having labour pains all morning, I didn't want to miss lunch at the Shingle Inn with Leigh's mother and grandmother, so I went into town, all dressed up – those were the days when being married meant you always wore a hat and gloves to town. I must have been clutching the table in pain because Mrs Atkinson said, 'You're in labour,' and whisked me out the door, into a taxi, and up to the doctor at Wickham Terrace. Then it was straight over to the

Mater Mothers' with Leigh's mother shrieking at the taxi driver, 'If this girl gives birth in this cab it'll be your fault,' and the poor man breaking the speed limit all the way. We swept into the Mater, me still dressed up for lunch in the city.

It turned out to be a busy and social afternoon because Leigh's father, his sister and her fiancé, and Leigh himself, were all on the staff of the Mater and people kept popping into the labour ward. One of the old nuns, seeing me doing breathing exercises from my book on natural childbirth said, 'What nonsense is this?' which was hardly helpful. As the pains got worse, I thought, 'Well, Mum said labour was unbearable and this isn't yet.' After six hours Nicola was born, to much cheering from the assembled multitude. The cheering would continue, at least metaphorically, as she got her first tooth, took her first steps, went to school, became school captain, and went off to university.

Damien, on the other hand, was born in the early hours of the morning and until almost the last moment I had only one of the elderly nuns sitting by the bedside with a beer and a cigarette, while Leigh and the doctor were having coffee down the corridor. I'm not sure whether the beer and cigarette were fantasies of my condition but they are a clear memory. The days leading up to the birth were eventful. I had recorded an episode of *Beauty and the Beast* on Saturday and felt I was in early labour, but had gone to a party that night with my hospital bag in the car, as well as 13-month-old Nicola in her carry basket. After a couple of gins at the party the contractions stopped. The next afternoon during mass my waters broke and I sat in my pew in a puddle. We had a Sunday night ritual where we went to Leigh's parents' house to watch *Rawhide* because we didn't have a television set, and when it was over at 10 pm Leigh stood up and said, 'We're off to the Mater now.'

Eloise had the most peaceful birth, in Edinburgh where we had no relations at all. As I had become pregnant quickly after Damien, I wasn't sure of her actual due date. We did a quick trip around Scotland after Leigh's exams, and then my Scottish doctor decided the time was right and she was induced. After the induction procedure I heard him giving the nurse his program for the day, which seemed to have every hour accounted for. I asked, 'When would it suit you for me to have this baby?' and he said, 'About 7.30 tonight.' And that's when she came, with Leigh and the doctor chatting about hospital statistics and me saying, 'Excuse me, I'm giving birth here!'

Genevieve and Stephanie were both born at the Mater Mothers' Hospital in Brisbane, and both were reluctant to come out and had to be medically induced. Genevieve was born three years after Eloise and the family joke was that I had learned by then what caused babies. After the induction it took all day for labour to start, and then it moved fairly quickly. I was actually in the labour ward, saying I was ready to push and the sister said, 'You're not far enough dilated.' I said, 'This is my fourth baby.' There were shrieks all round: 'Nobody told us that!' As though it was my fault. It was a chaotic beginning.

Stephanie was born three years after that. She took even longer after the induction procedure, and in the middle of the night I was alone in the labour ward with a very young nurse saying, 'I haven't delivered a baby. I won't know what to do!' To which I was able to reply, 'Well, I do.'

By about 2 am the doctor, having arrived, was impatient. But we had talked of this being the last baby, and I really wanted Leigh there, so they had to keep ringing him up. He didn't quite make it.

But I'm getting ahead of myself. Leigh and I had both been

the first babies born to nervous mothers – one of them, either Leigh's or mine, used to boil our orange juice to kill the germs and with it the vitamin C – and with our first child we were determined to be sensible. When it was time to come home from the hospital with Nicola, Leigh picked me up and took me to his mother's where we had some lunch before he went back to the hospital saying, 'I've got my squash game tonight, I'll be home after it.' Mrs Atkinson dropped me at the flat and not wanting to interfere didn't come in. There was no food in the flat, so I had to ask the woman next door if she would watch the baby while I ran down to the butcher's. When Leigh came home he brought his squash partner for dinner, an embarrassed chap who later became a psychiatrist and often told this story. But I was lucky in one sense. Having had babies at home when I was growing up meant I was never fearful with my own.

New Farm was home to a strong Italian community so when I took Nicola to the baby clinic we were among the young Italian mothers with their babies in layers of frilly lace. In the February heat I took Nicola in a singlet and nappy. My embarrassment was reduced by the doctor saying, 'Very sensible mother', but perhaps he just felt sorry for me.

There was an extra layer of tension in those days for young Catholic women, as I now was, and that was birth control. Contraception was a mortal sin, so while our Protestant friends were happily on the pill, I was not. I got the gold star for Catholic womanhood when I became pregnant with Damien four months after Nicola was born, thus busting the myth about breastfeeding being a natural contraceptive. But life was also difficult for the young women who couldn't get pregnant, not because they were practising contraception but because it simply didn't happen. And this did cause distress and feelings of failure.

Young Catholic wives were allowed to take the pill to regularise our periods, so that we could practise the rhythm method, a bit of mental manipulation on the part of the church. The rhythm method involved calculating those days when ovulation was likely and avoiding sex then. The calculation involved temperature-taking and note-making and a lot of tension. A friend confided to me that she stayed up late ironing on those days to avoid difficulties in the bedroom.

For the first few years of our married life I was always pregnant and Leigh was working long hours, often sleeping in the hospital, and studying for the degree that would qualify him as a surgeon. I was actually studying too, to finish my Arts degree, though not with the same amount of dedication. I now think that one of the problems for our marriage later was that we didn't have the chance to get to know each other as friends. We were married young, and Leigh went straight from his parents' home to married life. As one of a family of girls, the only male underpants I had ever seen were my father's on the clothesline.

THE SCOTTISH 'BEAN CLUB'

WE ALL HAVE turning points in our lives, and some of us have several. They're not necessarily the most important events, but they change you – or at least part of you – from being one person to being another. I guess my first was my sister's birth, the next realising that with Dad losing his job our circumstances were changed. The death of my baby brother Charles meant leaving one stage of my childhood behind.

But going to live in Scotland with small children and no family support marked the first time I had real responsibility for other human beings on my own. Twelve thousand kilometres away from my mother, I was free to question her rules and opinions and make decisions based on what I thought and I knew. It was not an easy few years, but I was exhilarated by the challenge. I discovered I could cope very well, and found a sense of purpose in helping Leigh study for his degree. And no matter how cold and uncomfortable it got, I knew we would eventually be returning home to the warmth and comfort of Brisbane.

We went to Scotland as part of Leigh's career plan, common to all young would-be medical specialists of the time. We were still living in the era when everything from overseas was considered better than at home, so young surgeons and physicians went to Edinburgh or London for their specialised training.

The Royal College of Surgeons of Edinburgh had been established in 1505 as one of the first such institutions in the world. It had produced such famous alumni as Joseph Lister, the father of antiseptic surgery. In our day, young medical hopefuls came from all over the world and it was a real melting pot of Asians, Africans, Australians and Canadians. Perhaps even more important than the fellowships they gained were the friendships they would not otherwise have made, from all over the English-speaking world. Edinburgh was also a very beautiful and cultured city, with its gracious and elegant New Town architecture and the annual Edinburgh Festival, which included everything from opera and ballet to country dancing in the gardens of Princes Street.

We arrived in Scotland in time for New Year's Eve 1966 and went to a hotel on the edge of the Bruntsfield Links close to the city centre. The hotel was a large and daunting pile and the weather was typically cold and grey. Daylight hours are short during an Edinburgh winter. My early memories are of being colder than I had ever been before in my life and the smell of wet disposable nappies. The nappies were thick pads impossible to dispose of. I had bought them for the flight over, which turned out to be an adventure in itself, though not in a good way.

At nine months Damien was a wriggling crawler and was filthy by the time we got on the plane after a two-hour stopover in Sydney. We had given both children some medicine to knock them out for the trip, but had obviously miscalculated the dose and given them too much, and they were both hyperactive.

The bassinet for Damien was not fixed to the front but swung hammock-like overhead so all the other passengers were treated to legs and arms waving and then the baby falling out. At one stage I asked the hostess to heat a bottle for me and she took it between her manicured fingertips as though it was contaminated.

We had never travelled with children before and during our three years in Edinburgh and holidays in Europe we never did again, with the exception of a driving trip to Ireland to see Dad's relatives. In those days nobody travelled for pleasure with small children; ours were looked after by friends, and we in turn minded their children when needed.

Our first priority in Edinburgh was to find somewhere to live. We were living on our savings and as many medical students took several attempts to pass the fellowship exams we had no idea how long we would be staying. (Luckily, Leigh cleverly passed the first time he sat, literally a few weeks before Eloise was born.) So I set off by bus while Leigh stayed in the hotel with the kids, and I found a flat that I thought we could afford in Pitt Street, Leith. Leith is now a very upmarket part of Edinburgh, but it wasn't then. Our first-floor flat in a grey stone tenement was one of the few that had a bath. For Alice, a 10-year-old girl who lived down the street, a special treat was being allowed to have a bath with our kids. I have no idea what her mother thought, but they were a relaxed lot in Pitt Street where the babies were put out in their prams in the street early in the mornings to watch the passing parade, and mothers came and went for a gossip and a chat. The flat was above a grocery shop which gave me my first taste of the convenience of inner-city living.

I had come from Australia pregnant with Eloise and with medical benefits so I was referred to a private consultant in Edinburgh. Dr Loudon had rooms in an elegant house in one of the very elegant streets in the New Town. The consultation was more like a conversation and I don't remember anything as crass as being weighed. I do remember him asking me if I would mind going to the Eastern General for the birth. I had no idea why I should mind but later discovered it was considered quite rough, and not like the Simpson or the Western General, but he was trying to make it more popular. It turned out to be fine. I had a private room and other women would wander in, assuming I was lonely. Of course with little ones at home it was blissful to be alone. I could almost relate to the Brisbane friend with eleven children who told me, 'It's so wonderful going to the Mater Mothers' every year for a holiday!'

Eloise was born at 7.30 one night and we gave her the middle name Margaret after the patron saint of Scotland and my mother's second name. The next morning a nurse came in with the baby and a bottle. I said, 'You can take that bottle away. I'll be breastfeeding her.' The nurse almost dropped the baby and five minutes later came back with the matron who said, 'What's this I hear? You're feeding her yourself?' followed soon after by Dr Loudon, 'What's this nonsense?'

I realised it was easier for the hospital to manage rows of mothers in the nursery with bottles, but I stuck to my guns. At the Mater Mothers in Brisbane, breastfeeding was almost obligatory. For days afterwards, young nurses would arrive in my room to study the phenomenon of a mother breastfeeding, one who actually knew what she was doing.

In his early days of study Leigh had one half-day off from the university and while he was looking after the children during their afternoon nap I would wander around Edinburgh and soak up its grey architecture and bloody history. In the evenings while he was studying and the kids were asleep I went out to the theatre, the opera and ballet and my cultural spirit really blossomed. One of my great finds was a small theatre in Leith that showed live plays. It was next door to a laundromat so I would pop my washing in the machine before the curtain went up and collect it at interval.

Life in Pitt Street, Leith, was like nothing I'd ever experienced. Much of it was lived in the street. Ten-year-old Alice was fascinated by Damien. I wrote home:

> I don't know where she comes from but she appears about every second afternoon to take Damien for a walk, which is very nice for me. The kids here seem to just wander around. The street is full of three and four year olds all day long, plus big lorries, and at the first ray of sunshine every house has a pram in front of it. Gladys next door leaves her 18-month-old in his pram on the other side of the street all day long so he can watch the children play. I've taken my children out and he's yelling, and come back an hour later and he's still yelling.
>
> Last night I took Nicola to the doctor at six, and told Alice she could walk with us to the bus stop, and the next thing she's on the bus too. I was frantic about her mother worrying but she assured me she never did and when Alice came round today she said her mother hadn't even noticed. I was really frightened Alice would be stopped coming as folding nappies is her greatest treat!

Gladys next door filled me in on the rules and customs of the street. One of the unwritten rules was that in each tenement building the residents took turns to wash the stone staircase between floors. Gladys told me when my turn was and I got out there on my hands and knees with a bucket of soapy water and a scrubbing brush. When I finally finished they told me it wasn't good enough. In a rare show of courage I emptied the bucket and flung it away with the brush, and that was the end of my community service in Pitt Street.

Leigh passed his primary exams and joined the Department of Surgical Neurology at the Western General, so we felt we could move up from Pitt Street. Through the university accommodation section we found a detached bungalow at Craiglockhart, on the way to the airport and not far from the zoo. The owner was a lady minister in the Free Church of Scotland (the Wee Frees) who showered us with kindness and baby clothes. But this bliss was not to last. When the local priest came to visit we were told that this was the first time a Roman Catholic priest had been seen in our street. I'd never experienced that kind of bigotry before. The house had a lovely garden tended by the landlady's father, who didn't seem to mind Catholics, the children could run around in it and we bought a little mini-van.

It was a happy summer but as winter approached we were told our lease would not be renewed, and we were on the move again. Unfortunately the minister asked for her baby clothes to be returned, which was indeed unfortunate because they were by no means in the same condition they had been when she lent them. We moved to Colinton, not far from where Robert Louis Stevenson grew up and wrote his verse, this time a two-storey detached house, and there we stayed for two years.

At first our social life took place at the houses of various professors ('… *we were the only people under 40*', I wrote home) and the parties were of the sherry-five-to-seven variety. And that's exactly what they meant. Used as I was to the Atkinsons' cocktail parties which would go on into the night with lots to eat and drink, when the first such invitation came I hired a babysitter and had the better of my two maternity frocks dry-cleaned in expectation of a proper night out. At the professorial home, a grand stone affair, there was only sherry and not even a peanut in sight. At the stroke of seven, I happened to be standing next to the professor who turned to me and said, 'So good of you to come,' and out we went into the Edinburgh night. But once we settled and had been there a year or two, we had a busy social life and I was writing home, *'I've just counted up and in the last fortnight we've been out nine nights and I've been out eight times during the day.'*

In suburban Colinton we had joined a 'bean club' for baby-sitters. No money changed hands, but every member was given five beans and when you needed a babysitter you rang around and paid the sitter with a bean. I think the fee was two beans after midnight but as we were all young mums we were rarely out late. The host member always left supper for the sitter and I came to appreciate those who gave you really good ones. As all the families in the club were young and usually away from their own families, we also had dinner parties at each other's houses. When we went to Ireland for a week Anna Taylor, a great New Zealand friend, took in eight-month-old Eloise, who sat up by herself for the first time in Anna's house.

I think it's difficult for Australian mothers, given our climate, to understand what it's like to be confined indoors during a British winter. I had the wooden playpen set up in our small living room and sometimes to get time to myself I would put myself inside it with a book and let the children roam happily through the house. It was in Edinburgh that I felt the first stirrings of resentment as I struggled through Scottish winters warming a house, cooking, cleaning and caring for small children with a husband who often had to be absent and living in the hospital. I started to think, for the first time, that it was unfair that men got to have a family at the same time as a chosen career but that for women it seemed to be either/or. Growing up in an all-girls' school, I had never felt disadvantaged being female. Oh, there were things that boys did, like playing football, and that girls did, like having babies, but these were delightfully hormonal differences.

Many women, and I envy them greatly, get enormous satisfaction from housework and cooking. I did enjoy making cakes and scones, and I did knit jumpers and make clothes on the old sewing machine in the house and felt a real sense of achievement from this, but the novelty wore off. Later I was to realise it made more sense for me to do what I was competent at and let someone else do what I was not. This was a good lesson for management.

In Edinburgh I continued to write as a freelance journalist for British and Australian publications. Being able to work was very important to me – it was a necessary contribution to my self-worth. It was also a chance to have an income of my own, however small, as we didn't have a joint bank account even in Brisbane. The income paid for the babysitters. And it was a chance to get out and meet people, to understand Edinburgh.

I wrote on subjects as varied as British prams (for the *Courier-Mail*) medical developments in Scotland for the London-based *Medical News-Tribune*, and the Australian Immigration Office. I also interviewed Maggie Smith on the set of *The Prime of Miss Jean Brodie* for the *Women's Weekly*. Daytime babysitters were sometimes a problem and I remember interviewing a bemused car dealer in his showroom for the Edinburgh *Tatler* magazine with the three children playing under my feet, and his. I did most of my work for the *Tatler* and the car dealer provided just one of many advertorials, paid advertisements disguised as stories.

I didn't have much respect for the *Tatler's* journalistic quality but it had surprising social cachet and got me into interesting places. The best was a week-long trip to Germany to cover fashion. For a young mother with three small children it was an offer too good to refuse, professional considerations aside. I can't even remember who moved in to mind the family; I think a nurse from the hospital or Leigh's sister Edwina who was living in London. I went to Berlin, Frankfurt, Munich, and through the Black Forest to Düsseldorf, attending the Igedo fashion fair. I was wonderfully looked after and wrote a story that filled five pages of the magazine when I got back.

Once, in some mad flight of fancy, I caught the train to Glasgow to audition for a newsreader job with the BBC. They later told me I hadn't got the job because I didn't have a west of Scotland accent, this being the days before ethnic diversity. How I ever thought I was going to do it I can't imagine, it can only have been the temptation of a day out in Glasgow for the audition that compelled me to try.

Leigh and I travelled a lot and I made my first visit to Paris. I wrote to my sister Louella afterwards:

I can't believe that something I'd looked forward to so much could not only have lived up to expectations but exceeded them. Everything about it was beautiful ... the streets, the buildings, the atmosphere, the people.

Like my first sight of London, it was the shock of familiarity, of everything you've read about and seen in movies for years suddenly being real. This was also the summer of 1968 and student rebellion was at its height, which gave an added frisson of unfamiliarity to the Paris trip.

We went to Scandinavia, taking our little mini-van by ferry from Newcastle to Stavanger in Norway. The first night, in full moonlight, we slept in the back of the car in an apple orchard close to Hardangerfjord. Another night we parked on a deserted Swedish beach, flat countryside all around and rain pelting down with us snug in our sleeping bags. We went to Gothenburg and saw *Fiddler on the Roof* in Swedish, and to Copenhagen where we saw the Tivoli Gardens. Through the local tourist office we booked into a private house, our first experience of bed and breakfast accommodation.

All this I wrote home in my weekly letters, the familiar blue aerograms in the days long before email and the internet. Phoning home was expensive and complicated. You had to book a call and around Christmas it was especially difficult. I would always have my conversation planned beforehand so as not to waste any minutes. I once rang Mum for her birthday and she spent several expensive seconds being surprised. Most of the letters were about the children and their doings, about bringing two-year-old Nicola home from town in her first taxi, a huge black London cab, which she had loved so much that she refused to leave it, and the driver had to haul her out; about Damien at eighteen months having me bailed up in a corner with a toasting fork; about Eloise being such a great talker that a bus driver said, 'Och the wee blether, was she vaccinated with a gramophone needle?'

When you have small children you develop all sorts of coping mechanisms. One of mine was asking for help on public transport. I'd stand at the bus stop, baby on hip and one on either hand. When the bus came, I'd say to the person standing next to me, 'Would you mind lifting a child on?' Stunned or bemused they may have been, but they always did. There were no thoughts of stranger danger then.

NO JOB FOR A WOMAN

By the end of 1969, our three years were up and we made plans to come home. Leigh did a quick trip to the US in December while I packed up the house. In the New Year we sailed from Southampton on the *Angelina Lauro*. I had wanted to come back by ship because I thought it would be an adventure, which it was, though not quite what I'd thought. I wanted to relive my childhood sailing adventures, as well as having the migrant experience of coming to Australia, and I thought it might be my last sea voyage for some time.

The *Angelina Lauro* was an Italian ship with a lot of 'ten pound Pom' British migrants. It called at Naples and then Genoa to pick up Italian migrants, and somewhere along the way Yugoslavs, who were Serbs and Croats. As the voyage got underway, they all fell into their national stereotypes. The Poms whinged, the Italians flirted, the Yugoslavs fought each other. There were always a couple of Yugoslavs in the ship's brig or jail and a few irate husbands complaining about the Italians. We had a couple of Yorkshire miners on our table who complained about the food, the wine which was free and the service which was given by waiters who spoke little English. The irony was that while they were having an almost free passage, our family was paying full fare and we were loving the pasta and free wine.

Somewhere between Naples and Genoa the ship hit a rock, was attacked by a Russian sub or sprang a leak – all rumours – and we limped into port at Genoa. There we sat for a day while chaos ensued and nobody seemed to have any idea what was going on. The water was turned off so there were no toilet facilities and no drinking water for the hundreds of families on board. We mothers just sat in the lounge areas of the ship, our children around us, looking for all the world like wartime refugees. Leigh demanded to be taken to the captain and came back to report that he was a quivering mess. Leigh had told him he should stick to making ice cream, a fine piece of nationalist insult that Leigh could get away with because he was a quarter Italian. Then we were all told we were going to be disembarked and put up in hotels in Genoa while the ship was being repaired. So off we went in busloads, our family to a typical Italian hotel with terrazzo floors. I remember the floors very well because while Leigh and I were at dinner one of the children filled the bidet with water, which overflowed across the floor and down the stairs in a torrent almost to our feet.

A few days after our arrival the owner of the shipping line, Mr Lauro himself, sent a car for Leigh to come to meet with him. He had obviously been keen to get rid of him and offered us flights home, which Leigh refused. While I admired Leigh's principles, I was regretting the weeks of the sea journey ahead. My spirit of adventure was much dimmed. After a week in the luxury of our Genoese hotel and seeing the sights we once again set sail for home. For me the most interesting part of the voyage, via Tenerife and Cape Town, was going to the classes for migrants. Immigration department people would tell them honestly all about life in Australia, its difficulties as well as opportunities. But talking to people afterwards, I found they had only heard the good bits and still had expectations of a land of milk and honey. It was a great lesson – sometimes we really hear only what we want to hear.

THE JUGGLING ACT

WE ARRIVED BACK in Brisbane as a family in the heat of February 1970, with the *Angelina Lauro* steaming up the Brisbane River. Nicola and Eloise wore red cotton frocks with white Peter Pan collars that I had made myself, while I wore a navy blue dress, loose fitting to cover a bump, though I was only two months' pregnant with our fourth baby. Eloise was a British citizen and, though not yet three, had to go through a separate line in immigration, much to some general irritation. I had deliberately not registered her as Australian in case she became a good swimmer and could compete for Scotland. Back then, the Scots were not champions in the pool; they have become pretty good since. Eloise had to be properly naturalised in City Hall some years later so she could vote.

It had been arranged that we would go to East Brisbane, to the Atkinsons' old house until we found our own. This was the large Queenslander that Leigh had grown up in. While Leigh's father's busy general practice surgery was located underneath, the house itself was empty. The only furniture was the dining-room table and chairs. We bought beds but had no dressing tables or sofas, and it was total bliss. There were vast areas of carpeted floor for the children to roll around and play on, and no housework.

Leigh started work at the Mater, Nicola started school at St Benedict's around the corner, which had a kindergarten for Damien, and I began house hunting with Eloise in tow. I took myself to the Catholic Education Office in the city to quiz them about class sizes and teaching standards. They were shocked that someone should query the system. It was typical first child syndrome. By the time I got to the end of the line with Genevieve and Stephanie I was pretty much opening the car door when we got to school and saying, 'Out you hop.' To be fair to myself, I did know much more about schools by then.

I looked at houses every day and I'm not quite sure why it took so long to find one we liked. I think now that it may have been because although we had decided we would live on the south side of the river in order to be close to the hospital, I had a hankering for Toowong or St Lucia near the university. We were also keen on Highgate Hill and East Brisbane. Early in the piece I found a great house in East Brisbane, a two-storey brick house designed by the famous Queensland architect Robin Dods. Leigh didn't want a wooden house or an old house like the one he had grown up in – 'too much upkeep' – and brick houses were not as easy to find. The Robin Dods house was in the path of a proposed highway leading from a bridge across the Brisbane River. In hindsight, if we had bought that house and stayed there we would not have gone on to later live at Indooroopilly and I would not have run for Council. East Brisbane was strong Labor territory.

With the baby due in August, we finally settled on a simple house in Holland Park about six kilometres southeast of the

CBD. It was certainly not the house of my dreams but because it was a blank canvas it had potential, as well as four bedrooms. And it was brick.

Genevieve was born on 20 August, and we moved house a few weeks later. I settled into the role of house-proud house-wife in our first real home. There was all the excitement of furnishing it, and choosing curtains and bedspreads. I found an oval dining table in a second-hand shop and carefully 'antiqued' it grey, in eighteenth-century French style with matching bent-wood chairs. I had one wall of the entrance hall painted shiny charcoal grey with co-ordinating patterned wallpaper on the opposite wall, and can still remember my chagrin when we were selling the house some years later and I overheard a prospective buyer saying to her husband, 'Who would have ever thought of choosing this frightful colour?'

In those days, we were indeed housewives. There was no thought of popping down to the local cafe for a coffee and a chat. Morning teas at friends' houses were deliberate occasions with careful preparations. We had our domestic routines, which seemed to take a lot of time. I attended to a different room every day. Monday I thoroughly cleaned the bathroom, Tuesday the bedrooms, Wednesday the kitchen, and so on. Then there were elaborate preparations for the evening meal and preparations for the husband's homecoming – young wives were still being advised by the women's magazines to tie a ribbon in their hair and put on lipstick to greet their husbands at the door. When I wrote my first column for the *Australian* newspaper I complained that men were never advised to spruce themselves up to keep their women.

The Brisbane version of the *Australian* was a tabloid wrapped around the broadsheet national daily. My friend Hugh Lunn was the editor and Harry Davis, another ex-*Courier* reporter, was the sports editor. I wrote a weekly column based on my life as a housewife and mother, covering topics such as my children's attitude to the tooth fairy and the trials of taking my son to football.

While we were camping out at East Brisbane, I had been asked to do some freelance work at the *Sunday Mail*: more of 'the woman's angle'. I wrote about baking bread, a project that seems extraordinary in retrospect, and some semi-advertising pieces on childrenswear and beauty products. I also wrote a few serious articles, one on the problems for parents of children with spina bifida, another on the lives of single older women in the suburbs.

Life was busy through the early 1970s. Nicola and Damien were at two schools, the convent and the state school, and while I was on the Parents and Friends' Committee at the convent Leigh became president of the P&C at Mount Gravatt State School, where Damien was enrolled. Leigh had also set up a private practice on Wickham Terrace.

Looking back I seem to have been busier than I needed to be. But, as the priest said at the funeral of a friend who had killed himself, 'We are all the victims of our own chemistry.' I liked being busy and I liked the variety of doing different things. I helped various voluntary causes by giving speeches and compering fashion shows. My friend Julien Beirne had a public relations business and I sometimes helped her when she had more than she could cope with. I was still contributing to medical news journals, and I had commissions from a couple of magazines.

I also joined the Liberal Party, and so did Leigh. Once we had become involved, I did some public relations for the Party in various elections and became Queensland editor of the *Australian Liberal*, the party newspaper. 'Editor' was a rather glorified title. I was the only person there and the position was honorary. I simply gathered and wrote stories about Liberal politics in Queensland. We had editorial meetings in Sydney or Canberra, with the 'editors' from other states, presided over first by Peter Coleman, who had been editor of *The Bulletin* and of *Quadrant* and was to become NSW Opposition Leader, and then by Grahame Morris who would become John Howard's chief-of-staff and later work with me at Barton Deakin.

Flying interstate, even for a day, was very exciting for a mother with young children. But totally blissful was the rare overnighter. The first time we had a two-day conference we all stayed at the Boulevard Hotel in William Street, Sydney. The boys made plans to spend the evening at the Harold Park trots. I said I'd rather stay in and have room service. They came past my room on their way out to persuade me to join them, but I was already in my nightie, having had a bubble bath, and about to wait for my dinner in bed.

The ABC in Brisbane got me to do radio interviews for them, particularly in April or May when various government departments had to use up their budgets before the end of the financial year. Leigh was not totally supportive of my working outside the home, so I tended not to tell him what I was doing, and I didn't tell him about the ABC. One day, as he was driving from somewhere to somewhere, he heard me on the radio and I was sprung.

If the 1960s had been the first stage of liberation through the advent of the contraceptive pill, the 1970s was a time when women started to consider what they should do with this liberation. There was a lot of discussion about being able to make career choices and I knew of women leaving home and running away to 'find themselves'. I wrote a column about the danger of that – what if you didn't like what you'd found?

Women were starting to think about different ways of working, so that we could combine responsibilities at home with job commitments. In spite of my working on a miscellany of projects, employers had not yet grasped the idea of flexible working hours or job sharing. I was asked to be the TV reporter for a Sunday paper, which would have meant working full-time. I suggested sharing it with a friend, which would have worked well, but that was a concept ahead of its time.

One thing that coping with small children, a busy husband, a house and outside work does for you is make you organised. I'm not a naturally tidy or organised person. But I am adaptable and flexible, good at juggling where necessary and fitting things in. Nicola and Damien were at school, and Eloise in kindergarten. In the early 1970s we only had one car, which I could use on Leigh's operating day, so I arranged any driving to be done on a Thursday. On other days I would go by bus to pick up Eloise from kindergarten and be back to meet the others walking home from school. When Genevieve was a baby, I simply took her with me. A friend from my ABC days remembers all four children sitting on the floor, colouring in, while I edited a radio story in the Toowong studios.

Another important part of our life in the 1970s was the advent of Terri as our foster daughter. She came to live as part of our family in 1970 and was to give me some vital lessons, as well as lots of love. One of three little girls whose mother had been killed in a road accident in Victoria, she had been with her sisters in St Vincent's Orphanage at Nudgee since shortly after their father had brought them back to his home city of Brisbane. When Terri was 14 and living in a family care home at East Brisbane, one of the nuns in the Catholic social work department rang in November to ask whether I would like to have a young girl to help me over the Christmas holidays. With four small children to look after it was an offer too good to refuse.

Terri arrived, a typically sullen teenager who didn't much want to do anything. But I was used to that, from school and home, and with so much to be done and Christmas looming there was no time for moods.

I was to discover that in just half an hour Terri could do what would take me a couple of hours and I was full of admiration and gratitude. When the holidays were ending the nuns told me that every previous family with whom Terri had spent Christmas had sent her back, and asked whether we would like to keep her. By this time of course we were all very fond of her, and she slotted into the family in the role of big sister, much as I had done in my own family.

The lessons I learned from her were manifold: that we are not all good at everything and she was much better at cleaning and cooking than I was; that to be praised and appreciated is a hugely important incentive; and that talking openly about issues is a major step in solving them. When I asked her why those families had sent her back for being difficult, she told me they had all talked sanctimoniously about 'having an orphan for Christmas' and it made her feel dreadful. Without meaning to, she showed me that because I was not very good at being domestic it seemed simple economics for me to work outside the home and have someone else working in it. So Terri stayed with us and finished her high school education, coming home from school to help me in the afternoons, much as I had done with my own mother. And then she went off to college and became a secretary.

When she married some years later, Leigh gave her away, Nicola was her bridesmaid and we had the wedding reception at our place at Indooroopilly. Now Terri and her husband, Ray, live in Melbourne with their two sons, one of whom is father to two little boys. The boys have called me Grandma Sallyanne and I guess the little ones will call me Great.

In 1973 I found I was pregnant again and we had to start thinking about a bigger house. It was a question of extending at Holland Park or moving. I had not stopped yearning for the western suburbs and I was also keen to build. We had several friends who were architects and the idea of choosing one was difficult, but Leigh had a patient who was a manager with a firm of project builders, which seemed a good compromise.

We built our house in Castile Street, Indooroopilly, between the Indooroopilly and St Lucia golf courses, and it was to be the family home for the next 15 years. It also provided the impetus for my political career. A Council drainpipe at the top of the street kept bursting and as ours was the first house in the street we suffered most from the flooding. Neighbours nominated me as the person to nag the Council, and I was certainly the most affected. When the pipe was finally replaced, after a relentless campaign, I felt great triumph and a real understanding of how local government worked.

My other motivation for a career in city government was a book about Brisbane I wrote in 1972. It was something I had thought about ever since our return from Edinburgh. The Scots were masters of national promotion and there were dozens of books about what to see and do in Edinburgh and all over Scotland. But when we had visitors to Brisbane, and there were lots, there was no literature to give them.

In 1972 Leigh went on a three-month Rotary group study trip to Pennsylvania in the US and this seemed an ideal project to undertake while he was away. I would be on my own with the children for those months, with no evening meal to cook for a husband and a car for my sole use.

With the children in tow, I set about exploring the city, its sights and restaurants. I included Toowoomba and the Gold and Sunshine coasts. The book, *Around Brisbane*, would not be published until 1978, and then by the University of Queensland Press, its original publisher having suffered in the floods of 1974. I mentioned a few hundred restaurants, many of them long since closed, and now there are thousands in Brisbane. In the introduction I wrote:

> *The essential Brisbane is still a city whose people have a relaxed and casual attitude to life and pride themselves on not having been caught up in the ratrace of their southern neighbours. But Brisbane is now a young-adult sort of city newly grown up. The city skyline has soared upwards and our citizens have acquired the confidence of coming of age.*

Getting to know my city so well led me on the path to promoting it and looking after it. I also found that Brisbane people, though feeling affection for their city, had no pride in it. I asked a taxi driver to show me the sights of Brisbane and he said, 'Ah, there's nothing much to see here, lady.' I wanted to change all that.

That time on my own, independent with my own car, managing my life, the four children, the house and running a project, changed me. I found new confidence in what I was able to do and knew I could do.

AN ACCIDENTAL POLITICIAN

I WISH I could say that my political life began with a grand and noble cause. It actually began in a laundromat in Edinburgh. We didn't have a washing machine in our flat in Pitt Street, Leith, so I would take the clothes to the local laundromat, sometimes going by bus at night when the children were asleep and Leigh was studying.

One evening the woman at the next machine asked me, 'Are you interested in politics?' Vaguely, I said yes, because it was after all one of those obvious questions. And she said, 'Because I'm a member of a Conservative Party Young Mothers' Group and we meet once a month with a guest speaker, and babysitters for the kids.'

Babysitters! I didn't need any more convincing, and off I went to a church hall along Ferry Road, two small children in tow. While the children played games I listened earnestly to speakers whose messages I have long forgotten. I became friendly with Jane Duff (who is still a friend) whose lawyer husband Ronald was a Conservative member of the Edinburgh City Council.

I helped them campaign, and that was really where my engagement in politics began.

When Leigh and I returned to Brisbane we decided to get politically involved. It was not an automatic choice to join the Liberal Party, and we gave it thought. The Liberal government had been in power for as long as I could remember and my parents never thought about voting for anyone but Sir Robert Menzies, who had been in power before they were married and – with some interruption – was still in power when my third child was born. I used to boast that I got three votes when I turned 21: mine and those of my parents, who would do what I recommended because I had studied political science at university. Leigh's parents had close friends who were actively involved in the QLP – that breakaway group from the Labor Party in Queensland – and his mother was later an active member of the Liberal Party's women's committee.

It was an interesting time in Australian politics because young Australians were starting to question politicians in a way that had not happened before. The Vietnam War had polarised Australia's youth, and Gough Whitlam was an inspiring Labor leader. But in the end, for me at least, it was the hold the trade unions had over the Labor Party that was a giant turn-off. The more I thought about Liberal philosophy the more I felt it was the right one. I have always believed, in the bringing up of my children and in all the organisations I've been involved with, that the best way to support people is to help them to be self-reliant and independent. At the same time, it's important to recognise that there are people who will always need the help of others and to them any civil society has a duty. I find phrases like 'social justice and equity' quite meaningless platitudes without thought for individuals.

After joining the Central Branch of the Liberal Party, Leigh quickly became branch president. He also became chairman of the Party's health committee and I was on the education and arts committees. We threw ourselves into every campaign for state and federal candidates in the Central Brisbane area, which was strong Labor territory. Our greatest triumph was the state election of 1974 when the conservative parties, Liberal and National, won all but 11 seats and our man Harold Lowes won the Labor-held seat of Brisbane. It came as quite a shock to poor Harold, a solicitor, who proceeded to run his electorate out of his legal office in Brisbane's T&G building. Sarina Russo, who later started one of the country's most successful training and employment companies, was his secretary. Harold rang me up one day soon after the election and said, 'Sallyanne, they tell me I have to go to school P and C meetings!'

I said, 'Yes, Harold, you're the state member now.'

My first involvement in professional politics came about, like so much else in my life, by accident. In 1975, the Liberal Party health committee had an important motion coming before the state Council in Townsville. Leigh couldn't go because he was on call, and sent me up instead. I must have been supposed to lobby delegates. The Party leader, Gordon Chalk, invited me to a small lunch, and I sat next to Jim Killen.

Killen, later Sir James, the federal member for Moreton, knew about my role as Queensland editor of the *Australian Liberal*. He asked me if I'd like to be his research assistant. The Whitlam government had recently decided that each federal member should have one as well as a secretary. I pointed out that I had a young family and wasn't looking for a job. Jim was the kind of man who having got hold of an idea was not going to let go, and afterwards he kept ringing me up to try to persuade me to take the job. I finally said that I could only do it part-time and Jim's immortal words were, 'Give it what you can, dear lady, give it what you can.' And so I did.

They were rough and earthy years in politics. Party conferences were not the bland and choreographed gatherings they are now. Year after year, a motion of no confidence was moved against Gordon Chalk, later Sir Gordon, state treasurer and the Party leader. It was always defeated but only after loud and noisy debate. There was a trade union element in the Party in the person of Noel Wilson, and he always had a lot to say on the floor of the conference.

At the Townsville lunch, I was both shocked and amused when Gordon Chalk said to Norman Lee, Minister for Transport, 'Of course, Norm, the only reason I made you a Cabinet minister was so I could look down your wife's dress.' His glamorous wife, Dorothy, who was also at the lunch, just laughed. In those days, women usually smiled sweetly at sexist remarks. Nor did Norm think it was casting any aspersions on his capability as a minister, and a good one at that.

I spent three years working with Jim Killen who was always known by his surname. It was a very useful apprenticeship in practical politics, although at the time that was not my intention. At first he was in Opposition, but after the 1975 election that followed the tumultuous dismissal of Gough Whitlam and his government, Killen became Minister for Defence under Malcolm Fraser. My role was vague and varied. Killen was a great parliamentarian, one of the few who spoke without notes and he despised others who spoke with them, and a great orator whenever he gave a speech. I would research and write speeches that he never gave; it was very frustrating. I remember once going to great lengths to prepare a speech to the motor industry, crammed full of facts and figures, not a single one of which he used. Nonetheless, the audience rose to its feet to cheer the speech he did give.

Part of my job was sorting out Killen's filing cabinets, which were stuffed with all kinds of interesting letters and documents. There were the notes he received across the floor of Parliament from men like Gough Whitlam and Fred Daly, friendships that cut across Party lines. He often used to quote Prime Minister Sir Arthur Fadden – 'All the best bowlers are not on the one team.' As a man who loved to go to the races on a Saturday afternoon, Killen had a wide circle of friends from all walks of life. He had a column in the *Australian* newspaper, which after he became Minister for Defence I would write for him. I knew his language and style. One day he rang me from Canberra and said, 'Are you sure I didn't write this? It's very good.'

To my surprise, what I most enjoyed was the social work aspect of every federal member's role: the constituents who came with a variety of problems. After Killen was in the ministry, a lot of these would be family problems brought by wives of service personnel and so I had my first taste of the frustration of dealing with government bureaucracy. I was also Killen's de facto press secretary in Brisbane, although media queries, even from a local paper, were supposed to go through Canberra. It was maddening to explain that the Brisbane *Telegraph* needed an answer before the lunch deadline, not the day after tomorrow. We had a call one day that the security arrangements needed to be assessed for the minister's home. This was a concerning proposition. Killen lived in an old wooden Queenslander in Yeronga and his office under the house was hardly the safest place for the defence secrets of the nation. I was able to explain that the guard dog was very fierce.

Actually, I had been checked out myself by national security when Killen became a minister. I was asked to give three character references. Among them I gave Sister Mary St Gabriel of the Mater Hospital, a formidable woman whose brother was a federal member of Parliament and whom I had first met on the day of my engagement. The man from ASIO was invited to tea in the convent, an event of great excitement for the nuns. He asked, 'Is Mrs Atkinson of good character?'

Apparently Sister Mary St Gabriel drew herself up and said, 'Sir, she is married to one of our doctors.'

Unexpectedly, one day in 1978 my local alderman, Lex Ord, announced he was not going to stand at the next election, and freinds suggested I should try. The ward was Indooroopilly, such a safe Liberal seat that years before when Clem Jones's Labor team had swept to victory in Brisbane, it was the only ward that did not vote Labor. I had never thought of running for office, or of local government. When I discussed it with Jim Killen he said, 'Oh, my dear, looking at life through a municipal drainpipe.' But I was involved in the local branch of the Liberal Party and people were urging me to have a go. Interestingly, although Lex Ord was one of the no-job-for-a-woman brigade, years later his daughter, Lecki Ord, was to become Lord Mayor of Melbourne.

Even though I hadn't considered it before, so many threads seemed to be drawing together. There was my newfound passion for Brisbane because of my book, and the discovery that helping people in the minister's office was very satisfying. The truth was, I knew about municipal drainpipes, too. When the pipe at the top of our hilly street had burst three times I had successfully campaigned to have it fixed. This had given me a sense of real power and achievement, but it also showed me how badly something as simple as a burst pipe could affect daily life.

There was one major snag: I was a woman. At this stage, there were no women sitting in the House of Representatives in Canberra (Elaine Darling, elected in 1980, was to be the first woman from Queensland). There had in fact only been four women elected to the House of Representatives since Federation and three of them had been one-termers. One, Dame Enid Lyons, had been the widow of a prime minister. So people said, 'They'll never give that seat to a woman. It's too safe.' One of the arguments used against me was that I was keeping a man out of a job.

Brisbane City Council (BCC) wards were roughly the same size as state government seats. In fact, BCC was like a small state government. It was one of the largest local authorities in the world and it had a unique place in Australian political life. Queensland had done away with its Upper House in 1921, making it the only unicameral state in the Commonwealth, so BCC was the only political entity of sufficient size to act in any way as a check or balance.

Unlike other local authorities in Queensland, Brisbane has always been political. The BCC was established in 1925 as an amalgamation of twenty-odd towns, shires and boards, by a Labor government that naturally assumed it would win the majority on the new Council. But the first mayor, William Jolly, had been a conservative businessman who brought his team with him. Since then the Labor Party has frequently won in Council elections and there has always been a conservative group against them. Until 2012, there had not been an Independent elected to BCC for 60 years. I had a good chuckle when, at my first Local Government Association conference, one of the elderly gentlemen from rural Esk Shire harrumphed, 'There are no politics in Esk Shire. We're all National Party.'

In 1975 the Liberal Party had decided to come out of the closet and officially contest the Brisbane Council elections. This move was not without controversy within the Party, some of which lingers still, but it was thought opportune to consolidate its place in the capital city. This was the year when its coalition partner changed its name from the Country Party to the National Party.

I decided to run, and I did it as a man would. I had learned that most women who had stood for local councils, albeit much smaller ones, had done so on a platform of community involvement such as fighting for a local swimming pool. But Brisbane was different. So I did the hard grind of contacting the branch members who would be delegates to the preselection and asking for their votes. I wrote letters and canvassed local issues. I sought the active support of influential Party members, and Ian Prentice, later to be the state member for Toowong and his wife, Jane, who was later elected to the Council and then to federal Parliament – they helped me write my speech for the preselection. There were nine hopefuls on that night in 1978, and in the end it came down to three of us. One was Margaret Hollingsworth, showing that women could indeed make it and the other, whom I only just beat, was Bob Mills. When I was declared the winner Bob immediately offered to be my campaign manager, which I thought was a very generous gesture. And he was to get his turn later, for when I stood down from Indooroopilly to run for the mayoralty I supported Bob as my successor.

Leigh had been supportive of my running, saying I would be focusing on one job rather than several. He was also very involved in the Party as vice-president and chairman of the Brisbane area. Having full-time help in the house meant I could concentrate on running for office. When babysitters were no longer necessary I had a daily housekeeper to do the cooking and housework. (That, by the way, is the second breakthrough moment in parenting – when babysitters are no longer necessary. The first is when your child is out of nappies, the third when your children can drive themselves.)

We ran a very serious campaign in spite of Indooroopilly being a safe seat. I was never one to take anything for granted, and we did everything that had to be done, such as producing brochures and putting up signs and raising money. Friends were wonderfully enthusiastic and supportive. Former journalist colleague Gary Stubbs was in charge of the brochures and even allowed himself and his family to be photographed for them. Female friends rallied around, giving lie to the old saying that women don't support each other. Lynn Everingham, who was to lead a group of friends through all my campaigns, organised all sorts of functions.

Indooroopilly was a huge ward in area, just under 150 square kilometres and the largest in the Council. There were 23,400 electors on the roll, taking in the populated suburbs of Taringa, Indooroopilly and Kenmore, and the less well settled, like Fig Tree Pocket and farming areas of Brookfield, Moggill and Pullenvale, which were just beginning to be gobbled up by developers.

I've always had an aversion to doorknocking, both as the giver and the receiver. To have a political candidate knocking on my door and wanting to have a chat has seemed just plain intrusive, and knocking on the door and trying to have the chat just as embarrassing. I used to carry a stash of cards on which I'd written, 'Sorry I missed you' or, 'Sorry you weren't at home' which I'd drop in the letterbox or under the door on which I had knocked, praying that it wouldn't be answered.

The BCC elections are always held in March, which means a long hot summer of campaigning. In the outer suburbs of Indooroopilly ward, Pullenvale and Brookfield the houses were isolated and the driveways long. If the householder was home one was more likely to have a slow cool drink or a cup of tea rather than a quick chat. So in that very first local campaign through January and February I was a doorknocking backslider and had moments of panic when my opponent used to boast he'd knocked on every door in the electorate. Later, when the results came in, the Labor vote hadn't budged an inch. So all that doorknocking, or my lack of it, hadn't made any difference.

My Labor opponent was a nice man called Denis Jackson, a bachelor. His marital status is significant because one of the Labor mantras was, 'How could a woman with five children represent us in the Council?' to which I was able to reply, 'How could a man who doesn't have any possibly know?'

On election night I won with 55 per cent of the vote. The next day I asked Denis, in a tactful way, if he had thought he could win. He said yes, because everyone whose door he had knocked on had said they were going to vote for him. In the matter of doorknocking, my case rests.

A win is a win and I was very excited. But I did have a moment of terror when it suddenly dawned on me that I'd made an enormous commitment and I was going to have to honour it for the next three years. But my panic did only last a moment.

My first day in the Council Chambers was unnerving, although not for the reasons I had expected. The only time I had been there before had been once when Clem Jones was Lord Mayor: with his 20 to one majority he didn't encourage debate and that Council meeting had lasted 15 minutes. With that in mind I went to my first Council meeting expecting that it would finish, perhaps not in 15 minutes, but certainly in a couple of hours. At 4.15 pm I went over to the Leader, Alderman Syd McDonald and said, 'I have to go, George the butcher shuts at five.' He was not pleased.

Council Chambers had been installed when City Hall was built in 1930 and hadn't changed much since. The benches were still darkly panelled though the picture of the King had been replaced by that of the Queen. Later, I was under pressure to put in air conditioning, which I resisted on the grounds of cost and interference to heritage, but also – although I didn't say so – because it would lengthen the time aldermen would talk by making them too comfortable. The room could be stiflingly hot in summer.

The early photos of the Chambers in the 1930s show the same desks and chairs as in my time and the aldermen are all male. The atmosphere was masculine and heavy. There was one other woman in Council, Dulcie Turnbull, a Liberal, and in the past half-century there had been at least three, but still no female toilet. The ladies' room was down the corridor towards the administration building and quite a sprint if you didn't want to miss anything. The gents, of course, was just outside the Chambers entrance. I would get one of the blokes to check there was no one in there, then guard the door when I went in. It was my first experience of what a urinal looked like.

Being an alderman is a cross between being a social worker and a community activist. I have a clipping of the front page of the local paper, the *Westside News*, which illustrates this. The main story is about my fighting Council's plans to establish a sewage treatment plant in a semi-rural area in my ward. Next to it, taking up the rest of the front page is a photo of me looking very young as I pinned badges on the captains of a local primary school. The reason I have the clipping is because of what became a common occurrence in Brisbane – people telling me about their school-age memories of me. I was to work years later with one of the school captains, Melinda Duncan, in Queensland State Development, and her mother had kept the newspaper in which little Melinda featured. One morning a man rang me to complain that his neighbour had the lawn sprinkler on and water was coming through his window. 'Why don't you just talk to him and ask him to turn it off?' said I.

He sounded affronted. 'Talk to him? I haven't talked to him in ten years!'

It was a steep learning curve, even though my years with Jim Killen had prepared me for much of it, particularly dealing with constituents. My background as a journalist had trained me to ask questions and process the answers. It had also given me the confidence to go and see people I might ordinarily think too important, and to seek their advice. Because I was pretty sure that having won the preselection I was going to win the ward, I could prepare myself as well as campaign even before the election. So I went to see Town Clerk Peter Thorley to get in-depth briefings and the Minister for Local Government, Russ Hinze, who had himself been a member of the Albert Shire Council and its chairman for nine years. This established a useful relationship in years ahead. During school holidays at the Gold Coast I also went in to see Sir Jack Egerton, the Labor renegade who would become Deputy Mayor of that Council.

Aldermen in Brisbane, today called councillors, worked full-time and were paid a percentage of a state member's salary. The amount was fixed by a formula, which was to give me grief later on. The demands of the job were too much to allow for another job, and few tried it. Business owners could have perhaps put in a manager as country state members did with their farms. Ray Smith, who was a barrister as well as the alderman for Chermside, tried to keep up his practice but found it impossible. About the time I came onboard Council aldermen started to have offices and secretaries; before that they had operated out of their homes with their forbearing wives taking calls and helping with the admin. We were given offices in City Hall, basically small cubicles. Today, councillors not only have offices and two staffers instead of one, they are also provided with cars and phones. I have been intrigued at the need for all this extra support when I had assumed that computers would lessen the load and the need to write letters, but I am assured that social media has increased the accessibility of councillors and the personal demands on them.

Any elected representative has to enjoy dealing with people and nowhere is this more important than in local government. Issues affect people's lives in a very meaningful way which makes them important, but no matter how large or small the council may be, the councillor is always going to bump into constituents in the street or shopping centre. I enjoyed going to the Boy Scout meetings and the CWA teas and found it stimulating to hear about a local issue and then prepare a submission to Council to have it seen to. I was lucky that I had a fantastic ward secretary, Narelle Cowan, who had worked for Council since she was 16. She had been a relief secretary for my predecessor and when told that his permanent secretary wouldn't work for a woman Narelle asked if she could have the job. She was only 18 and I was told she was far too young to be in charge of a ward office, but I wanted to give her a go and I was rewarded. Quite often constituents don't realise how much of the real work is done in the local office, at every level of government.

I received lots of phone calls at home, and often at night. We had a second phone line installed so that the main line would be always free for Leigh's urgent calls from the hospitals. The kids used to refer to the two phones as the Brains and the Drains. I didn't believe in having an unlisted number, for the constituents' benefit, and the children wanted to be listed for the sake of their social life, and there were some funny calls. One night, after I had become Lord Mayor, I answered the phone to a young man who said he was in the pub and he'd had a bet with some mates that he could get the Lord Mayor on the phone. I said I hoped the bet had been a good one. Another call, about one o'clock in the morning, was from a distressed gentleman at Murarrie, on Brisbane's south side, where residents had been complaining about the dreadful smell from the local abattoir. 'I'll hold the phone out the window so you can smell it,' he said.

There were serious and difficult issues. I went to court to fight the Indooroopilly Golf Club selling some of their land for a housing development. The land in question was the Sir John Chandler Park which the Club had been given in a land exchange with the Council back in the mid-1970s, but it had been designated parkland since 1949. We lost, and it had been difficult because the Club membership was made up mostly of the Liberal males in the area, including my husband. This being Brisbane I knew John Gallagher, QC, the barrister on the other side, so when I asked him to repeat a question and he said, 'With your Arts degree I thought you could understand English.' I was quick to reply, 'With your Law degree, I thought you could have put it properly.'

I went to the March 1982 Council election, my second, with Orme Olsen as Liberal Party leader and me as his deputy. Orme was a typical old-style alderman, a successful businessman, determined to give back to his community, in this case the City Council. He had had a furniture company called Olsen and Goodchap. After the election, which the Liberal Party lost but gained one extra ward to give us 10 seats, there was a move in the Party room to replace him with me. I obviously had the advantage of looking different – I was a woman, I was younger, and I was also a mother of five. The media had been kind to me during the campaign, looking, I suspect, for an easy story. I had also topped the polls in the election. In Indooroopilly, I won with 75 per cent of the vote. The closest was Len Ardill, the Labor Deputy Mayor in Sunnybank. Numbers in Council were now close. Labor had 11 seats to our 10, and they included that of the Lord Mayor who had been elected by the Labor majority.

The new Lord Mayor, Roy Harvey, the alderman for Mitchelton, had been vice-mayor under Frank Sleeman who had retired. But Orme was keen to stay on as leader for the Commonwealth Games in August, and this I totally understood – as Leader of the Opposition he would have an honoured place in all the Games events. And I wasn't in a hurry, I was going to be the fourth Opposition leader in a little more than three years. The first had been Syd McDonald, known as Syd the Pieman, because that had been his business, the second John Andrews, a well-respected surveyor. Syd was to resign in a huff from the Liberal Party later that year and to stand unsuccessfully for the next election as an Independent.

The Commonwealth Games was a hugely important event for Brisbane, the largest we had ever held in the city and responsible for what everyone described as our 'coming of age'. Part of the success for Brisbane was giving lie to the 'Great Southern Putdown' – the belief that we couldn't do it. (When I launched my book on Brisbane a Sydney journalist had quipped to the publisher's publicist, 'How long is it? One page or two?')

Our facilities, funded by Commonwealth and state governments as well as Council, were ready so far ahead of time that I joked they might be worn out by the time the Games started. They were used for swimming and athletic events of all sorts the year before and we were proud of our achievements. In the weeks before the Games started there were athletes running around our streets, Africans and Asians, not a common sight in suburban Brisbane then. I had to go to Sydney for a meeting a few weeks before the opening, and was having withdrawal symptoms just being away from the excitement.

The Games were opened by the Duke of Edinburgh and there was a civic reception in City Hall when he asked one of my children what it was like to have a busy working mother and she replied, politely but frankly, 'Just like yours!' My best memories are of the athletes' village, in the halls of residence at the newly established Griffith University where friends, David Williams and Reet Howell, were the commandants of the athletes' separate male and female quarters. I was able to spend time with the athletes and experience the Games from the inside. There was a cinema in the village where I went to see the movie *Gallipoli* sitting between a German professor of sport and a New Zealander, so that the film really underlined the futility of war. In the final dramatic scene the heroes had to sprint for the Turkish trenches. As we left the cinema I heard one young man say casually to another, 'D'you reckon that was a one-hundred-yard dash or two?'

After the Commonwealth Games, life got back to normal.

Except that I became Leader of the Opposition. Almost as soon as I was appointed I began to understand what sexual harassment is, in the non-physical sense, when Labor aldermen nicknamed me Tinkerbell. One day I was speaking in Council Chambers and Ian Brusasco, actually one of the more intelligent on the Labor side, called out, 'Are you pregnant, Alderman Atkinson, or just fat?' This was a particularly telling barb because I was self-conscious about my increasing weight. Eating is a definite political hazard; Clem Jones told me once that he put on four stone (25 kilograms) while he was Lord Mayor.

Lord Mayor Roy Harvey was quoted in the press as saying, 'Alderman Atkinson has yet to realise that there is more to running a city than running a house.'

Young women would now simply refuse to put up with a lot of what we had to endure then. Not all the barbs were meant unkindly, and sometimes the sexism was quite unconscious. At one stage I took to wearing flat-heeled shoes to better manage all the walking around I was doing. Orme Olsen took me aside and told me that 'the boys' would prefer I got back into my high heels because they looked better. And I'm embarrassed to say that I did.

But there were defenders too, and some surprising. Some years later as Lord Mayor, I was the subject of debate in state Parliament. Labor member Bill Prest, a former mayor of Gladstone, said the only job I was fit for was as a TV weather girl. Sir William Knox, hardly the most radical of parliamentarians, chided him for making a sexist remark. (I actually had been a weather girl for a week in the 1970s, filling in for someone who was on holidays.)

There was formal sexism then as well. Back in 1979, Indooroopilly Golf Club was still at St Lucia on land leased from the Council and when I went to call on the Club manager, I was unable to step inside the clubhouse. Women were banned;

it was for men only. As the local alderman it was inconvenient, but something I accepted as how things were.

Life in Opposition was always going to be a slog, particularly as there was no extra staff support for the role. In the year before the election a group of businessmen, understanding the handicap I was under, paid for an extra staff member in the form of Digby McLeay, son of a former federal minister. Digby was quick-witted and entrepreneurial and great with the media. He had worked on radio and one of his more successful tricks was to record an interview with me on a tape recorder, and then give the tape to a radio station who would play it just as it was. After a while the radio stations woke up to what was happening, but I had been able to spruik a lot of policies on air.

Looking back through the newspaper cuttings of those years, it is amazing how much space is given to City Hall and local government matters. In my days on the *Courier-Mail* there had been a City Hall roundsman, senior journalist Peter Trundle who had been famously banned from City Hall by Clem Jones, which of course only increased his stature. The newspapers in the early 1980s, and there were three dailies in town, were full of stories about buses and dogs, the visit of Prince Charles and Princess Diana, the venues for David Bowie's concert and petty squabbles with the state and federal governments. The squabbles were petty, even if their causes were not, for intergovernmental funding was always contentious. But the big and ongoing issues of the early 1980s were garbage, heritage and Games, both student and Olympic.

It could not be denied that everyone cared passionately about garbage disposal, especially in Brisbane's hot and steamy climate. The Council began moves in 1983 to change the way our household garbage was collected. The 'garbo' had always been a picturesque character in Brisbane's suburban life and the efficient collection of rubbish a vital contribution to its good health.

Brisbane's Olympic aspirations began with the Commonwealth Games. No one seems to know exactly when the light-bulb moment happened, but Lord Mayor Harvey stood in Brisbane's Queen Street mall late in 1982 and said that the Council was considering Brisbane bidding for the Olympic Games. Everyone acknowledged that the Commonwealth Games had been a huge success so trying for the Olympics was almost a natural progression. But then the administration decided to bid for the Student Games or Universiade, a lesser and perhaps more reachable target. These Games somehow lacked the brand appeal of the Olympics and all through 1983 and 1984 there was controversy, with renegade Labor aldermen holding out on the decision behind closed doors, while others were taking investigative trips that were spotlighted in the full glare of the media.

The Universiade was indeed the second largest multi-sports event in the world after the Olympics, but the competitors were university athletes and because no one had ever heard of them it was hard for the Council to sell the benefits of bidding for and hosting the event.

In January 1984 Primo Nebiolo, the Italian president of the Universiade's governing body, the International University Sports Federation, came to Brisbane and held a press conference to push Brisbane's case for hosting the Student Games. In an unfortunate case of timing the tenders for Brisbane's multimillion-dollar refuse collection had been called a few months earlier in September 1983 and almost immediately there was trouble. Services were disrupted and this meant that during the Brisbane summer household garbage bins were filled to overflowing, smelly and maggot-ridden. Regrettably, when the

Italian Universiade president made his visit the journalists only wanted to talk about garbage. Primo stormed out of the press conference saying, 'I didn't come here to talk about garbage!' (My favourite Primo Nebiolo story was during the Barcelona Olympics in 1992. He was in the royal box at the tennis when he noticed Princess Anne, the British International Olympic Committee (IOC) member sitting in the stand below with her children. He grandly sent a note down to the princess suggesting she join him in the royal box. She is supposed to have sent a note back: 'Wherever I am, that *is* the royal box.')

Despite the political posturing, Brisbane's bid for the Student Games was unsuccessful.

I do find it extraordinary looking back at the amount of media I was able to get as Leader of the Opposition. In part this was because I was, put simply, a good story. I was young and a woman. And as the mother of five children I was not the stereotypical career woman. Because I had been a journalist I knew what made news. I knew, for example, that talking about Council finances was never going to spark the interest of reporters, but that issues concerning their own lives and those of their readers would. In one sense this was to create a rod for my own back later, when I would be accused of being a lightweight and not interested in Council finances and inter-governmental relations. These were matters to be dealt with seriously, but they were not made for the media. And because of the Labor administration's paranoia and policy of secrecy, we on the Opposition side of the Chamber were never allowed to look at the real figures on any of the important issues, such as the garbage contracts.

To attract media attention, we offered up lots of initiatives, and interesting ones. For example, I had been in correspondence with American planning lawyer Richard Babcock who was visiting Australian cities in early 1983 and was to lecture at the University of Queensland in early April. His visit to Brisbane coincided with Easter and the university had to cancel. He was still keen to come, so I invited him and his wife to stay at our house in Indooroopilly and asked him whether he would give a seminar in City Hall. We organised a venue, and invited planners, developers and business people – it was a great success. Even more successful was the publicity. Mr Babcock held a press conference in our front garden and told the media, who were having a quiet Easter, that warm weather was bad for the brain and all the great thinking of the world had happened in cold climates. This of course went national, and Melbourne and Adelaide were particularly excited. Mr Babcock's special field was transferable development rights, a planning concept allowing the sale of unused rights from one site to use on another. It never quite took off here, despite my attempts, and I can only think of one example where it was used, the preservation of Naldham House in the city.

In Opposition we had to take initiative, and did. The visit of Richard Babcock also showed how unexpected opportunities can lead to friendship. He and his wife, Betty, became great personal friends, and I was to visit them in Chicago several times, as did some of my children. It was on one of those visits that I learned something new about Brisbane. Introduced to Dempsey Travis who had written a book called *An Autobiography of Black Chicago*, I heard for the first time that black American servicemen in Brisbane during World War II had been segregated on the south side of the river. We had never been told about this.

The editor-in-chief of the *Courier-Mail*, Olympic historian Harry Gordon, who happened to live in our street, asked me to write a column. There were complaints about this from the Council administration, though one of the other columnists was radio personality Janine Walker, who had been a Labor candidate. I was told not to write about politics or local government. Instead, I wrote articles on all kinds of things, from cricket to the new Chinatown mall, and could be as whimsical as I liked. I once suggested we move Christmas to Easter, saying I was sure that God wouldn't mind. Christmas in December, with all its gaudy decorations was a necessary relief in a Northern Hemisphere winter, but here the heat of summer, the end of the school year and Christmas were all inconveniently timed together.

Heritage became the defining issue of my early political career. Once, after I had made a particularly impassioned speech to Council, Lord Mayor Frank Sleeman called me in and told me I had been clever to take up this cause. He was not congratulating me, he was being cynical. Frank happened to be the only person in my professional life who has ever made me cry. I don't remember exactly why, but I do remember feeling very upset by his scathing attack because I respected him; he actually reminded me of my father. He was small and understated and had been a surprise choice as Lord Mayor by the Labor Party room. But he was strong, as were all the men like him who had survived as prisoners in Changi during the war, and he was authentic. His nickname was Sandbank Frank; fishing from his dinghy, he had been stuck on a sandbank in the middle of Moreton Bay and had had to be rescued.

Throughout my political career I never minded being criticised or attacked by people I didn't care about or respect, but I would be upset by comments from people who mattered to me or whose opinion I valued. There's a lot of criticism you take on the chin, without appreciating the effect it can have on others. I remember one of my daughters coming home very upset during my first aldermanic campaign because one of my posters had a moustache painted on it.

I really discovered 'heritage' when I had been researching for my book, *Around Brisbane*. The first house I loved had been 'Hazeldene', a lovely old Queenslander in Southport and the first house my parents had bought, 14 years after their marriage, and sold when Dad lost his job in Colombo. Hazeldene was a true Queenslander, painted white with verandas all around and rooms on either side of a central hallway, and a big garden. It is a house that features a lot in my dreams. Like so many of the lovely old Queenslanders it was knocked down years ago to be replaced by a brick apartment block.

As I was driving around Brisbane researching for the book and really thinking about the city, I came to realise how unique was Queensland architecture and how it defined and contributed to our identity. In early 1978, I went to Rome with my friend Julien Beirne and it struck me how important the very old buildings were to an understanding of that city and the appeal to tourists and economic development. When I came back to Brisbane I was invited to speak to a group of architects by a friend whose husband was the organiser and I talked about the value of our heritage. It struck a chord of sympathy for some and surprised others. And this was to be part of Brisbane's dilemma. In prosperous postwar Australia we wanted everything to be modern and many people couldn't understand why we should cherish the old.

This was Frank Sleeman's criticism also. He was surprised that his son in Sydney was keen on old houses rather than the brand spanking new ones replacing them. I remembered my own surprise as an eight-year-old when I first saw the flimsy timber and tin houses of suburban Brisbane from the train and thought them so awful after solid redbrick Sydney.

After *Around Brisbane* was published in 1978 and I was preselected for Council, I continued to talk about Brisbane's heritage and how vital it was to the city. Nobody seemed to be very interested but it was a good issue for the media. Then came the demolition of the Bellevue Hotel by the Deen brothers in the dead of night in April 1979 under the direction of the Bjelke-Petersen state government. This galvanised the press and the community, although I suspected then, and still do, that this was more about the way the demolition had been done than for what had been demolished. The Bellevue Hotel was a grand and elegant old building on the corner of George and Alice streets and on the corners opposite were Parliament House, the Queensland Club and the Botanic Gardens. In its day it had been the smartest place in town for weddings and balls and many famous people had stayed there. I had interviewed Yehudi Menuhin and his sister Hephzibah at the hotel, memorable for me because when the famous violinist opened the door of their suite he cried, 'Look Hephzibah, it's a teenage reporter!'

The Queensland government bought the hotel and used it as a sort of boarding house for country members of Parliament. The building fell into disrepair, there was much discussion about the cost and worthiness of restoration, and the lovely old cast-iron railings were taken away for 'safekeeping'. There was a small rallying to the cause. Our Liberal Party branch passed a motion calling for the Bellevue's preservation and Liberal members of Parliament waxed eloquent. In the mid-1970s we had organised a street corner rally opposite the Bellevue where there were more media than protesters. We were just a handful, including the Anglican Dean of Brisbane, Ian George, eminent barrister

John Greenwood, later to be Minister of Survey and Valuation, and me with Stephanie in her stroller. The National Trust was loud in its protest. However I realised to my dismay that the general public was not really interested in preserving heritage buildings, and this was later proved true when we tried to save other public buildings, including Her Majesty's Theatre.

However, the 1979 demolition of the Bellevue did spark outrage and focused media attention. When I was elected to the Council that year I was able to continue the campaign with calls for heritage legislation for the state, and regulations for Council. There was a lot of networking. Allen Callaghan, the premier's former press secretary and an old *Telegraph* colleague, who was then head of the Department of Arts, National Parks and Sport, was sympathetic and came to a lunch I organised at the Queensland Club with Professor David Yencken as speaker. Professor Yencken was chairman of the National Heritage Commission, established in 1975 after Australia became one of the first countries in the world to sign up to the International Heritage Register the year before.

During my research on *Around Brisbane*, I had found that a funny old building in Ann Street had once been the stately Brisbane School of Arts but had long been boarded up with a fibro front, and I was able to point this out to Council. The building was subsequently restored with the frontages ripped off to reveal the old building behind, and it still stands today. The Council set up a heritage committee and I was appointed. I became vice-president of the National Trust and later was made a life member. State heritage legislation finally came in with the *Queensland Heritage Act of 1992*, but before that we had lost many valuable buildings. Our Town Plan, with its heritage conditions and regulations, could only go so far.

It makes me very happy today to see that Brisbane residents are valuing old houses. The grand houses around the city and suburbs have always been considered desirable, but now we are seeing little cottages painted so that their railings stand out in white, while in the inner suburbs we can admire the ornamentation that was part of building styles of a more leisured time.

Not having access to research resources in Council led to looking for opportunities outside. My Council ward, as well as my home, were not far from the University of Queensland where I had always kept up my contacts. I was able to tap into academic expertise in planning and engineering, for example, and get help with projects. This was before the university realised it could sell off its expertise to the world outside and I managed to convince various lecturers about some useful projects for their students. Dr Bob Pretty from the School of Engineering had his students draw up a bikeway plan for Brisbane, and I even managed to convince Minister for Transport Don Lane to make his first visit to the university to have a look at it. These were the days when government and university were at loggerheads, the days after the years of anti-Vietnam protests and the Springbok tour of 1971 and continued student unrest. In 1986 when the university announced they were awarding Premier Bjelke-Petersen an honorary doctorate there was a riot at the graduation ceremony, to which Sir Joh did not turn up.

As Opposition leader I was awarded a US Visitors Grant, given to up-and-coming young leaders to study American political trends for a couple of weeks. It was a wonderful opportunity and in November 1983 I went to Los Angeles, Chicago, New Orleans, Atlanta and Texas. San Antonio was famous for its river development and its mayor Henry Cisneros, who was touted as a future-first Hispanic president.

New Orleans was preparing for Expo 84 – though non-preparing would have been a better description, as everything was way behind schedule. In New Orleans I was introduced to the mayor as 'Mrs Atkinson, the Leader of the Opposition in her Council. We don't have an Opposition in our Council.' To which the mayor replied, 'Oh yes, we do. It's called the Council.' Atlanta, which I was to visit again for the 1996 Olympics, had some charming historic neighbourhood programs.

In Los Angeles and Chicago I was to see public participation in action, with local citizens actually taking part in Council committee meetings. There were lots of ideas to bring back to Brisbane. I had also seen firsthand the strength of American volunteerism, for in each city I was escorted by a local volunteer who drove me around, had me to dinner and made me feel like a friend. These are the experiences that make a visitor remember a place, and something we always emphasised when talking about tourism in Brisbane.

At the end of my US tour I took myself off at my own expense to Edmonton, Canada, which had been the site of the Student Games. My strongest memory of Edmonton is of a cold even more biting than Edinburgh's. Just flying in was a shock, the blinding whiteness of snow as far as the eye could see and covering everything. On my first evening I was about to walk out of the hotel, bare-headed, to go to the theatre, when the doorman said, 'You can't walk outside in this cold.' I thought this was nonsense, but after three steps in the frosty air I felt as though my ears were being sliced by knives.

As leader of the Liberal Party in the Council, I became a member of the Liberal Party State Executive and witnessed some turbulent times, including the break-up of the marriage between the Liberal and National parties that formed the Coalition governing Queensland. The political events of 1983 were to have a direct impact on my future. In August, Terry White, Minister for Welfare and member for Redcliffe, led a group of rebel backbenchers across the floor of the Legislative Assembly to vote against the premier. As a liberal Liberal, known colloquially as a small 'l' Liberal, I sympathised with their principles if not the practicalities of upholding them. In the days and weeks after, Joh Bjelke-Petersen showed himself a cunning tactician, closed down Parliament and called a state election for October. Out of the Coalition the Liberal ministers had resigned their portfolios and the party had lost all the practical benefits of ministerial offices.

At the election the Liberal Party was almost wiped out and held just eight seats. The National Party won 41 of the 82 seats and, when Liberals Don Lane and Brian Austin defected to it, was able to govern in its own right. The National Party, until a decade earlier called the Country Party, had run at least one candidate in the 1982 City Council elections without success. There was now new confidence and pressure to try again, a move resisted by the National Party hierarchy despite Minister for Local Government Russ Hinze being quoted in the press as saying, 'We'll take City Hall.' For the first time the National Party held state seats in Brisbane, Toowong and Aspley.

In April 1984, after months of rumour, discussion and controversy, Russ Hinze changed the *City of Brisbane Act* to have the Lord Mayor elected at large and the number of Council wards increased from 21 to 26. The Brisbane City Council was important to the Labor Party because it had held it for 23 years, and during a time when Labor had no power in state government.

Much of the debate was around the fact that the change reversed an earlier change to the mayoral election process, made by the same government in 1972, apparently for good and proper reasons, to have the Lord Mayor chosen by the majority in Council, following the method used by premiers and prime ministers. However, the obvious and improper reason had been to get rid of Labor Lord Mayor Clem Jones, and that hadn't worked.

Now the plan – which Russ Hinze revealed to me but not to the public – was to run a National Party candidate who would win and have the unique power under legislation of the Lord Mayor of Brisbane, including control of the budget without being beholden to the majority in Council. He said he had candidates in mind and Test cricketer Greg Chappell was rumoured to be one.

Labor MP Eric Shaw said during the debate, 'It would be fair to say that the bill is politically motivated. It is a cynical attempt to manipulate the democratic procedure for the election of the Brisbane City Council.' Eric Shaw had himself been an alderman in Brisbane.

Another amendment, little noticed but significant, was that after the word 'his' in the Act, the words 'or her' were to be inserted. I rather felt this might be an omen.

As a party, we protested the changes. Certainly I was then, and would continue to be, firmly against state government interference in matters pertaining to the Council or local government. But I knew our protest would make little difference to any government decision. And privately I was excited and ready for the new challenge. The proper title of the original Act, assented to in 1924, is *An Act for the Good Government of the City of Brisbane*. I was ready to do what I could to carry this out.

LOOKING AT LIFE THROUGH A
MUNICIPAL DRAINPIPE

IN SOME WAYS my life experiences had prepared me for my role
as Lord Mayor of Brisbane. When I came back from living in
Edinburgh I felt that Brisbane was a better place than its residents
thought it to be. Researching for my book on it confirmed that
view. At my first preselection I had said it had the potential to
be one of the great cities of the world. Grandiloquent as that
may sound, a great city is not one with the tallest buildings, the
largest population; it is a city that is a great place to live, and that's
what Brisbane is. But for that livability to be sustained there has
to be growth and prosperity. I saw city government as being
about more than just the provision of services, I saw civic pride
as a tangible economic asset. I also knew that good financial
management was necessary to look after all the other assets and
provide services. Brisbane was very much a collection of suburbs
and I had been living a suburban family life, and knew it well.

In many ways Brisbane was also preparing itself for me,
or for someone like me, immodest as that may sound. A city

government, unlike other levels of government, is not so much about politics as about managing the structure of people's lives. Cities have distinct identities and characteristics that determine the feelings their citizens have for them. The development of a city is determined by those feelings. A city ideally chooses to be led by a government that reflects how those citizens feel about themselves.

Local government in Australia, unlike in other parts of the world, has never been given the respect and recognition it deserves. It is, after all, the level of government that most affects the daily lives of ordinary people.

When I chose my campaign slogan 'It's Time for a Change' I was reflecting what people were saying to me, what I was hearing on the streets. There was resistance in some quarters because it was a similar slogan to Labor's 'It's Time' in the 1972 federal election, but I was insistent. I knew that people in Brisbane were feeling different about themselves, and I knew I represented something different. Every great city (think Paris, Rome or New York) has its own personality and Brisbane was a city in the process of defining itself, a city that was changing.

I never actually thought of myself as a real politician, despite my interest in politics. I was involved in local government, the management and nurturing of places where people live and how they live. Politics produces outcomes, and I do love outcomes, real achievements that make a difference to people's lives. I was chatting one day to a bricklayer who was working in the Chinatown mall, and he said, 'I can bring my kids here and actually show them what I've done at work. It gives me a great feeling.' I knew exactly what he meant.

Despite my optimism and determination, running for the mayoralty was a huge risk. Labor had been in power for 23 years and under the Liberal banner we had tried and failed in three consecutive elections to unseat the incumbent Lord Mayor. The recent changes to the *City of Brisbane Act* meant that I would have to give up my seat of Indooroopilly, not only the Council's safest conservative ward, but a constituency that I had identified with and cared about for the previous six years. If I lost the mayoral election I would be out of Council altogether. The changes to the Act also meant that I would have to secure the support of the majority of the three-quarters of a million people living across Brisbane's 1200 square kilometres. A few years later, and after I was in office, Russ Hinze introduced further amendments to the Act that gave the Lord Mayor even more power. Prime Minister Bob Hawke was to remark to me, 'You're the most powerful politician in Australia, with more voters than anyone else and control over more money.'

The decision to run for Mayor was both tough and easy. It was tough because there was a risk of losing and having to give up the ward of Indooroopilly, where I could have stayed as long as I wanted to. It was tough because I knew it would not be easy for the family. Leigh was not only busy with his practice and at the hospital, but also the various medical and neuro-surgical organisations he was involved with, usually as chairman or secretary. The children also needed attention. In 1984, Nicola was 19 and Damien was 18 – both were studying Arts/Law at the University of Queensland, Damien after a year's jackerooing in far western Queensland. Eloise and Genevieve were at All Hallows' School and Stephanie, aged 10, was at Ironside State School. They were all used to me being out a lot and in the media, but becoming Lord Mayor would take it to a new level.

The decision was easy because I was Leader of the Opposition, and it was a natural progression to take on the administration that I had been so actively attacking. To do otherwise would have made a mockery of my efforts thus far. When I went into Council I had never in my wildest dreams thought about being in charge. As with everything else, I had focused on the present, doing the best job I could, without any clear thought about where it would lead me.

As I came to know Brisbane as one of the city's aldermen, I really came to understand the city it was and its potential. I felt a sense of excitement for what Brisbane could be. I had been learning about local government in every way I could. I had been to all the annual local government conferences, at my own expense. I had accepted invitations to speak whenever I was asked, usually to planning conferences or women's functions, including in other states, and I would always make contact with city government people in whichever city I was in. These were not always without friction. In 1983 I was asked to be a speaker at the Institute of Municipal Management conference in Canberra, and Brisbane's then Lord Mayor, Roy Harvey, had made a formal complaint to the organisers that they had invited the Leader of the Opposition and not him. My speech itself caused controversy, which also surprised me. As I remember, I talked about being able to be more effective as a councillor if you went and talked to council workers at the local depots. My saying I sat on a desk and had a chat to the workers seemed to convey sexual overtones. At any rate, Roy Harvey made a long speech in the Chamber the following week accusing me of embarrassing Council. However, it was the Lord Mayor of Wellington, New Zealand, the charismatic architect Sir Michael Fowler, who caused real excitement. Warming to the theme of the conference 'Managing With Less', he said he could certainly do with fewer women in his Council. There was uproar.

I was endorsed by the Liberal Party to run for Lord Mayor in May 1984. The standing ovation from the delegates to the preselection was not a true indication of behind-the-scenes enthusiasm, but I didn't know this at the time. The general view, apparently, was that I couldn't win.

This was to be a new kind of campaign right across the whole city and the Liberal branches were all involved with fundraising and campaigning for their local candidates. Even some of my own branches in Indooroopilly resented the fact that I would have to skip meetings to go to functions in other parts of the city. The Liberal Party president told journalists I wouldn't win. My mother agreed, pointing out that Brisbane was a Labor town. The business community who should have been my best supporters for an unashamedly free enterprise candidate were too afraid of retribution from the Labor administration.

I often had to fight Liberal Party headquarters in matters of campaigning. I have always believed authenticity is one of the most important qualities in life, and certainly in politics, but the campaign gurus wanted me to portray myself as someone with business skills, taking part in boardroom discussions. I resisted because I had no business experience and wasn't going to pretend I did. I felt that common sense and intelligence plus a will to learn were more honest attributes. They also complained about my wearing pearls as too bourgeois. In campaign pictures, where I was actually photographed wearing them, the pearls were removed from the image. (It has amused me in recent years that at least two prominent Labor female politicians, Prime Minister Julia Gillard and Premier Anna Bligh often wore pearls in office, which is some indication that times have changed.)

Despite the naysayers, I did have supporters in the business community who helped with fundraising and offered advice.

I have never been afraid of asking for advice and I have found it is almost always generously given; it's something I often suggest to young people now. It was difficult to raise money from businesses in Brisbane, constrained as many were by fear of the incumbent Labor Council. I had seen this in action when a prominent town planner asked an aggressive question of Roy Harvey at a Brisbane Development Association lunch and was blacklisted by Council thereafter.

Instead, we turned our attention to the southern states. Some of the Queensland state government's tax reforms coupled with lower land prices and wages were making Brisbane an attractive place to do business, despite difficult dealings with a Labor Council. With Party treasurer and shoe magnate, Sir Bob Mathers, and my campaign director, Rod Samut, I went to Sydney and Melbourne and hosted lunches and dinners. I rang trucking magnate Lindsay Fox from a public phone box (no mobiles then, of course) to ask for an appointment to talk about his business in Brisbane. He would have known I wanted campaign funds and said, 'I'll give you money, just because you've had the guts to ring me yourself.'

I wrote in my Economic Blueprint:

Sallyanne Atkinson and her Liberal team know the economic health of Brisbane depends on a free enterprise system which encourages business to provide jobs prosperity and growth.

We believe that it is a Council function to encourage business to expand and develop, and to attract industry to re-locate here by having practical consistent policies to ensure co-operation between Council and the private sector, and by instilling attitudes of positive encouragement and helpfulness in all Council staff from top management to the most junior levels.

I did write all our policies myself and I'm appalled at the length of that second sentence, but they were important messages. It was very radical stuff back then, because most people didn't think that economic development was a function of local government. There was a view that Councils should stick to the three *r*s: roads, rates and rubbish (or what the mayor of Katherine in the Northern Territory called the three *d*s: drains, ditches and dunnies). Nowadays Councils see economic development as very much part of their remit.

Political campaigning has changed over the years. When my old boss Jim Killen went into politics in the 1950s he addressed street corner meetings, often from the back of a truck. If he wasn't actually pelted with tomatoes he was certainly heckled, and he gave back as good as he got. It made for lively entertainment, if not for actual votes. When I was growing up, every election campaign meant a car or truck with a loudspeaker on top and big placards on its sides slowly cruising the neighbourhood blaring a candidate's message. Usually, it was the candidate himself doing the blaring, or perhaps one of his team. I say 'him' and 'his' because this was not a campaign style suited to women, even if there had been any female candidates.

By the time I came along campaigning was a bit more genteel. We were much given to pamphlets with photographs of the candidate and the candidate's family, and a text listing achievements and promises. We went door to door in shopping centres, and I discovered that the best places for campaigning were butchers' and barbers' shops. These were effectively community centres where people stopped to talk, and even wanted to: 'I'm trying to decide between chops and mince for dinner, Mr Brown, and why do you think the government's doing such-and-such?' I think it was the process of deliberation that encouraged conversation, and butchers always seem such people-friendly folk. Customers waiting at their local barber shop were always up for a chat, whereas bakeries and green-grocers were not places where people lingered. I remember one Saturday morning Digby McLeay, my only paid campaign advisor, carrying an armful of purchases from the butcher and muttering, 'This is going to be a leg-of-lamb-led election win.'

One of my favourite campaigning ploys was to approach a line of cabs at a taxi stand and engage each of the drivers in conversation. If the driver was affable or even sympathetic I would give him a handful of pamphlets to put on the seat beside him so that he could hand them over to interested passengers. These were the days before we had so many drivers from over-seas. Most of our cabbies were born and bred Brisbanites and because they drove all over the city they knew it well and were usually happy to talk about it.

One of my least favourite campaign activities was standing on the side of the road waving at motorists, which is now common practice. Back in the 1980s we used to stand at railway stations and engage commuters. John Moore, the federal member for Ryan, said voters liked it because it was 'an exercise in humili-ation of the candidate'.

Our Liberal team had lots of policies. There was one about making Brisbane the convention and sports capital of the Southern Hemisphere:

> For too long tourists have by-passed Brisbane in their desire to see North Queensland and the Gold and Sunshine coasts. Last year only 20 per cent of inter and intra state tourists to Queensland visited Brisbane ... Pride in our city, generated by an enthusiastic City Council, will act as the catalyst for this goal.

The purpose of Town Planning is to ensure that a city is a good place for its citizens to live, work and enjoy themselves ... Town Planning aims at the guided development of the future while providing for the proper management of the present. It aims to safeguard the environment and to conserve the best of our heritage both material and man-made.

When I first became an alderman in 1979 it was accepted that City Hall was the centre of the city and all would radiate outwards from there. But in the meantime free enterprise had taken over and significant new development was happening on the river at the other end of the CBD. Town planning had become a particular passion of mine. I had never known much about it until I went to the seminars that the University of Queensland's Planning Department held for people in local government. They were run by Victor Plavinski, a war refugee from Poland who migrated to New Zealand, where his pre-war qualifications as a town planner were of no use. Instead, he got a job as a labourer and told me that one day a group of Council road engineers were huddled over a problem and Victor had helped solve it for them. I am not quite sure how he got from there to the university, but I'm glad he did. He ran stimulating seminars for councillors, most of whom would never have set foot in a university. The very first one was my 'St Paul on the road to Damascus' moment and I was to get a lot of inspiration from town planners who were not necessarily of my political persuasion. One of these was Phil Heywood, a lecturer at the Queensland Institute of Technology (QIT, now the Queensland University of Technology), who was so far to the Left he almost fell off the edge, but together we worked on some exciting projects.

A colonial couple, circa 1939 – Mum (Ruth Kerr) serving afternoon tea in the garden in Colombo, Ceylon, and Dad (Terry Kerr) relaxing with a smoke.

Mum, just 23, with me aged four months, Sydney.

My sister Louella and me enjoying the sunshine in our garden in Vijaya Road, Colombo.

The rollers that carried boxes of tea in the factories 'up-country' made great slides at children's parties. Dad's firm, Davidson & Co, made the Sirocco brand in Belfast and shipped the machinery to Ceylon.

Posing for a family portrait in Sligo, Ireland, 1946. Mum with Louella (left), Jill (middle) and me sitting on Dad's lap.

Left: While most of the women were evacuated, Dad and his friends joined the Ceylon Planters Rifle Corps to defend the island from the Japanese, circa 1942.

Snapped by a street photographer in Surfers Paradise, January 1957. I'm reluctant to be part of the family and Dad is lingering behind. Baby Charles is in the stroller.

At 11, I regarded younger sister Holly as my own and a replacement for the dolls I had left behind in Ceylon. I'm playing Mother here in the garden at 'Hazeldene' in Southport.

Holidaying with my Sydney grandparents, Will and Helen Helmore.

I was the only girl in my Senior class whose mother had given birth that year. My one-year-old sister, Kim, sits on my lap. Louella (right) is 15 and Holly (left) is seven.

Enjoying a day at the beach in Surfers Paradise, 1962. On my first date with my future husband, Leigh Atkinson, we joined a group of friends including Bill Everingham (pictured) who would later become Liberal Party president.

The College Players were students from the University of Queensland's Women's College and St John's College. I was a fairy in the chorus of Gilbert and Sullivan's *Iolanthe*, 1960.

Training as a cadet journalist included evening classes to learn shorthand. Seated third from left, I am beside fellow cadet and good friend, Hugh Lunn.

Leigh Atkinson and I were engaged on 12 December 1963, which happened to be his birthday. We were married the following year on 1 May. Leigh's grandmother, Nora Keane, made my wedding dress.

With my mother-in-law, Edna Atkinson, at my eldest daughter Nicola's christening on 28 March 1965. Babies were baptised very young, a legacy from the days when infant mortality was high. I am wearing my going-away outfit from my wedding day the year before.

Looking my best, with my hair and make-up professionally styled, for for an episode of Channel Seven's *Beauty and the Beast*. The panel were tasked with answering viewer questions. I was pregnant with my second child, Damien, at the time.

Raising a young family in Edinburgh, Scotland, was a challenge. Eloise was born not long after we arrived. We travelled many miles in our little van.

Nicola and Damien travelled on my passport. It was only when I was issued with my first passport that I discovered my name on my birth certificate had been misspelled; my grandfather was obviously flustered when he registered me in 1942.

I love this photograph – Nicola, Damien and Eloise are wearing outfits I made myself. I knitted the navy blue jumpers to match their tartan skirts and shorts.

What do YOU expect from your local alderman?

These brochures were used in my 1979 bid to become Alderman for Indooroopilly. We handed them out, stuffed them into letterboxes and gave bundles to willing taxi drivers to help promote my campaign.

As alderman I was often in the media spotlight. This promotional shot was a bit deceptive. The happy children are authentic, but that saucepan looks rather empty. From left to right: Genevieve, Nicola, me, Damien, Eloise and Stephanie.

Premier Joh Bjelke-Petersen and I helping to celebrate the first five years in business of good friend and 'Jobs Queen' Sarina Russo in the mid-1980s. Three decades later the Sarina Russo Group is a global leader in education, employment and training.

Local government minister Russ Hinze and I make a toast with tea cups on top of the Gateway Bridge as construction is finalised in 1986.

As Brisbane Lord Mayor I helped promote the Olympics. Pictured here with Simon, a koala from Lone Pine, launching a book about the city.

SALLYANNE ATKINSON: "Keep your options open. If you want to be a housewife, be one. But make sure it's what you want and not something that's been thrust upon you. Make sure you don't feel trapped."

Vogue Australia did my hair, clothes and make-up for a shoot with photographer Richard Bailey in 1982. I was featured as a woman of achievement in an article by Marion von Alderstein. My advice: 'Keep your options open. If you want to be a housewife, be one. But make sure it's what you want and not something that's been thrust upon you.'

All of my children and their grandmother lined up to meet Pope John Paul II in the foyer of City Hall during his visit to Brisbane in 1986.

Holidaying on the Gold Coast with the kids at Northcliffe beach. From left to right: Eloise, Genevieve, Damien, Stephanie (front), Nicola and me.

Prince Philip, Duke of Edinburgh, came to Brisbane and City Hall in 1990 as President of the Word Wide Fund for Nature.

The interior of City Hall was restored to its former glory in 1986. Always willing to pitch in, I got up on the scaffolding to help paint the final gilded rosettes.

The Lord Mayors from each of the Australian capital cities, gathered in Melbourne in 1985 for their annual conference. From left to right: Doug Sutherland (Sydney), Mick Michael (Perth), me (Brisbane), Brian Broadby (Hobart), Ed Beacham (Melbourne), Jim Jarvis (Adelaide), and Alec Fong Lim (Darwin).

THE AUSTRALIAN *magazine*

February 24-25 1990

THE MOST WANTED WOMAN IN POLITICS

Designer Keri Craig made this evening dress for a formal mayoral function. I was proud of the dress, but always felt this front-page contributed to the party girl image that the Labor party used so successfully in my defeat.

Farewell from City Hall, taken following my final press conference as mayor, 1991.

DEFENCE SUPPORT TO DROUGHT AREAS

In 1993 I headed up the Drought Funds Co-ordinating Committee, which brought together various organisations to assist farmers struggling in rural communities. I travelled around Queensland to see the work in action.

The proud family of the bride celebrated my daughter Nicola's wedding to Ted at St Patrick's in Fortitude Valley, 1992. Pictured from left to right: Genevieve, Leigh, Nicola, Ted, me, Eloise, Damien and Stephanie.

Paris was the perfect place to explore my newfound status as a single woman. The Australian Embassy where I lived and worked was on Rue Jean Rey and within waving distance of the Eiffel Tower.

The Brisbane Broncos established a team in Northern England and came to play a team in Paris. As Number One jersey holder I hosted an official reception for them.

Joined by members of both political persuasions the morning after Sydney won its bid to host the Olympics in 2000.

I first got to know Gough Whitlam through notes he and Jim Killen wrote each other in Parliament. We later became friends on the Olympic trail.

Nelson Mandela visited the South African team at the athlete's village during the Sydney Olympic Games. As deputy mayor of the village I acted as escort. He asked if he could put his arm around me so it wouldn't look as though he needed support.

In 2004 ABC Learning was growing at a fast rate. An agreement was signed for a new facility in the presence of Maha Sinnathamby (left), chairman of Springfield and developer of Australia's fastest growing city, and CEO Eddy Groves (behind). I was acting in my role as Chairman of the Board.

With girls from my old school, St Hilda's, at Women's College where I am now President as well as alumna. This was at our annual Academic Dinner where we recognise the extraordinary achievements of young women.

In 2015 I was Ceremonial Naming Lady for the Australian Border Force cutter *Cape York*, which was launched near Freemantle, WA. Pictured here with Richie Ah Mat, Chairperson of the Cape York Land Council.

The growing Atkinson family gathered for Christmas in 2010 at the Vaucluse home of my daughter Stephanie. I am the proud grandmother of 14 grandchildren.

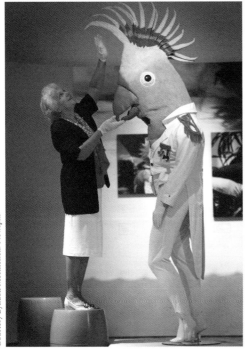

In 2015 the Museum of Brisbane hosted an exhibition to celebrate the 25th anniversary of Expo 88. Pictured here, in my role as Chairman member, with Major Mitchell Cockatoo. This was a brief grey hair phase for me.

I had policies on everything – open government; bus transport; sport and recreation; a 'Back to the Suburbs' proposal, which included establishing regional Council centres so that people wouldn't have to travel into the city; and another inelegantly called 'Rates Rip-off', where I promised to freeze general rates for 'at least the first year after assuming office'. This was to give me grief when I did assume office and bring down my first budget because the Liberal Party advertising had omitted the word 'general' in key advertising. I was accused of breaking a promise when the other charges – water, sewerage and cleansing – rose in line with inflation. The general rates charge, the largest component of what people paid to Council, was the only area in which we had real discretion. The others were charges based on cost recovery.

Despite the distance to be covered on the campaign trail and the number of shopping centres to be visited and babies kissed, metaphorically if not literally, we kept to a tight schedule. Ironically, it was a better campaign than those we ran later when I was seen as a winner and by then had to put up with the full gamut of Party interference.

That first campaign did have the support and involvement of Gary Neat, the Liberal Party state director, and Digby and Narelle from my own office, but otherwise it was run by volunteers, people like Rod Samut and Lynn Everingham who were both with me for several campaigns – 'the coalition of the willing' someone called it. Rod, who was a former president of the Queensland division of the Building Owners and Managers Association, was to continue volunteering as the chairman of the Lord Mayor's Economic Strategy Committee and later as chairman of the Office of Economic Development. Lynn and I had had babies at the same time in the Mater and had been young wives in Edinburgh together, so we were good friends. She organised women from all over Brisbane – some friends, some strangers – to hold morning teas and assist with fund-raisers. There was a core group of about 20 friends who did everything from hosting teas for the elderly to cocktail parties for 400 guests. It was very hands-on, the women cooked for the parties, our daughters helped address the envelopes and were waitresses at the functions; we didn't wheel in the caterers. Apart from being grateful, I was pleased to be able to prick the balloon of 'women don't support women'. In addition to the campaign support, I was always able to count on friends if children needed ferrying about.

It was an interesting time. Chicago-born university lecturer, Joe Siracusa, was a political enthusiast, a great motivator and intellectual energiser on the campaign trail. He would insist on writing my biography in 1987. Thinking he meant in the distant future I had agreed during the campaign that he should write it. He wrote it quickly, and it was published far too soon to be a considered examination of my political career. The result was that he positioned himself as a self-appointed spokesman on my life. He also became involved in the Joh-for-Canberra push and disgraced Police Commissioner Terry Lewis's travails, which did nothing for his reputation, or mine by association.

During the election campaign advice sprang from another surprising source: Clem Jones, the long-serving Labor Lord Mayor. Word was that Clem hated current Lord Mayor Roy Harvey – they had come to blows, literally, back in the 1960s. I was willing to listen to what he had to say and we had a lot in common – we were the same age running up to election, we had both been to Anglican grammar schools and we had both studied local government in the US. Clem gave me copies of his campaign launch speeches, which were long and detailed. Then, one day he called me and said, 'I won't be able to help you anymore, the Labor Party has just made me a life member.' So I think I might claim some credit for Clem's life membership of the ALP!

One of the good things about local government elections in Queensland was that they were always held at the same time: every three years on the last Saturday in March. This made for a very long campaign, or at least mine certainly seemed to be. I had a couple of campaign experiences that have stuck with me. One was at a Local Government Association conference in Cairns, to which I had taken myself because I was never the Council's delegate. Roy Harvey took me to dinner one evening with the other Liberal female alderman, Dulcie Turnbull. Once we were seated he proceeded to show off, asking the waiter to bring the best wine in the house. I suddenly realised he didn't take me seriously. I thought, 'He has no idea what he's up against!'

The other experience was later in the campaign, when I was starting to feel so exhausted that I wondered whether I would last the distance to the election. I went to the tennis at Milton in December to watch Pat Cash play. A high ball came over the net from his opponent and looked as if it was going to be out, but Cash still ran to the back of the court to take the ball, which was just in. It was a light-bulb moment. I thought, 'That's what you have to do. You have to run for every ball.'

I don't remember much about election day. I think it was sunny. I would have spent all day visiting booths, but I don't think I could have visited them all because there were so many. The owner of the Coronation Motel, Mario de Vivo, had given me a room there to rest during the day, and I did. The

Coronation had the best coffee in Brisbane and I would often stop there on my way home from the city to have a coffee and assess the day before braving the domestic front.

When the results came through that evening they were decisive. I had won with 52 per cent of the vote, a clear win without worrying about preferences. Importantly, the Liberal team had won 15 of the 26 wards, so there was no concern about having a hostile Council. (It was this concern that led Russ Hinze to amend the *City of Brisbane Act* again in 1986 to strengthen the powers of the Lord Mayor.)

There was great excitement on the night and lots of shrieks from the children. They had all been involved, more or less, in the campaign. I have always let the children be as active as they want in my work. Sometimes the younger ones enjoyed going to school fetes. Stephanie, our star tennis player, has a photo of herself with Ivan Lendl. The older ones did surveys of commuters at railway stations. When they were small and I was a working journalist I would often have to cart them about with me. I've never thought that work was something you would hide from your children. Some years before, when I was a fairly new alderman, I had been walking through Surfers Paradise with the children when I heard Damien say to one of the younger girls, 'Behave yourself or people will criticise Mum for having badly behaved kids.' There are indeed sacrifices that political families have to make.

Our house in Castile Street had been the setting for every election night party, and the next day people were still coming around to celebrate and this time even more than there had been for the Alderman for Indooroopilly. Among those celebrating the Lord Mayoralty were senior members of the Liberal Party executive who started to give me lectures on how I should be doing things, and insisting on being given access to Council books. I had to remind them that I knew exactly how Council functioned and had a very clear idea of what I intended to do.

There was a fair deal of excitement among the city's conservatives about the new look in City Hall and a lot of advice to be given. Senator David McGibbon, a former dentist who was one of my Indooroopilly neighbours, rang to tell me the first thing I must do was take down the 'Nuclear Free Zone' signs through the city. These had been erected by the Labor administration and of course were a total nonsense, and would hardly be a deterrent to a nuclear attack. I have always disliked empty gestures, so I told David they would indeed disappear, but in good time.

I'LL TAKE CITY HALL

WINNING THE LORD Mayoralty created as much of a shock as losing it six years later. There was a difference. I had thought I would win in 1985 and though I was not so confident in 1991 I didn't think I would lose. But in 1985, in the lead-up to the election, I had no idea what to expect. Knowing the polls would not be declared immediately, I had made all kinds of personal and domestic appointments for the days after and of course they were not fulfilled.

The media calls came from all around Australia. Brisbane's first female Lord Mayor was a big story, and there was surprise that it should have happened in Brisbane at all. I was an unusual kind of female politician – young, married and with five children. Nowadays there is discussion about work–life balance, and how both men and women juggle their careers with having a family. But in the 1980s it was still assumed that men went to work while women stayed at home or, if they didn't, at least took responsibility for the house and children. The only real exceptions were professionals – lawyers, doctors, teachers.

There was a lot of interest in the election of a new kind of political figure, and after its recent woes and poor performance on the hustings a new Liberal Party had emerged. Labor had come to power in Canberra two years earlier in 1983, vanquishing Malcolm Fraser's Liberal government, and the Liberal–National coalition in Queensland had foundered later that year. The Liberal Party in the Queensland Parliament had been reduced to six seats. The headline of the *Australian* that Monday was euphoric: SALLYANNE BREATHES NEW LIFE INTO THE LIBERALS. 'By demonstrating that there is room in Queensland for a free enterprise party which is not committed to the premier's style of government,' the article stated, 'the Liberal party has helped the federal Coalition parties as a whole as well as strengthening its own hopes of revival.'

Adrian McGregor wrote in the *Courier-Mail* about 'an invigorating new era in Queensland politics', adding that, 'Alderman Atkinson actually represents the first alternative style of government Queensland will have seen in a quarter of a century'.

But for me, there were more immediate issues at hand. We now had 16 seats in the Council Chambers and 26 wards, thanks to Russ Hinze's new boundaries. Unlike my three predecessors, I had been elected by all the people of Brisbane and a fair number of them had switched political allegiance. Nine of my aldermen were newly elected as were several on the Labor side, so there was need for induction and training.

My first day in the office I came to work by bus. Well, not actually from home but from The Gap, a nearby suburb where I had arranged to meet the Council's Transport Manager, Ken Davidson, who might well have been catching a bus for the first time and who looked uncomfortable in his formal grey suit. It was a symbolic gesture and one for the cameras, that awaited my arrival at City Hall. I was very aware of symbolic gestures.

I had briefing books prepared for me by all the departmental managers, and a couple of big events to plan for in the near future: the visit of the Duke and Duchess of Kent in April, a trip to East Berlin to launch our Olympic bid, and the annual budget to be brought down by June. I observed to a friend that I felt like a white mouse on a wheel – the faster I ran the faster the wheel spun.

I made my first speech as Lord Mayor in the Council Chambers on 16 April, and began by thanking the people of Brisbane:

> *Thousands of whom changed the voting habits of a lifetime to give me and my team the strongest mandate for more than ten years to guide and direct this city. We will not let them down. As Lord Mayor I represent all Brisbane people, of all political persuasions, from all walks of life … We take office with their permission, we seek to continue in office with their approval and on their behalf I will ensure that Brisbane is run with common sense, sound management, dedication and imagination.*
>
> *Today we are neither Labor nor Liberal but citizens of a common place in pursuit of a common goal … the growth and prosperity of Brisbane.*

When I look back now at that first term, the clearest pattern is of reaching out to people and involving them in the workings of Council. I set up the Lord Mayor's Citizens' Advisory Committee, a Student Representative Committee and community advisory boards in each ward. We held Cabinet meetings outside City Hall in the suburbs, an initiative later followed by other levels of government. Council officers had the new experience – not always a happy one – of having to talk to ratepayers, and local residents had the chance to put questions and comments to me and the chairmen of the various health, works, finance, planning, traffic and transport committees. The Labor administration had started outdoor concerts in the City Botanical Gardens and we took these into suburban parks. The establishment of regional Council centres meant that people could pay their rates close to home.

In the early days, the big and pressing issues facing me were the garbage, the budget and the Olympics, and not necessarily in that order.

The garbage problem, with its series of strikes and go-slows, had really begun in 1983 with the proposed introduction of the now-familiar wheelie bins. Back then the 'garbo' was a common early-morning sight and sound in every neighbourhood as he rattled the garbage can and slung it over his shoulder before jumping fences between backyards. The process of change ended up in court, over the validity of contracts between Council and the private enterprise contractors. Nothing had come before the Council Chambers as it should have and we in Opposition were allowed neither input nor information. The unions complained about lack of consultations and conditions for the men. It was a challenge. I realised that the Labor Council had always been hampered by the close relationship between the Party and the unions. It was rather like a family argument with everyone trying not to offend. I came into office with no political strings attached.

Premier Bjelke-Petersen had offered emergency legislation that he had brought in the year before to end the electricity strike, when he had 'confiscated' workers' superannuation. I said I wouldn't need it and I thought he had been cruel and heartless. He said, 'They deserved it'; the only time I saw the really hard side of Sir Joh. He did bring in an Act, in December, allowing us to vary the workers' contracts if necessary, which included some fairly draconian fines for both contractors and workers. We never had to use it. Given that the fine for non-performance was $50,000 for an individual worker and $250,000 for a company, I wasn't sure we really could, there would be few garbos able to stump up that kind of money.

Meetings were held in the boardroom beside my office. I told union officials we would remain where we were, drinking cups of tea, until we made some progress.

I realised I had the edge when I started getting phone calls from the garbos' wives saying, 'Get the bastards back to work', and, 'I'm sick of having him at home.' I wanted to talk directly to the men myself, but was told by Council officers that the proper way was for our industrial relations people to talk to the union officials. One morning in frustration, I got into the Mayoral limo and was driven out to a southside depot where the men had finished their shift and were sitting about drinking coffee in the autumn sunshine. There was a bit of banter about what a great life it was (from me) and nobody else would want to do this dirty job (from them). I replied by saying that I could gather up a mob of women friends with utes to go around picking up the garbage 'just like Dunkirk!'. I don't know if that in itself had any real effect, but over the months ahead things gradually improved.

I was starting to realise how unusual my role was among mayors. The Lord Mayor of Brisbane was really the Council's executive chairman, part-chairman of the board, part hands-on manager of a big company – Brisbane City Council (BCC) had 8000 employees when I was elected, and, after restructuring, about 7000 when I left. Mine was a role of great actual power and one of great symbolic strength. For many people, the Lord

Mayor *is* the Council. I realised pretty quickly that I had to beware of my views being taken as commands. One morning in the first few weeks I commented on a pot of geraniums on the reception desk outside my office. 'I do love geraniums!' I said. The next morning the corridor was lined with geraniums. When I protested I was told, 'But Lord Mayor, you said you loved geraniums!' Well, yes, but only up to a point.

I also learned pretty quickly that my most important task was making decisions, and that people in a bureaucracy often didn't like making decisions for fear of getting them wrong. Mayors, like all politicians, get no training for the job. I was a journalist by background, a housewife and mother by experience, thrust into a huge management role. What I did have going for me was six years as an alderman and an enormous passion for Brisbane, the city and its people.

As an Opposition member, with only my ward secretary as staff, I had had to find my way through the bureaucratic maze that was the BCC and I'd developed lots of good and useful contacts, among them young professionals who were keen for change and progress. Importantly, I knew what I didn't know and was constantly seeking advice on management and leadership, which are not necessarily the same thing.

The television comedy *Yes Minister* could have been written in Council. One of my first public appearances was the opening of Heritage Week. I rang up a Council planner Terry Conway, who had specialised in the area, to get some pointers. About an hour later I had a call from the manager of the department.

'I understand you have contacted a member of my staff? I wonder why you did that, Lord Mayor?'

'Well, I needed some information,' I said.

'I wonder why you didn't ask me, Lord Mayor?' he asked.

I explained that I knew he wouldn't have the information I needed, to no avail: the manager was offended. I had ignored protocol. It was the job of the head of the department to pass the request down the line, which could take some days. I'd had some experience of this frustration when I worked for Jim Killen and the answer to a journalist's question had to be cleared with Canberra regardless of deadlines. Often, if it was a simple question I would just give the journalist the answer.

Common sense does seem to be a commodity undervalued in organisations. In so many of the decisions I had to make, serious as well as superficial, I found it to be the guiding determinant. I also found that running a house with five children did indeed equip me with useful skills that I could utilise at work. Balancing a budget, delegating tasks, jockeying with competing interests, and adjudicating family disputes all work on the same principles in a domestic situation as in the largest companies in the country.

That conversation with the planning department manager was my first parting of the ways with a bureaucrat, and a difficult one because I liked and respected him. I had known we were on different wavelengths; during the campaign he had said that if 'she' got elected he would have to resign because he couldn't work for a woman. However, that was not our eventual point of rupture. One of my concerns had been Council's plans to build a freeway along the river and under the Harry Seidler–designed and recently built Riverside Centre. It was the first modern building in the Eagle Street precinct and the first to relate to the river. The proposed freeway would have cut off that building, and all others, from the river.

The manager was head of planning and an engineer. We had many discussions about the freeway and its purpose and I was not convinced. Finally, he said, 'If that freeway doesn't go ahead I would have to resign.'

I said, 'Well, obviously one of us has to go, and I've just been elected.' This happened on a Friday afternoon and the manager went into his office and locked the door.

On the Monday morning he came into my office all smiles and told me that his wife had said, 'Thank goodness, and sixty-two is a very good age to retire.' I was able to give him a six-month task of evaluating major Council projects, a job that would allow him to retire with dignity. He was concerned about keeping the large car that came with his manager's role so that his neighbours wouldn't think he had been disgraced. I understood that men, in particular, measured status by externals such as car and office size, and I agreed that he could keep the car. This provided another insight into management-think, for management protested that if this man kept his big car and was no longer a manager, everyone else at his new level would be entitled to a big car. I dismissed this, of course, as nonsense.

One of the great traditions in our democracy is the Westminster system, whereby public servants have no overt political allegiances and can work on either side of the political divide. Sadly, this is a tradition that seems to have disappeared in Australia in the past 40 years. But there are other differences, not to do with policies but more with practices. Many of the Council managers and directors were men who had been with the Council for many years, they were accustomed to doing things in certain ways and had difficulty accepting change.

Early in my Mayoral career I had a taste of dealing with intransigent men, but from another sphere of government. Russ Hinze as Minister for Main Roads was chair of a policy committee for planning transport in the Brisbane region. Minister for Transport Don Lane, myself and a number of bureaucrats, who were all male and mostly middle-aged, would also attend. At one meeting, when I was protesting some plan or other, Russ ordered the microphone to be turned off: 'You can complain all you bloody-well like, but it's going to happen,' he said, and then the microphone was turned back on. Another time when we were discussing a planned main road through some houses on the north side, I suggested we should go out and consult with the residents. The ministers both looked at me in amazement: 'What, go out and ask people what we should do? That's what we were elected for, to make decisions.'

I understood Russ for what he was, an old-fashioned country gentleman. So when he called me 'girlie' or 'pet', I didn't protest. I knew there were bigger issues at hand. And I saw the value of 'rising above it' as witnessed in his dealings with Maha Sinnathamby an entrepreneurial Sri Lankan who had come to Brisbane in the early 1980s. Sinnathamby came with me to meet the minister with a big idea for extending the Queen Street mall underground. In those days, Maha, later the developer of Springfield, a master-planned city on the outskirts of Brisbane, was called Ted. In meetings Russ would say, 'Let's hear from Mr Sin' or 'What have you got to say Black Ted?' Maha wouldn't blink an eyelid. Now he is one of Australia's richest men and Springfield, with a population of 32,000, is the fastest emerging city in Australia.

But Russ Hinze and I did form a good working relationship. I could always depend on him for a quick decision. In Opposition, I had fought against a proposed sewage treatment plant at Moggill in my electorate. Now as Lord Mayor, I had to find a site for it somewhere. Council officers had found a suitable one at Wacol, but some government departments – Primary Industries had a research centre nearby and Corrective Services had the Wacol prison – were objecting. I appealed to Russ as the minister and we had an on-site meeting. Russ arrived in his car and lumbered out on walking sticks. He asked the men from each department what their concerns were. The man from Primary Industries said the research centre would be affected by the smell and the man from Corrective Services said the inmates wouldn't like it. Russ nearly exploded and uttered some choice expletives. 'Listen, fellas, this little girl needs a sewage treatment plant and we're bloody-well going to give it to her,' he said, before lumbering back to his car.

Trying not to smirk I said, 'Well, gentlemen, you heard what the minister said.'

I had known before the election that I would have to tackle bureaucracy but once in office I realised the Council admin-istration needed serious attention. After 24 years of Labor in power there was a certain complacency about how things were done. One of the most obvious and pressing needs was setting up what amounted to a register of Council assets. No one could tell me how many parks the Council owned or where they were. Despite our increasing number of libraries there was no City Librarian. I had chaired an international library conference in Brisbane the year before I came to office, and this was a need I had discovered and a promise I had made. I was told there was no proper map of the sewerage system of Brisbane, the infor-mation was all in the head of one man.

The advantages of having already been in Council for six years were that I understood its structure and I had built a network of bright young men (and they were all men) who had ideas and were keen to make changes. I wanted to restructure, but I didn't want to get in consultants from a large and equally unwieldy organisation, so I chose a company headed by John White, a former army officer who I had known at school. John was someone I could talk to easily, and he understood organisational problems and my concerns. We chose a group of second-tier managers and with John and a couple of his colleagues they formed a small team. There was resistance from people who thought I should have involved the managers of the departments, but if they had thought change was needed they would have already made it, and they would more likely be defensive. I wanted people who were young and had a vested interest in and commitment to the future of the organisation.

I brought in an internationally recognised firm to advise on the financial management of Council. One of the great holes in the structure was the lack of a personnel department, an extraordinary gap in an organisation of that size. We set one up and appointed a manager. We also appointed a City Librarian, an obvious position as we had one of the most extensive library systems in Australia.

A year after I was elected I had to deal with my first public sacking, that of the Town Clerk, the title then of the Chief Executive Officer of the Council and someone I liked and respected. It was to be both public and painful.

The actual break was complicated by unfortunate circumstances. Paranoia was rampant, and people were telling me my office was bugged. I wasn't terribly concerned as I couldn't understand why anyone would want to listen to my conversations. I didn't really have any secrets and I'm not a secretive person. When I mentioned this in passing to Premier Bjelke-Petersen he said, 'Get Terry to send down some of his boys who specialise in that sort of thing.' Police Commissioner Terry Lewis, later to be famous for all the wrong reasons, sent two tall young policemen to my office. What was most memorable about this was that to my embarrassment I blurted out to one of them, 'Oh, you're far too good-looking to be a policeman.' This was to be significant later.

The police didn't find any listening devices, but this didn't satisfy the worriers. Digby McLeay, my executive assistant, called in a specialist de-bugger without actually telling me, under the authority of the vice-mayor Denver Beanland. I was in Sydney at the time, dealing with the awful circumstance of one of my sister's baby's cot death. When I returned I was told that a bug had indeed been found and that, surprise, surprise, the man who had found it was the very man who could protect me against further such intrusions and for serious money. I didn't take any of this very seriously and dismissed any such suggestion.

When I was to state later that the police had looked for bugs and couldn't find any, the police immediately denied ever having been there. But I knew I wasn't mistaken, because of my remark about the good-looking policeman. I was mystified by their denial but could only assume the unit from which they had come was a 'Commissioner's Own' and wasn't supposed to exist.

These events unfortunately coincided with discussions among senior aldermen, the Civic Cabinet, about our working relation-ship with the Town Clerk. There was absolutely no connection between the two events, but two days after we spoke with him, asking for his resignation, a story appeared in the *Sunday Mail* about the bugging of the Lord Mayor's office which looked as if there might be.

So a process that was never going to be easy became extremely difficult. The Town Clerk didn't want to resign, so was then dismissed at a meeting of the full Council after loud opposition from the Labor Opposition. There were unhappy months ahead with appeals to a tribunal, public controversy, and a final vote in Council to confirm the dismissal. At the heart of it all was an elemental aspect of government – the elected and bureaucratic arms, represented by their respective leaders, must be able to get along.

The role of the Lord Mayor, of any mayor, is to plan and direct the future of the city. The word 'planning' usually meant town planning, and in the narrow context of zoning and development control. To me it meant more than that: it meant deciding what kind of a place we wanted Brisbane to be, and then working out how we would get there.

We set up a series of studies and reports on important aspects of municipal life. In 1987 we launched the Brisbane Traffic study. The planned freeway in front of the Riverside Centre had shown me that there was no overall traffic plan for the whole city, a sort of helicopter view of where traffic was coming from and where it was going. This was important to Council in its dual role as public transport operator and major planning authority. Such was the importance and detail of the study that it would take two years to complete. There were several committees, two of technical experts from the Council, the state government and the planning profession. My steering committee, which took the overarching view, was more community-based. It included Gail Chiconi, the alderman for Holland Park, Len Ward from the Transport Workers' Union, Phil Heywood my socialist planning mate from QIT and Alan Goodridge, executive director of the Taxi Council. I had actually wanted a taxi driver because they seemed to know exactly what was wrong with the traffic, but that proved too difficult. The committee handed down its recommendations in 1989 and an immediate furore ensued because it included a recommendation for a couple of bridges across the river, which put local residents offside. I have always taken the view that recommendations following a study are just that: recommendations, albeit very considered ones. The receiving authority is not bound to accept them, but should use them to make plans.

Bridges seem to have always been unpopular in Brisbane. Back in the 1920s there was a bridge proposed between West End and St Lucia but the Council dithered and by the 1940s the pylons were still lying in the grass at West End and the bridge was never built. Years later the growing populace understood the need for bridges to get across the river and we got several.

The Council budget was another daunting issue. I knew from my years in Opposition that the budget process was likely to be as unwieldy as the bureaucracy itself. When Roy Harvey was Lord Mayor, he used to walk about clutching very large black folders and saying cryptically, 'This is the Budget.' As soon as I got into office I was excited to get my hands on the magical black folders, but to my disappointment I found they just contained reams and reams of figures.

And this was the problem with the Budget as it was. It was just about numbers, and those numbers were simply last year's numbers plus a percentage (from memory I think it was 10 per cent). One by one I met with the departmental managers, and one by one they presented their departmental budgets as a done deal. Many of them were quite stunned when I asked them to talk me through the details and explain why they wanted a particular amount. We held meetings far into the night. The BCC Budget was large – at one stage bigger than the state of

Tasmania's, although we lost that distinction in 1977 when the state government took away electricity from us, for it had been a generator of funds as well as energy. In 1985 the Budget was to be $551 million to cover a range of services from parks and libraries to buses, water supply and sewerage. Our single greatest item of expenditure was interest on loans, over which we had no control. Interest rates that year were around 14 per cent; they were to go up later to 18 per cent.

By the following year we had introduced program budgeting techniques, which emphasised the importance of words as well as numbers. Descriptions of programs and measurements of their success became as important as expenditure and revenue allocation. This proved successful generally, and it was a great source of personal satisfaction for me to report in 1986 that we had been able to resurface 22.2 kilometres of road with the money allocated for 15.8 kilometres. 'That's 41 per cent more road for our money,' I declared proudly in the *Annual Report*. 'With concrete footpaths we got 64 per cent more for our money.'

There were practical policies to implement, sometimes at the cost of some personal angst. Backyard incinerators had always been a feature of Brisbane suburban life, but they were a source of pollution and as a former local alderman I knew they were weapons in suburban warfare. I'd get a phone call from an irate housewife saying she had sheets hanging on the clothesline and her nasty neighbour had deliberately lit his incinerator, sending smoke and sparks her way. The personal angst took me back to childhood, as visiting the incinerator had been a daily ritual for my dad: 'I think I'll just go down and do some burning-off.' We banned backyard burning, and the air of Brisbane was grateful.

MORE THAN ROADS, RATES AND RUBBISH

THE ROLE OF Lord Mayor requires much ceremonial duty: in the English system of local government the Lord Mayor is the first citizen. The government of the City of Brisbane was more like the American system, with an executive function. However, I attended many memorable and important formal occasions, including celebrity visits. The first, just a few weeks after I was elected, was by the Duke and Duchess of Kent who were in Brisbane to officially open the new Queensland Performing Arts Centre. We organised a civic reception at City Hall for them. Brisbane designer Keri Craig made me a couple of beautiful evening dresses and the mayoral robes had to be altered in a hurry. The robes, dark and heavy, are modelled on the traditional English ceremonial robes and worn with chains made up of medallions, each inscribed with the name of a lord mayor. Roy Harvey was a big man, so hems had to be taken up to fit me. I was always curious to know if there had been an allowance of material for all the taking up and letting down; Frank Sleeman had been a small man. Later the Lace Guild of

Queensland designed and made for me special cuffs and jabot to go with the robes.

The public aspects of the office brought their own problems, peculiar to women. I had never been particularly interested in clothes and fashion but now needed to be. There would be a Letter to the Editor in the *Courier-Mail* one year complaining that I had been photographed in the same dress twice in one week. Steve Ackerie, Australia's most entrepreneurial hairdresser and so successful he became known simply as Stefan, would send one of his staff up to City Hall to make sure my hair looked good. Stefan is one of the few entrepreneurs from the 1980s who continues to be successful to this day, and continues to contribute to Brisbane.

Sometimes the details of ceremonies were not so public. The electricity authority had offered the Council a special promotional deal to install lights across the Story Bridge, which had loomed dark in the night sky since it had been opened in 1940, designed by John Bradfield of Sydney Harbour Bridge fame. We had a lighting ceremony which involved me attending an event at a riverside restaurant in the city to press the switch and turn the lights on. In reality, a man behind me phoned a man on the bridge, who pressed the actual switch and illuminated the bridge.

The visit of Pope John Paul II in 1986 was a major event for the city, but also for me both publicly and privately. Months before the Pope's arrival I had sat on a plane next to the priest in charge of the visit and suggested to him that it would be a nice idea if the Pope waved from the balcony of City Hall à la St Peter's in Rome. The premier did not think it was a nice idea and knocked it on the head, pointing out that this was a state visit, not a Church visit, the Vatican being a state in its own right. Sir Joh had a record of being not only anti-Liberal but also anti-Catholic, and there had always been stories about senior public figures whose careers had suffered because of this. But I dug in and insisted that my plan go ahead. I pointed out to the planning powers that I had become a Catholic and had diligently brought up my five children as Catholics, and that my mother-in-law, the Lady Mayoress, was a devout Catholic, too. (I should explain how Leigh's mother came to have this title. My being Lord Mayor meant that there was no title for Leigh, of course, and so I conferred the title of Lady Mayoress on his mother, Edna Atkinson. She was wonderful in the role of hostess at official functions and chair of various committees.)

In the end I got my wish, but it did not go smoothly. The plan was that the Pope would come to City Hall where he would meet with me and the family. Then I was told that on his tour no politician's families were to be included, so again I had to protest and again I won. A couple of days before the visit, I was talking to the children about what they were going to wear and one or two said, 'Oh I don't want to meet the Pope.'

'You certainly do,' said I. 'I've put in a lot of effort to make this happen, and it will.'

We had made grand plans for the pontiff to go out on the balcony of City Hall to wave to the masses gathered in King George Square. A couple of days before, the head of the Works Department, in effect the city engineer, came to my office and said, 'The Pope can't go out onto the balcony. I have a report that says it is structurally unsound.'

I said, 'Mr Wood, I do not want to see the report, I don't want to know about it. The Pope *will* go out on the balcony.'

With a note of panic in his voice he said: 'But what if the balcony collapses and the Pope is killed?'

'It won't,' I reassured him. 'The Pope is God's man on earth, and God will look after him.'

On the day, after we had all been to mass out at QE II and the children had the great thrill of being whisked back to the city in police cars with sirens blaring, we all lined up in the foyer of City Hall. We were blessed, received rosary beads and had a few words from a rather dazed Pope. When he started moving towards the grand staircase, a great crowd of cardinals and bishops made to follow him. In alarm I said, 'Where are they going?'

'To the balcony,' was the reply. And up they went. The Brisbane faithful got their papal wave and the balcony laden with the Catholic hierarchy did not fall down, although the balcony was quietly removed not long afterwards.

Actually, that papal visit destroyed my confidence in security arrangements. We had not been used to overt security measures in Brisbane but it was laid on for the Pope. There were sniffer dogs in my office, and I presume the rest of City Hall, for days before his arrival. On the day itself there were snipers on the tops of buildings around King George Square. As the Popemobile pulled up at the front door and the Pope opened his window to acknowledge the vast crowd, a little old lady threw a rose, which landed at the Pope's feet. Of course, there was a mad flurry from security, but I couldn't help thinking it could just have well been a grenade.

There were quasi-ceremonial occasions, too. The Queensland Irish Club each year had a St Patrick's Day dinner the night before on 16 March, and a grand occasion it was. It was an all-male dinner and there were 16 speakers, including the Anglican and Catholic Archbishops, the premier and the Lord Mayor. I had heard all about it from Jim Killen who was always the fifteenth speaker by which stage most of the audience were more than slightly inebriated and he may well have been, too. The food was minimal, but the beer was not.

I was told that a special committee meeting had to be held to discuss the problem I posed for the 1986 dinner. The Lord Mayor of Brisbane had always spoken at the dinner, but they had never had a woman. After two hours' deliberation they decided I was to be invited, 'but only as Lord Mayor and not as a woman'. When I arrived on the night in the lovely old dining room with carved shamrocks around the ceiling, I found that of the two toilets at the back of the hall one had been set aside for my use. This meant that, with the copious amounts of beer being drunk during the evening, there was a continuously long queue at the other.

It was a pretty riotous night, with speakers being cheered and booed, though apparently less so than usual on account of my presence. I'm sure the regulars were relieved when sometimes in the years ahead I would send along my (male) deputy. And then some years later the format was changed and women were invited. And so they are today.

Local government exists by virtue of the state and its Acts of Parliament, and much of its funding ultimately comes from the Commonwealth government. Thus, relationship with premiers and prime ministers, and their ministers and officials, became important and necessary. At times a political divide must be crossed.

Joh Bjelke-Petersen was the first premier of my mayoralty. I felt I knew Joh before I actually met him. He was, of course, frequently in the newspapers, but in 1971 I had also been to his home 'Bethany', near Kingaroy, to interview his wife, Florence.

Hugh Lunn, editor of the wraparound *Australian*, had sent me up to discover the power behind the premieral throne. Flo, as she was always called, was also well known locally as a strong community worker, she played the organ in church on Sunday and who kept up a presence in Kingaroy while her husband ran the state of Queensland as he had done since 1968. But she had always kept a low public profile and this was her first detailed interview. The photographer and I had a wonderful afternoon, which included sampling her soon-to-be-famous pumpkin scones, and before we left for the four-hour drive back to Brisbane we collected some manure from the farm for my garden back at Holland Park.

In 1981 Flo was selected by the National Party for the Senate and went off to Canberra – she would become Senator Lady Bjelke-Petersen when Joh was knighted in 1984, although she was always known affectionately as Lady Flo. I have always thought that Sir Joh's eventual unravelling began when his wife left Kingaroy and was no longer the steadying influence by his side. There was also a lovely story, perhaps apocryphal, that the plan had been for Flo to hold the seat for her husband but that when she was later asked to stand aside for him she said in effect, 'No, thank you very much. I like it here.' And there she stayed until 1993.

I first saw Joh on stage at City Hall for a campaign launch in the early 1970s. What I remember most was his holding up his arm and saying, 'On my right' but it was actually his left. I've always believed this was a political ploy, Joh seeming dumber than he really was so that ordinary folk could relate to him. As a public speaker he was often almost incoherent, stumbling over his words. But in private all of this disappeared. In all my meetings with him Premier Bjelke-Petersen was focused and articulate.

It was widely understood when I was elected, just a few years after the rupturing of the Liberal–National Party coalition, that Joh was aggressively anti-Liberal and the National Party wasn't at all keen for me to win the Mayorship. Even so, he rang me to congratulate me, and he always treated me like the old-fashioned country gentleman. He was smart in meetings, usually with his senior advisors Sir Leo Hielscher and Sir Sydney Schubert in attendance, and would turn to them, 'What do you think, Leo? Should we do this, Syd?' Leo Hielscher was the Under-Secretary of Treasury and Syd Schubert the Co-ordinator-General. Leo was particularly helpful to me during my mayoral career, giving me advice on intergovernmental loans and Council finances.

When Joh resigned during the corruption controversy that led to the establishment of the Fitzgerald Inquiry, Mike Ahern became premier for two years and then Russell Cooper for a little over two months before the government fell in 1989. Both were contemporaries of mine; Mike Ahern was a month older than me and Russell Cooper a year older. The only Cabinet minister with a university degree (in agricultural science) Mike had been a very young member of Parliament, succeeding former Premier Frank Nicklin when he retired in 1968 and Joh became premier. Mike's father had been President of the Country Party and an enemy of Joh's, an enmity apparently fuelled by Joh's anti-Catholicism. Russell Cooper was a traditional Country Party politician with strong and clear traditional values. A grazier from a prominent Queensland family, he had done a stint on his local shire council before entering Parliament and had been a very effective Minister for Police.

My early relationship with his successor, Wayne Goss, was difficult. This surprised me, because this being Queensland, we had a personal connection: his mother-in-law Bridget

Hirschfield had been my brother-in-law's godmother. At one of our early meetings tensions were so high that I asked him if all the staff present, which probably included his chief-of-staff Kevin Rudd, could leave the room. I asked, 'Why are you being so difficult?' and he said, 'Well, you've criticised me publicly.' I replied, 'Of course I have, that's politics.' It cleared the air.

During my time in local government I dealt with two prime ministers – Malcolm Fraser and Bob Hawke – and they couldn't have been more different from each other. Malcolm Fraser was a patrician grazier from Victoria's western district, tall and aloof. At early Liberal Party conferences I was one of several young women prevailed upon to take it in turns to sit beside him at lunch and struggle with conversation. It was hard work. His wife Tamara 'Tamie' Fraser, on the other hand, was delightfully warm and bubbly. The first time I heard her speak in public she said she had been nervous about doing so because she had always been the person at the back of the room making snippy comments about the speaker, and now that she was the speaker she was wondering who was at the back of the room.

Malcolm was an interferer, took a paternalistic interest in everything, and it didn't stop with his retirement. As Lord Mayor I was at a board meeting of the Australian Elizabethan Theatre Trust in Sydney, and the chairman Sir Ian Potter was handed a note that he passed down the table to me. It was from a then-retired Malcolm Fraser (which did impress Sir Ian) and it read: 'Sallyanne, you should buy Brisbane airport.' Brisbane City Council was not quite ready for this, but years later Malcolm's instruction was obeyed when Jim Soorley took a percentage share for the Council in the Brisbane Airport Corporation.

In contrast, Bob Hawke was a classic Australian larrikin and the living definition of the word charisma: he was great fun, a terrific flirt and never shy about demonstrating it. I had got to know him in my Killen days when he was President of the ACTU and then went into federal Parliament as member for Higgins. Once, when I was in Canberra, I was waiting with a group of capital city Lord Mayors outside the chamber for the prime minister to emerge from Question Time. Also waiting was a small group of war veterans. Bob burst out, nodded to the veterans then clasped me in a waltz embrace and whirled me around the lobby space. There was spontaneous applause and varying degrees of surprise and bemusement.

But in mid-1986 there were public concerns about the Queensland government and allegations and charges soon necessitated the Fitzgerald Inquiry into Queensland Police Corruption. From my earliest days in Council I had heard about corruption, and once in charge I made it very clear that I wanted to hear about any suggestions of bribery and would not tolerate it. In fact, I had only come within breathing distance of bribery once, and that had posed an unusual moral problem, although the money wasn't being offered to me personally. A shopkeeper in my electorate had wanted an extension to his shop and had offered me $10,000 for the Salvation Army if I could get it through. For a split second I felt really bad at depriving the Salvation Army of such a donation, especially as I was leader of their local Red Shield appeal. But I consoled myself with the fact that as an Opposition alderman, albeit the local one, I couldn't even have guaranteed to get through what he wanted.

My immediate concern with the state government was not about corruption but about interference in Council matters. Sir Joh announced in May 1986 that Brisbane was going to get the world's tallest building. As BCC was the planning authority this was news to us, and it cut right across our planning guidelines, so I said no. The developer, John Minuzzo from Melbourne, came to see me, and begged and pleaded. The proposed building was 108 storeys high and quite out of scale for our city. I continued to say no, but it was a worry that the state government would try to override Council on planning matters. The state did have the authority. After all, we existed under the *City of Brisbane Act*, but back then it was generally accepted that the state ran Queensland and the Council ran Brisbane. Our roles and responsibilities were clearly defined. Nowadays the lines are blurred and there seems to be duplication in matters such as transport and planning.

After saying no to the building, we had to defend our decision in the Supreme Court when Mr Minuzzo appealed. I had told City Solicitor Paul O'Brien that I'd be happy to give evidence, at which he visibly paled and said, 'No Lord Mayor has done that before.' I said brightly, 'I'll just go in there and tell the truth,' to which one of his lawyers said, 'With respect, Lord Mayor, that's not what the law is about.'

It was a daunting experience, to go into the wood-panelled court, overwhelming in its atmosphere. There, in front of me as I gave my name and swore the oaths, were twelve barristers in robes and wigs. I knew one was ours but I didn't know which one. Sitting in the body of the court was Paul O'Brien looking like a nervous parent at a school concert.

In the end the court found that the application had not been properly made, because of various gazettal changes to the Town Plan and the building never went ahead.

THE SECOND TIME AROUND

In 1988 I won my second election as Lord Mayor. I had a clear win with 63 per cent of the vote and an increase in the number of Liberal aldermen to 17.

I had already moved into my new office in City Hall, which had been opened up to the public with concerts held in the King George Square foyer and refurbished function rooms. The Lord Mayor's office had been in the Brisbane Administration Centre (BAC), linked by an overbridge to City Hall. The BAC building had been built in the mid-1970s and all Council departments, including management, had moved there. With them went the Lord Mayor like some captive bird. When I first got there it was dingy and brown, and not somewhere you would proudly bring visiting dignitaries. It would have been pretty impossible for an ordinary ratepayer to even find it.

Brisbane City Hall, by contrast, was and is an important building. Council literature has described it as 'the finest civic and cultural centre in Australasia'. Its clock tower was once the highest edifice in the city, and when I was a child we would be taken up in the lift on our school-shopping days in Brisbane. Not long after I took office we embarked on its restoration, which then was really a matter of opening up more rooms and refurbishment. The structural problems requiring the building to be closed for three years were not yet evident. City Hall had been built on a swamp and 55 years later this would be a huge problem. The auditorium that had always held school speech days and concerts was acoustically defective, and the solution was large panels made of wool on the walls to absorb the sound. The 1891 Willis organ, considered one of the finest in the world, was restored.

There was some controversy within the heritage community about taking City Hall back to its original state, but sadly this had been fairly unattractive in the financially reduced days of the depression of the 1930s. The building was in the English neo-classical style made famous by Scottish architect Robert Adam and his brother James, and the interior should have reflected this. The Adams used light colours, pale blues and greens, with cream and biscuit shades. The Brisbane Room which had already been refurbished was in pale green. We continued to use this and a pale blue theme throughout. I would say to critics, 'This is how they would have liked it to look in the 1930s if they had had the money.'

Another neglected asset in the city was the river. Brisbane is the only Australian city named for the river on which it sits. Both the river and the city, originally an outpost of Sydney, were called after Sir Thomas Brisbane, Governor of New South Wales and an Ayrshire Scot, who is remembered in the city's emblems by the Staffordshire knot for his regiment and stars for his interest in astronomy. Brisbane doesn't so much sit on its river in the way that, say, London sits on the Thames. Brisbane sprawls across its river as it winds through the urban centre and out through the suburbs, as befits a relaxed subtropical city. A visiting young Englishman recently observed that 'Melbourne is a European city, Sydney an American one. Brisbane is really Australian.'

I believe a city takes its personality from its origins and history. Brisbane was established in 1824 as a convict settlement for the worst of the worst, to be as far away from Sydney as possible. Free settlers were not allowed until the 1840s when they came as rich squatters from the Darling Downs, or as poor migrants. It became a municipality in 1859, the same year that Queensland became a state. Most interesting to me is the fact that so many grand buildings – Parliament House, the Treasury, the Queensland Club – were built in the half century after this, showing the confidence the city and the newly gazetted state must have had.

After World War I Queensland took some steps that set it apart from the rest of the country. The Municipality of Brisbane joined with the 26 small councils and boards around it to become the Greater Brisbane Council in 1925, the largest in Australia and one of the largest in the world. This put out of office all the mayors and aldermen from the other councils. But it was right in line with another stepping down, when members of Queensland's Upper House or Legislative council allowed themselves to be voted out of office in 1922.

With the advent of World War II and the threat of Japanese invasion, Brisbane saw an influx of troops from the United States, Dutch Indonesia and Great Britain and the floating population doubled. (The permanent population in fact increased by 21 per cent between the start and the end of the war.) The Brisbane Line was the farthest north that Australia was to be defended should the Japanese invade. Forty years later in City Hall I would come across elderly American couples who were making sentimental visits to the city where they had met – at tea dances arranged for the troops in the auditorium. The Brisbane-born grandmother of Kristina Keneally, the first woman premier of New South Wales, had met her American husband there and gone back with him to the US.

Nevertheless, Brisbane and Queensland were always disparaged by the rest of the country, with Queensland called the Cinderella State. We were the capital of an agrarian economy, and a sluggish one at that.

All this would change in the 1970s with the discovery of oil in western Queensland, the abolition of death duties and other taxes by Premier Joh Bjelke-Petersen and a new attitude, born of affluence, that lifestyle was important and to be valued. There would be a great flood of southern migration.

Brisbane's character and personality derive from the river, but it had always been taken for granted, certainly in my lifetime. Once the river had been the lifeblood of the city – ships sailed up it, merchants built stores and warehouses on its banks, children swam in it. Yet until the 1980s, buildings along the river had their backs to it, with their windows and balconies facing away from the views.

We designated 1987 as the Year of the River to focus attention on its recreational potential and how we developed its banks. It was a major exercise in community involvement, with groups working on riverfront parkland and developers being made aware of the importance of river views.

We had a committee comprised of a wide range of people who would all bring different perspectives. The chairman was Jerzy Kozlowski, Head of Town Planning at the University of

Queensland, and his deputy was Susan Davies, a public relations consultant. The committee included Trevor Bryan, master mariner, Gary Balkin, who gave us the *Kookaburra Queen* paddle steamers, Stefan Ackerie, hairdresser and successful businessman, and many more. It produced a report *The Brisbane River: A Strategy for Our Future* which is still worth reading today, backed up by a whole lot of technical information.

The river was to get even more attention in 1988, the year of the World Expo, which was centred on its south bank across from the city centre. Expo was a great party for Brisbane and much has been written about it. It was generally accepted to be Brisbane's 'coming of age' and that meant different things to different people. For most Brisbane people, it meant eating later and often outside at cafes. Typically, people like my parents had their dinner which was called 'tea' at about 5.30 or 6 pm and then they watched television and went to bed. There were not many restaurants in Brisbane.

At Expo, people discovered the joys of eating out, of not having to cook. Another reason for its great success was the six-month pass for public transport. You bought your pass (we gave each of the kids one for Christmas) and then you could go whenever you liked, even every day, which many people did.

Expo also meant that the world was coming to our door, and liking it. There was a wonderful feeling of smirky triumph when southerners waxed lyrical and surprised. A city bus driver said to me, 'Now I think I never have to travel, because with all these foreign passengers I feel I've been overseas.' Brisbanites had discovered a newfound confidence, the confidence that comes with external approval, rather like a girl at her coming-out party who is surprised at being told she's pretty. For those of us who had believed in our city, Expo was an opportunity to showcase all those things that are best about Brisbane – the climate, the friendliness of people, the river in front of the Expo site and the green hills of Mt Coot-tha that formed a backdrop to it.

For me, the best parts of Expo were the national days; each nation brought in a special dignitary and celebrated with a lunch. So, for example, we had the King and Queen of Spain for Spanish National Day, British Prime Minister Maggie Thatcher, and Ranasinghe Premadasa the prime minister of Sri Lanka. To each lunch, which was hosted by the Commissioner-General of Expo, Sir Edward Williams, were invited local guests, and others not so local. Former Prime Minister Gough Whitlam was one, just after former Labor leader and former policeman Bill Hayden had been announced as Governor-General. Someone asked Gough what he thought of the appointment. With hardly a blink he said, 'Well, he is that rare phenomenon, an honest cop from Queensland.' This, of course, was the time of the Fitzgerald Inquiry into police corruption.

I saw a different side to Margaret Thatcher from her public persona, and that extended to her husband Denis, who had always been faintly ridiculed as a meek and ineffectual figure. Towards the end of a long and tiring day we had gone back to their hotel and were having a drink. Mrs Thatcher started to complain noisily that the whisky, or perhaps the gin, wasn't what she wanted. Denis put his hand on her arm and simply said, 'Time for bed, dear', and like a lamb she got up and followed him. Earlier in the day we had been in the British pub, one of the highlights of Expo and usually full of British tourists. I asked Denis if he'd like a drink and immediately he shot back, 'If a picture appeared of me with a drink in my hand, I'd be labelled a drunk!'

I had first met Mrs Thatcher back in 1976 when she was Leader of the Opposition Conservative Party in Britain and I was doing my stuff for the *Australian Liberal*. I followed her around all day on various engagements in Canberra, but waited until the end of the day to do an actual interview. Other journalists needed to talk to her and it was a case of 'family hold back'; I was the in-house reporter. It was late in the afternoon when we sat down with a cup of tea and she asked, 'Do you mind if I kick my shoes off?' Of course, I didn't. We chatted about a lot of things, including women in politics and the problems they faced. The evidence was before us. There were currently no women in the Australian House of Representatives. She pointed out that it had been easier for her because she lived in London and that's where the British Parliament was. When she asked me, 'Why don't you have a go?' I quickly pointed out that I lived in Brisbane and had five children. Nowadays it's an accepted fact that young women with children are members of Parliament and have even given birth during their time in office. Then, it was not even a consideration; the Labor Party had used the fact that I had kids against me in my first campaign for the Brisbane City Council.

I met Mrs Thatcher again, or rather caught a glimpse of her on stage, at a Conservative Party conference in Blackpool in 1989, the year before she stood down as prime minister. I was a guest of the British government on a trip to the UK, meeting with government people in various places. I went to Belfast and to the Sirocco Works where Dad had begun his working life, and I met interesting people across the political divide. I had input into where I would go and when I had asked if I might visit Northern Ireland the official reply was a definite yes, because no one ever asked to go to Northern Ireland.

I was introduced to Prime Minister Premadasa as someone who had grown up in Sri Lanka. He suggested I should visit while he was still in office so he could 'guarantee' security. The civil war in that country was at its height. I took myself there in 1989 on a private visit, the first time I had been back since my childhood. It was very emotional and somewhat disturbing, for we were not used to personal security in Australia. When I went for a dip in the Galle Face Hotel pool where I had learned to swim 40 years earlier, a man in a suit stood on the edge, arms folded, watching me. Mr Premadasa, son of a low-caste washer or dhobi man and now president, was assassinated a few years later by a suicide bomber as he watched a May Day parade in Colombo. About ten others, including his bodyguards, were also killed.

In my role as Lord Mayor I also hosted various members of the royal family. Some occasions were more memorable than others. We held a lunch for Prince Philip in City Hall in his capacity as President of the World Wide Fund for Nature. Before his arrival we had found, in the great caverns below City Hall, two chairs specially made for his first royal visit to Brisbane in 1954. We got them out, and at lunch I sat on one and he on the other. I said, 'Sir, these are the chairs on which you and Her Majesty sat in 1954.' And he said, 'Bloody uncomfortable then and bloody uncomfortable now.'

Prince Charles and Princess Diana made a visit to Brisbane in April 1983. We were all upset that they didn't bring Prince William to Brisbane, and everyone wanted to talk about him to Diana at the reception. I remember Prince Charles being quite cross when they did a walkabout in King George Square. He went to one side of the gathered crowd and she the other. The crowd on his side were obviously disappointed and showed it. I was to be told by people in the royal circle that this was one of the strains on their marriage, that she was obviously more popular than he.

The Duke and Duchess of York came to Brisbane in 1990 and to City Hall. In 1920 the foundation stone for city hall had been laid by the Duke's great-uncle (later Edward VII and then the Duke of Windsor). The current Duke was to unveil a commemorative stone. The Duke and Duchess were a jolly couple, generally known as Andrew and Fergie. We had a lunch for the great and good in the Balmoral Room and the entrée was decorated with flowers. My son, Damien, who was sitting in for his father, said to the Duchess beside him, 'You can eat these flowers,' and proceeded to do so. She started to follow his lead when the Duke leaned across and sternly said, 'No!'

I asked the Duke to speak after my words of welcome at the lunch but he said he was speaking at the unveiling afterwards and that was enough. I was disappointed for the guests at the lunch who were not going to be outside for the unveiling, which may have explained my later irritation. The Duke said as we were walking out, 'Why wasn't your husband here?' I explained that Leigh was operating. The Duke said, 'I always thought surgeons could get someone to replace them?' To which I replied, 'You wouldn't like that if it were your brain!'

The visit had its oddities. I was told that the Duchess would want to wash her hair after she came up the Brisbane River and before the lunch. That seemed strange to me, but we dutifully had a hairwashing hose put in the sink in the bathroom off my office. When they arrived I asked the Duchess, 'Do you want to wash your hair?' She looked absolutely stunned, and of course I told her of the request and we had a good laugh.

When Expo finally ended we all had withdrawal symptoms, but for those of us who had a concern for the city and a responsibility for it, the hard work was just beginning. In Council we had long been thinking about what would happen afterwards.

Premier Bjelke-Petersen had made a promise that Expo wouldn't cost taxpayers anything and its site would be sold off at a profit due to the improved value of the land. But this meant that the south bank of the river would be turned into a second CBD, another North Sydney, and we didn't want that. The people of Brisbane didn't want it either, because they had come to know the pleasures of parkland close to the central city where you could eat outdoors. So for a few years and through several iterations of planning proposals I argued with Sir Llew Edwards, chairman of Expo 88, and three premiers: Mike Ahern, Russell Cooper and Wayne Goss.

The South Bank Development Corporation was established and the legacy of their work has been South Bank, that green strip of parkland with its picnic areas, swimming pool, playgrounds and cafes that make up the 40-hectare site, with the cultural precinct, including the Queensland Performing Arts Centre, state galleries, library and museum at one end. I don't think there is another city in the world with such a green public facility within walking distance to the centre of town and bordering the river. I look out at it every day from my balcony and my heart sings.

Expo certainly changed the way people thought and felt about Brisbane, but it had also involved a lot of Council staff in providing infrastructure to the site and re-routing of traffic. There were changes to the inner suburbs, places like West End and South Brisbane but also New Farm and Paddington. We established the Inner Suburbs Action Project, which was to be hugely important for the way planning was to be done in Brisbane and accessibility to suburbs. Town planning was always seen as technically driven, using technical expertise to find theoretical solutions. But in my mind it was really about people's lives and how they lived them, and it should focus on quality of life, including a whole range of social and environmental issues.

The director of the project was an urban planner from New Zealand, Kevin Yearbury, and I chaired the steering committee, which met monthly. It comprised people from all walks of life, for example social worker Ian O'Connor who would years later become vice-chancellor of Griffith University. The project reported directly to me and the Establishment and Co-ordination Committee, or Civic Cabinet, so that Council staff would know and understand that this did not belong to one particular department but was across all Council activities, including traffic, parks, water and sewerage; this was very important.

Probably the most important aspect was engaging community involvement, and not just for their reaction to plans put forward by Council planners. People were involved right from the beginning of the process, and so were keen to be part of the implementation. We used the word 'action' rather than 'study', because we wanted things to be happening as a result, rather than having a series of studies which might just gather dust in drawers. The Brunswick Street Mall in the Valley and the work on Norman Creek were recommendations that were put in place immediately.

Resulting from the Inner Suburbs Action Project were five local area action plans and then an overall strategy project, known as the Brisbane Plan. A first for Australia, it was a city plan that looked at all aspects of the life of the city, now and in the future, and understood that a city was also affected by events beyond its borders. Professor Bob Stimson came to Brisbane as project director and after a year of work the plan was released in February 1991. This was bad timing, particularly for me as it turned out. I was defeated in March so I didn't get to see the Brisbane Plan implemented, although I was pleased to see in following years that various recommendations popped up in Council policies and practices. The Plan was re-released in September 1991 as the Stimson Report and called Brisbane–Magnet City. It covered all the vital aspects such as economic development, community engagement, traffic management and land use.

Two major projects were classic examples of the balancing act of government, particularly local government, which is closely linked with people's lives and the things that matter to them on a daily basis. The balance is between what's necessary for the community good and what is politically popular.

The projects were about waste disposal and treatment, and road building and traffic management, and both were to play a role in my later defeat.

The upgrading of Hale Street in Milton came out of the Brisbane Traffic Study as part of the means of improving traffic flow in the city. It would later connect with the Inner City bypass. But the widening of Hale Street was going to take in some of the land of the Anglican Church at Milton and of the Lang Park football field, home of Rugby League. Both were sacred in their own way and in fact part of Lang Park had been a cemetery many years ago. We had done research which showed there were no graves affected by the road. My private view was that Christians believed that the spirit left the body on death and the remains were mere dust, but I kept that to myself. The controversy was highly charged emotionally, with parishioners saying that Sunday services would be affected by traffic noise and residents of long standing having their homes removed. The emotion was heightened by one parishoner, an articulate state member and future premier, Peter Beattie, who was loud in his opposition. It's hard now to imagine Brisbane's traffic network without Hale Street.

In a fast-developing city like ours, waste management was a problem we had addressed for some years and we were looking at a range of different solutions. We had finally decided that landfill was still the best option and that current technologies could handle all the concerns of pollution, odour and noise. We spent a long time looking for a site, in and around Brisbane, and settled on land at Gardner Road, Rochedale, whose clay soil base was geologically ideal. We could have all the right safety and environmental protection and a guarantee of no toxic waste. There was strong community opposition, including from the local Liberal alderman, Graham Quirk, later to become Lord Mayor, who resigned in protest from his Finance Chairman's position.

There was a lot of dishonest Labor propaganda in the lead-up to the March 1991 elections, nonsensical statements were floated that the landfill would rise to the height of an 18-storey building. Politicking from the Labor state government forced us to make a decision in February rather than delay it until after the election.

I was confident it was the right thing to do and the Rochedale Engineered Sanitary Landfill went ahead. It's ironic given the Greens attack at the time; it now generates 130 MWh of renewable solar energy and Labor Prime Minister Julia Gillard was to praise it in 2011 as an example of green energy production. Over the years, local residents have told me it wasn't what they thought it would be and they're happy with the result. So I'm glad of that, although they all voted against me in the election. Since then new estates have been established in surrounding areas.

While all of this was happening in the broad scope of Council, 1989 was also a difficult one for me personally. I made the painful decision to separate from Leigh, and my mother died. I moved out of the family home in Castile Street and into an apartment in St Lucia with Genevieve and Stephanie. My office issued a statement to the media and said we wouldn't be giving interviews.

Leigh was surprised by my decision and I was surprised by his surprise. From my perspective we had lived for many years in an atmosphere of tension and low-level bickering. Home was not a comfortable place to be. To the world outside we presented unity and this was not a front. We did have lots of interests in common, especially the five children. A mutual friend said 'People who know you understand and the rest don't really matter.' In many ways my move into public life had been a way of side-stepping my lack of emotional satisfaction.

A few years earlier Mum had moved from Southport to Brisbane and was living at a nursing home in Indooroopilly, around the corner from where we lived. I was surprised at the intensity of grief I felt upon her death. She had been in a vegetative state for some time before she died and it had been many months since I'd had a real conversation with her. Even so, I had got into the habit of visiting her on my way home from City Hall and telling her about my day. Her eyes were closed and she never responded but the nurses would tell me she knew I had been there. I took comfort from this. It reminded me of when, as a schoolgirl coming home on the bus I would think of interesting things to tell her because I knew she would be sitting on the veranda knitting, waiting for me to share news of the day. Now she was not there. We all know that losing ageing parents is inevitable, but somehow it is like losing part of yourself.

When Dad had died of cancer ten years earlier he had been in such pain that in the end it was a relief that he was finally at peace. The odd sayings he was always fond of kept coming back to mind again and again. And so, even though he was not there, and Mum was not there, they continued as a presence.

But 1989 proved difficult in other ways as well. It was to be the beginning of what seemed to be a concerted effort to move me out of City Hall, and by my own party. In one sense I could say I was the victim of my own success, though I didn't see it like that. There appeared to be an assumption that I would naturally want to move up from local government. Nobody seemed to believe me when I said I was content with the role of Lord Mayor, I had a job to do and no intention of going anywhere until I had finished it. By the end of that year I was working on the Inner Suburbs Action Project and moving towards the Brisbane Plan which would naturally come out of it. There was to be a state election at the end of the year and the Liberal Party's recent history had been gloomy. In fact, the state of the conservative parties was not good after the Coalition split of 1983, followed by the Fitzgerald Inquiry and Bjelke-Petersen's demise.

Senior members of the party came to see me, in the flat in St Lucia. They proposed a bold scheme that seemed quite hare-brained to me. They suggested I stand down from the mayoralty and run for a state seat, and then after the election Angus Innes, the parliamentary leader of the Liberals, would stand down and I could replace him. Apart from the fact that I had no interest in state Parliament and had things to do where I was, there were a few flaws in this scheme. Angus showed no inclination of stepping down and I certainly wasn't going to knife him. The seat they had in mind for me was Yeronga, from which Norm Lee would retire. I knew Clem Jones had run for that state seat unsuccessfully years before, so the omens were not good. I could see that the Liberal and National parties, running side by side, were not going to do well at the election, and they didn't. Wayne Goss became premier of Queensland.

In early 1990 a similar plan resurfaced, but this time they were attempting to coerce me with a federal seat. It was an attractive one; the seat of McPherson on the Gold Coast where I had grown up was safe, the sitting member Peter White was going to retire but again I said no. I was being manipulated on two fronts, by the federal heavies on one side wanting me to run and the state hierarchy on the other wanting me to stay. Andrew Peacock, leader of the federal Opposition, told me I would have a ministry in his government. But I told him the time was not right for me. I had just separated from my husband, I had teen-aged daughters at home and Canberra was a long way away. Perhaps the most bizarre aspect of the whole episode was a coercive phone call from Melbourne businessman John Elliott who was then the federal president of the Liberal Party. He called me from his private plane as it was flying over Brisbane; a call from the heavens, quite literally.

Looking back, I obviously wasn't strong enough in my denials to run for state or federal office, because the media were always saying I intended to. I think, because I am basically honest, I wouldn't say 'never'. Who could know about the future? But I think the media particularly, and people involved in politics generally, could not understand or believe that I felt deeply about the importance of local government. I used to say that the three tiers of government were horizontal rather than vertical. That is, they should be considered side by side rather than one above the other. Local government is important because that is where people live and is representative of how they live.

At one stage late in 1990 I decided not to run for Lord Mayor again. The Brisbane Plan would be pretty much in place and my work would be done. But the reasons were mainly personal ones. Leigh and I had reconciled and he had moved out of the house in Castile Street, which we sold, and into the apartment where I was living at St Lucia. I wanted to try to get our marriage to work.

I typed a statement of my intention to stand down. I said I felt I had made the changes needed for the good government of the city and put in train the necessary reforms for the future. I called my media advisors into my office in City Hall on a weekend to discuss the best ways of making an announcement, and also told my plans to Phil Denman, the Deputy Mayor and Bill Everingham, the Liberal Party state president. They reacted very differently. Phil, who was almost at retirement age, said he would be ready to run himself. Bill was aghast at the suggestion of my leaving and said that without me there we would lose City Hall. Bill was an old friend, the husband of Lynn who had been such a campaign stalwart, and had been at school with Leigh. He came to the apartment and argued fiercely with Leigh and eventually persuaded me that it was my duty to stay. My announcement was never made, and very few people ever knew it might have been.

THIS SPORTING LIFE

MY PASSION FOR sport was inspired by the 1982 Commonwealth
Games in Brisbane, though not then or ever as a participant. It
was during those few weeks in October that I realised there is
more to sport than actually playing it.

The Olympics have been a thread running through my life
for several decades, which is perhaps surprising seeing I'm so
unsporting. The Commonwealth and Olympic games are not
just about young people participating in sport. For me it has been
watching the happiness that comes with athletic success, the thrill
of achievement, the qualities of teamwork and fair play.

My love of Rugby League stemmed from a chance last-minute
invitation when I was Leader of the Opposition to replace Mal
Meninga as a guest speaker at the Shaftesbury Community
Centre. A few days later there arrived in the mail a very nice
thank you letter from Mal and two tickets to the Grand Final
in which his team, Souths, was playing. It was my first Rugby
League game (I had been brought up as a Rugby Union girl)
and the most exciting sporting event I had ever witnessed. I've

always said it is the last of the gladiatorial sports — the atmosphere at Lang Park (now called Suncorp Stadium), the pure thuggery of the game and the visceral feelings as a spectator are unique.

When I became No 1 jersey holder for the new Brisbane Broncos team, one of the owners, Barry Maranta, had the bright idea that I should kick off the first ball. Bright idea it was not. I can still see the look on captain Wally Lewis's face when I walked out onto the field after the national anthem muttering, 'It's not my idea!'

The ball was placed, I kicked … and my shoe flew off, travelling higher and further in the air than the ball.

Any interest I might have had in cricket was stymied back in Colombo. In those days the English and Australian cricket teams would travel to each other's country by ship on alternate years, and the ship always passed through Colombo. Each team would play a match at the Colombo Cricket Club. All the local cricket lovers would be there, including my father, and we children would be forced to spend a couple of very boring days accompanying him, although we never liked to tell him that for us it was not a treat. Later in Southport, during the January holidays and in the days before car radios, Dad would insist we listen to the Test on the wireless so that we could give him the score when he popped home through the day. Later still, I made a memorable faux pas when Hugh Lunn introduced me to his hero Ken 'Slasher' Mackay. I said brightly, 'I went to the cricket in Sydney recently and it was so boring. There was one chap out there for hours and he only made four runs.'

Slasher said, 'That was me.'

My father only ever wrote me two letters. One was before Leigh and I went on our first visit to Belfast and he said, 'Please don't tell my sister you married a Catholic.' The other was to congratulate me when I was a reporter on the Sydney *Daily Telegraph* and I told him I was going to interview Richie Benaud.

As far as sport is concerned, I have done my best. I swam breaststroke in a relay at the World Masters Swimming in Brisbane in 1988. I have batted in a charity cricket match. I have played tennis with former Wimbledon tennis champion the late Ken Fletcher after whom we named the park that has the Brisbane Tennis Centre. I continue to play with another Wimbledon champion, Daphne Fancutt, whose name was given to an amphitheatre in that park. I have tried to ski at two Winter Olympics, in Albertville and Lillehammer – naturally not as a competitor but at the hands of kind and patient volunteers. Still, the most of my sporting triumphs have come as promoter or facilitator.

The Olympic Games are the world's greatest sporting event and my involvement began with the Brisbane bid for the 1992 Games. After I was elected in 1985, I realised that the garbage problems and the Olympics were inextricably linked. The same manager was in charge of the garbage issue and the Olympic bid, and there were no prizes for guessing his focus. I rang Kevan Gosper, President of the Australian Olympic Committee (AOC) and later the vice-president of the International Olympic Committee (IOC) and asked for help. He flew up to Brisbane from Melbourne and we talked about setting up a bid office within Council, but independent of it, with a professional sports administrator in charge. John Coates, a young Sydney solicitor with a background in rowing who later became president of the AOC was our choice. He and his wife, Pauline, moved to Brisbane with their five little boys. They spent Christmas with us at Castile Street.

Initially I had been ambivalent about bidding for the Olympics. For one thing, it had been impossible to get firm costings out of the Labor-dominated Council. And there was no firm commitment from the federal government either: something vital for the IOC to accept the bid. I had not forgotten that a few years before, Melbourne had decided to bid for the Olympics, and Prime Minister Malcolm Fraser had refused to give the go-ahead, causing embarrassment among Australian Olympic folk and rage from the internationals, or perhaps both.

The Olympic bid process has gone through many changes over the years. When Los Angeles held the Games in 1984, it followed in the footsteps of Munich, Montreal and Moscow, all of whose Games were troubled, financially or otherwise. Los Angeles was able to make its own rules and no money was spent on fancy facilities. The LA Games were considered a commercial and a sporting success, so in the lead-up to the 1992 bid there was a veritable troupe of bidders from around the globe.

This bidding contest was a new phenomenon for the IOC, and so were the later scandals and allegations of bribery that led to a plethora of rules and restrictions on the bidding process. The 1992 bid was good-hearted and friendly, with lots of wining and dining and visiting, although everyone involved was fully aware of the financial aspects of the ultimate goal and the magnitude of the project. We spent just under $6 million on our bid, as opposed to Sydney's $20 million for the 2000 Games. I honestly don't think we could have spent any more, unless all the IOC members we had invited to visit had come.

I always saw our Olympic bid for what it was, a marvellous marketing exercise with an outside chance of getting the Games. One of my lobbying lines was 'In Australia we have a famous race called the Melbourne Cup, which the favourite never wins'.

But I did believe, and passionately, that we would have run a very good Olympics. Australians are excellent organisers, and in Brisbane we had the climate and the space for the necessary facilities, plus the Gold and Sunshine coasts. This was our chance to show the world that there was more to Australia than Sydney and Melbourne.

A couple of weeks after taking office, I led a delegation to East Berlin for an IOC meeting, where the candidate cities for the 1992 Games would declare themselves. Our competitors were to be Amsterdam, Barcelona, Paris, Belgrade and Birmingham; New Delhi had pulled out. I should point out that the Olympics are awarded to a city, not to a state or a nation, which is not always obvious when politicians at all levels want a piece of the action. In our case, of course, the state of Queensland had the money, and so with us to East Berlin came the state Minister for Sport, Peter McKechnie, who happened to have been at The Southport School when I was at its sister school St Hilda's. For our final foray in Lausanne a year later we would have federal Minister for Sport, Recreation and Tourism, John Brown, attend. Peter was National Party and John was Labor: the three of us provided a fine example of political ecumenicalism.

At this first IOC gathering I found to my surprise that I was a bit of a star, simply because I was young, female and not the archetypical Australian sporting figure. I also spoke French, not well, but my accent was good. As Henry Higgins says in *My Fair Lady*, 'The French don't care what they do actually, as long as they pronounce it properly,' and there is some truth in that. So when I gave a speech in French at a lunch party held by Rupert Murdoch, the elderly gentlemen of the IOC – and they were nearly all men and nearly all elderly – fell about in astonishment.

At two o'clock one morning a few days before the IOC lunch, I opened my hotel bedroom door to find Rupert Murdoch's man Wilf Barker standing there in a state of mild hysteria. Wilf was rather a large chap and the sight of him in his shortie pyjamas almost reduced me to hysterics, although of a different kind. He had just discovered that the invitations we were about to send out for lunch at the Australian embassy in East Berlin would not be accepted by a large number of our intended guests because the Communist bloc did not recognise 'East' with 'Berlin'. So I got dressed and we all set about obliterating the word 'East' on the invitations so they could go out the following morning.

Hosted by Rupert Murdoch and his wife, Anna, in a marquee in the grounds of the embassy, the lunch was a typical 1980s extravagance. The food by leading Melbourne caterer Peter Rowland had been flown in specially, and there was drama when the seafood was held up for a bit at the East German border. The IOC members feasted on Australian crabs and prawns, seated at tables with tall centrepieces of native Australian wildflowers. Afterwards, as we were leaving, I saw the poor East German staff eagerly stuffing themselves with the leftover food behind the marquee.

At the lunch there was another potential crisis. Prime Minister Bob Hawke had sent a video, which I was told we couldn't use because it included a reference to 'our embassy in East Berlin'. The prime minister's endorsement was obviously vital for our bid, so I needed to come up with a solution. I played the video at the hotel beforehand and discovered that the offending words came very near the end of the tape. At the presentation I had someone hidden under a table near the power point and at just the right time the plug was pulled out.

'Oh, dear, technical fault!' we said. 'Sorry!'

Still, behind the Iron Curtain in 1985 it was scary and depressing. The shops in East Berlin were full of locals queuing for everything, and there wasn't much for sale anyway. In my hotel suite I met Horst Dassler, the highly influential head of sporting company Adidas, who gave me to understand in sign language that the room was bugged. When I suggested we go for a walk in the garden he looked taken aback.

I hosted a lunch for the female IOC members, a small gathering – Princess Nora of Liechtenstein, Pirjo Haeggman of Norway, Mary Glen-Haig of Great Britain and Flor Isava-Fonseca, the very glamorous Venezuelan who had been an Olympic equestrian champion. Flor was in her sixties, which seemed very old to me then, and announced that she kept young by taking lots of lovers. Mary, later Dame Mary and a former British hospital matron, looked suitably shocked. I'm not sure what the Communist listeners thought. On another occasion Princess Nora complained about the awful toilet paper in the hotel. We had obviously been warned about this in Brisbane and had brought our own, so later in the day I had some gift-wrapped in our special 'Brisbane 92' wrapping paper and sent around to her.

On Sunday I asked to go to mass and was told that it would be difficult in Communist East Berlin, where Christianity was banned. However, we found a Catholic church in which were a clutch of Catholic IOC members. Going to mass, which I did regularly at the time, was going to be an integral part of my Olympic lobbying during the year ahead, for all the Latin American members and many of the Europeans were diligent attenders. It was very moving in Berlin because the local Catholics were clearly part of an underground movement, and very brave.

My mass-going strategy only once went awry. In Lausanne some years later as part of the Sydney bidding team I was given directions to the cathedral. Former Prime Minister Gough Whitlam said he would like to come too, and so did my son, Damien, over from Cambridge where he was doing his Master of Laws. Halfway through the service, having noted there was not another IOC member in sight, it dawned on me that we were not in a Catholic cathedral at all, but the Protestant one. Gough, of course, had great fun with this story, telling everyone: 'There hadn't been a genuflection in that church for at least five centuries!'

In our 1992 bid, one of our arguments was that the Olympics had only been held in the southern hemisphere once before – Melbourne in 1956 – and that they should be held in the southern hemisphere again. Barcelona's strong selling point was that the Games had never been in Spain. I asked Eduardo Hay, the IOC member for Mexico, 'Are the Latin Americans going to vote for Barcelona?' He looked at me directly and said, 'Yes.' So when the announcement came and President Samaranch declared Barcelona the winner I was ready. We were able to do the Australian sporting thing and congratulate the Barcelona delegation on their success. We had come third in a six-horse race, Paris came second.

In recent years the Olympics, and it seems all major sporting bodies, have been tarred with allegations and evidence of bribery and doping on a grand scale, but back then none of this had surfaced. As newcomers to the world of sports administration, our naivety was tempered with surprise and cynicism at the accepted lavishness of the IOC world. In Lausanne for the final announcement of the 1992 winner, Denis Howell who had been Britain's first Minister for Sport and was the leader of the Birmingham bid, said to me, 'I'm just disappointed that our young athletes have had to witness how the IOC operates.'

As we were all sitting together in the hall waiting nervously for the announcement of the successful bidder, someone in one of the teams whispered, 'Have you heard what Paris has done? They've given all the IOC members fur coats!' Someone else said, 'But have you heard what Barcelona has done? They've put girls in them!' We all laughed uproariously.

For Brisbane, we had several Olympic lobbying forays: we also went to Moscow, Sofia in Bulgaria and Belgrade in then Yugoslavia. Sofia was bidding for the Winter Games, and Belgrade was bidding against us, but part of our strategy was to get second votes for countries who might not put us first. The Olympic voting system was preferential, just like the Australian political system. Joining John Coates, Wilf Barker and me in Moscow was long-distance swimmer Michelle Ford, the only Australian to win gold at their Olympics, and part of the team that had defied the Australian government's official boycott in 1980. Boycotts then seemed to be a regular feature of athletic events. The 1986 Edinburgh Commonwealth Games had been boycotted by 32 of the 59 eligible countries over the British government's acceptance of apartheid in South Africa. Michelle's presence in Moscow gave us official access and we were shown the city's sporting venues with great pride. At the stadium she whispered to me to ask to see the athletes' facilities, which I did, and they were indeed awful.

In the months leading up to the 1992 bid decision we hosted about 25 IOC members in Brisbane. We wanted to show our sporting facilities, mainly built for the Commonwealth Games and our plans for the future, as well as Brisbane's touted attractions like our friendly people and lifestyle. We made a series of videos extolling the virtues of Brisbane's climate, culture and sporting facilities, and explained how we would overcome certain problems such as quarantine for horses. We hosted dinners for the IOC delegates. These were not always trouble-free events. The Ethiopian IOC member was a doctor of medicine, wearing a lot of gold jewellery, while his country was in a crisis of famine and civil war. Damien asked him whether he felt guilty about being here. The doctor didn't seem to take offence. He replied that his country was a very rich one but its people were lazy, which shocked us all.

Lausanne in October 1986 was abuzz with delegations from the bidding cities, involved in rounds of parties and meetings. The Winter Games were also being awarded so there were people from Albertville (France), Lillehammer (Norway), Cortina (Italy), Sofia (Bulgaria) and Falun (Sweden). Royals were reduced to humble lobbyists. At dinner one night I sat next to Crown Prince Haakon of Norway, with Australian Olympian Herb Elliott on the other side. Queen Silvia of Sweden was in attendance. The Italians hosted a cocktail party at which Gina Lollobrigida was the star. When I met her in the receiving line she was very disappointing, old and lined with far too much makeup. Minister for Sport, John Brown, rushed over and said to me, 'Where's Gina?' I had to say, 'You've just passed her!' When a photographer asked to take a picture of me with the famous Italian film star, I was quite pleased. When I later saw the photo she looked gorgeous and I looked drab. I learned a lesson about makeup that day.

When Melbourne lost to Atlanta for the 1996 Games, there was great and public disappointment. Crowds gathered in the city, expecting that even if Melbourne didn't win, at least Athens' success would give the city's huge Greek population something to celebrate. Athens was of course the city of the original Olympics and the sentimental favourite among the six bidding cities. The party turned into a wake. In Brisbane we were more fatalistic, and certainly on my return I had letters of congratulations from all over Australia.

In 1987 I was invited to speak at the International Olympic Academy in Olympia, the actual birthplace of the Games in Greece and a deeply spiritual place. I spoke of Barcelona's 'emotional argument', that no Spanish city had ever hosted an Olympic Games. I avoided mentioning the emotional attachment between Barcelona and the IOC President Juan Antonio Samaranch. I ended my speech by saying, 'Although Brisbane did not win the vote of the IOC, the city won other things that were perhaps just as important.' The bid had succeeded in strengthening community spirit and civic pride, it focused world attention on our city and its potential for tourism and investment, promoted Brisbane's sports facilities and highlighted its ability as a sports administrator, dramatically demonstrating the ability of the public sector and private enterprise to work well together.

There was talk of a future bid but I was sensitive to the fact that a percentage of the population were opposed to the Olympics (despite the warmth of the welcome home) and to the next election. Early in 1988, the Australian Olympic Federation (later to become the AOC) invited all Australian cities to bid to be the candidate city for 1996. Brisbane, Sydney and Melbourne threw their civic hats into the ring and what ensued was a ridiculous mini-rerun of the Olympic bidding process with all kinds of allegations of behind-the-scenes shenanigans. When Melbourne, the chosen candidate city, lost the bid for the Games, I wrote to the AOC suggesting that they should make the decision on the next bidding city rather than allowing a competitive process. I have to say that part of my joy on that dark and stormy night in Monte Carlo in October 1993, when Sydney was declared the winner for 2000, was that I would not have to front up for Hobart, Adelaide or Perth.

For the girl who was always the last chosen for ball games at school, my Olympic experience has ironically been long and deep. I was in the presentation team for Melbourne in Tokyo in 1990. I went to the Winter Games of Albertville and Lillehammer as a member of Sydney's lobbying team and then to the Summer Games in Barcelona where I had persuaded the mayor, Pasqual Maragall, to host a lunch for the mayors of all the bidding cities of 1986.

I kept up my Olympic connections as Vice-President of the Australian Paralympics Federation to John Brown's presidency, and chairman of the AOC's Sport for All Commission. I was also Deputy Mayor of the Athletes' Village at the Sydney Olympics in 2000.

Interestingly, Brisbane is now considering bidding for the 2028 and 2032 Olympics, this time in a kind of consortium with twelve councils in southeast Queensland, including the Gold and Sunshine coasts and Toowoomba, which would work very well. We had discussions about this in our bid to be Australia's choice for the 1996 Games.

AN UNEXPECTED LOSS

Losing the mayoralty was a great shock, mainly because everyone said I couldn't; it would require a double-digit swing against me, and that's what I got. On election night in March 1991, with 75 per cent of the vote counted, I had suffered a swing of 18 per cent.

I didn't concede defeat that night, despite being 3000 votes behind Jim Soorley and with a clear loss of Liberal wards. The absentee and postal votes usually favoured us, and I was hopeful of Green preferences after our environmental initiatives – Australia's first Green Levy (which by 2015 had protected 3000 hectares of bushland) and the Boondall Wetlands, internationally recognised as important by the Ramsar Convention. We had undertaken several major studies of the environment which were pioneering in concept: the Brisbane Wildlife Study, a 1989 study into the implications of the Greenhouse Effect on the Council and climate change, and the Conservation Atlas. The Conservation Atlas, the first of its kind, was an inventory of all the significant natural areas around Brisbane. It was used by Council planners to assess development applications and it identified land that Council would buy through our Bushland Acquisition program.

We had declared 1990 the Year of our Environment to underline its importance, but the Green preferences went to the Labor Party. Some years later the Green candidate, Drew Hutton, apologised to me personally, which, as I pointed out then, was hardly a comfort. When the figures were finalised a few weeks later I had been ahead in the primary vote (185,395 to Jim Soorley's 184,557, with Drew Hutton on 30,137) but in the final count Soorley gained 211,124 votes to my 198,232.

I was stunned beyond belief. Earlier that evening we had been at a cocktail party at a friend's house, planning to have a few drinks and then go into City Hall to hear the results and celebrate. But people at the party were listening to the radio and it became clear the results were going to be bad. Instead, I went to my office and they didn't get any better. My personal staff were close around me because it had been their campaign, too. People came and went, some offering commiserations, some just slinking away.

I hardly slept that night. I had made two commitments for the next day, both of which I fulfilled. One was to help out with Clean Up Australia, where I was to do a stint at the Breakfast Creek reach of the river. As the mayoral limo pulled up to collect me Alderman David Hinchliffe, the smartest Labor member of the Council and my bête noire, stuck his head in the window. Heavily disguised in his Clean Up gear of towelling hat and sunglasses, he offered his condolences. The other commitment was to an Italian community function in New Farm. We had a family rule of no functions on Sundays but Graham Clay, the sitting Liberal alderman and a friend, had cajoled me into it by saying that the promise of my appearance would save his neck.

It might have saved his, but it hadn't saved mine.

Under electoral rules, I would be Lord Mayor until the polls were declared, and they were not declared – published in the *Government Gazette* – until Saturday 13 April. I was criticised for not leaving immediately, but rules were rules. In 1985, though I had won decisively on election night, I hadn't been able to take up office until the polls were officially declared. The new Lord Mayor was not in office until then, and the old had a responsibility to soldier on. And so I did.

I had taken care not to show my emotions in public, and I did maintain that stoicism. I had shed tears in private, grieving for a role that I had never seen as a job. I had always felt such a strong personal and emotional connection to the city of Brisbane. What I felt after the election loss was an acute sense of abandonment. Strongest of all was the feeling of rejection and a sense of injustice, upset that the very good things I'd done, the changes that I'd help bring to the city of Brisbane, hadn't mattered in the face of what I felt was a very dishonest political campaign against me. I was also concerned for my staff, who had been so dedicated and who had worked so hard and, in the way of politics, would now be out of jobs. I also had to consider my family. With Genevieve and Stephanie still living at home, it was going to be a major disruption to their lives. I was going to have to take stock and look to the rest of my life, or at least the immediate future. One night I said to Steph, still at school, 'Now I'll be able to do tuck-shop!' She looked quite horrified.

In the lead-up to the election, everyone had seemed to believe that my win was a foregone conclusion. The Liberal Party hadn't bothered to do any major citywide polling. At a big dinner at the Sheraton Hotel some months before, American basketballer Leroy Loggins, over here with the Brisbane Bullets, said in his speech, 'I don't know why this city even bothers having an election.' My heart sank. Anything that smacked of complacency would turn people off and have the electorate thinking you took them for granted.

In hindsight it is easy to see there had been signs that things were not going well. When I passed by the City Hall pre-polling booth where people lined up to vote the day before the election, there was an air of sullenness in the queue. The media had lost its enthusiasm for me; I could pinpoint the moment. When I announced that I was not going to run for a federal seat I could almost hear the collective sigh of disappointment: the media had lost their 'Sallyanne goes to Canberra' story. Almost immediately I became 'Atkinson' instead of 'Sallyanne', and unflattering photos became the norm. I did feel cross at the lack of attention to what I felt were serious matters. For example, a few weeks before the election I opened the city's, and probably Australia's, first asphalt recycling plant where we would re-use bitumen, but this got no coverage.

But these were signs, not reasons. Like most grand disasters and failures these were many and complex. Even at school when we learned, for example, the reasons for the French Revolution or the outbreak of World War I, I always felt there was a lot more behind them than we were told. There were people who said that voters had wanted to slap me down, given this widespread assumption that I was going to win – a sort of 'We don't want her to get too big for her boots' reaction. Academic Doug Tucker was later to talk of the 'phenomenon of pluralistic ignorance' where many voters who, thanks to the media, believing me to be invincible, cast a protest vote without actually wishing to see me lose. They didn't realise that if enough people did that I would be out of office, and so I was.

The campaign certainly managed to portray me as someone who was arrogant and out of touch. I suppose that, as I knew I wasn't, I didn't take as much notice of it as I should have done. There were ads showing me drinking a cup of tea while I looked over King George Square or gliding graciously down the marble stairs of City Hall – those were the Liberal Party television ads. The Labor Party ran an ad showing me, laughing, with a frangipani in my hair, implying that my life was nothing but parties. The original photo had Prime Minister Bob Hawke beside me at an official Gold Coast function, but he had been cut out of it for the propaganda exercise. Labor successfully painted me as being above the people, and the Liberal ads just fed them.

Much was made of my salary, and my name lent itself to the nickname 'Salaryanne'. The Labor campaign promoted the lie that my salary was bigger than the prime minister's; it wasn't. Mine was $110,000 and his was $164,000. There was the question of the allowance, which before my time had been paid directly to the Lord Mayor. I introduced a system where money from the allowance was allocated only on production of expense receipts. It had been an urban myth that Labor's Clem Jones, a wealthy businessman, had worked for nothing, having forgone his salary and taken only the allowance. What was not mentioned was that the allowance then had been tax-free.

There were two further facts that were ignored or not properly debated. One was that aldermanic salaries were tied by some formula to those of state members, and Alderman Bob Ward who handled the salary review had looked at this. The irony was that I had never been particularly interested in money and hadn't paid enough attention. The other fact was that in a previous salary review I had recommended to the team that they should forgo any increase and the electorate would thank them. They did, but the electorate hadn't noticed and the media hadn't reported it. The team weren't going to make the same mistake again, and it made the recent salary increases look high in percentage terms.

There was also a lot of propaganda about my overseas travel. The word 'trips', which has a certain superficial ring to it, was used a lot. It's interesting to look back now when politicians at all levels do travel a lot and I always considered it part of the job, about learning my craft and marketing Brisbane. Most of my travel was in fact paid for by someone other than the Brisbane City Council. I went to Britain as the guest of the UK government and to Israel as part of a conference of mayors from all over the world, an annual event organised and paid for by the City of Jerusalem and the US League of Cities. It was designed to give the rest of the world a better understanding of Israel and for me at least a deeper understanding of our Christian heritage. Ironically, Jim Soorley was to go to the same conference some years later.

There were other issues. A statewide referendum was being held on the same day as the council election, for four-year terms and daylight saving. Labor Premier Wayne Goss had campaigned hard for the 'yes' vote. He had been premier for a little over a year and as the media pointed out, 'the Goss gloss' was still there.

There were persistent headlines that I was aiming for Canberra. Because the story was not true I didn't pay it enough heed. But I can see now that people might have thought that I wasn't interested enough in local government.

I had another problem, too. In all political campaigns, which are adversarial contests, it is natural to feel animosity towards the Opposition. I had been thrown off balance by my opponent who until a few years before had been a Catholic priest. The normal goings-on of a political campaign somehow just didn't seem right. In a television debate the camera showed me tapping my foot in irritation under the desk. It was not a good look.

Following the electoral loss, after my initial distress and dismay, with flowers and phone calls pouring in, I went into a euphoric phase. I started to get my life back. I could make my own decisions without a daily timetable. In the previous year a friend from the bush had called me to say she was coming to Brisbane and to ask whether we could have lunch. I had had to say I couldn't for the next six months. Now I could catch up with friends and do nice things, like going to the movies. And there were reminders of public acknowledgement, which was balm for the soul – when I went to the local movie theatre at Indooroopilly Shoppingtown, the lady at the ticket counter said she had been told that if I ever came in I was to be given a free ticket.

There were a few problems dealing with life's practicalities. It had been many years since I had had to go to a post office to buy stamps or post a letter. Sir William Knox, former Liberal leader and state government minister, had once remarked to me that one of the hardest things he found with losing office was having to drive a car after a dozen years of being chauffeured.

One of the positive results of my defeat, was rediscovering true friends and finding out who were not. People who had been ardent supporters suddenly didn't really want to know me and there was a real sense of 'out with the old and in with the new'. But real friends were still there, even some I had probably neglected in the busyness of City Hall. I learned some salutary lessons about human nature.

I had been given very good advice about not rushing into future commitments, but that was not quite my nature. I took up a couple of things fairly quickly. One was to be an Australian-based consultant to the International Council for Local Environmental Initiatives, the UN-based body whose inaugural meeting in New York I had chaired the year before and on whose board I had sat. And I was approached to be a co-chair with Sir Gustav Nossal of a new organisation called Sustainable Development Australia (SDA).

That first meeting of what is now called ICLEI-Local Governments for Sustainability had about 200 local governments from 43 countries coming together for a conference called 'World Congress of Local Governments for a Sustainable Future' at the United Nations in September 1990. It now has more than 1200 members from 84 countries and its basic premise is that local initiatives are the best way to achieve global sustainability. My role was to assess projects in Australia and Asia.

SDA was really ahead of its time. The brainchild of Geoff Allen in Melbourne, it sought to bring together environmentalists and the business sector, but I found the mutual suspicion was too big a hurdle to overcome. This was despite the eminence of Sir Gus, a world-renowned science researcher, and our enthusiasm. We tried to raise funds from the business establishment, but at this time there was not the recognition of the economic importance of the environment that there is today.

Losing the election meant that now I was able to travel as a tourist. I went with Leigh to a neurosurgeons conference in Moscow, and wrote a piece for the *Courier-Mail* about it. My strongest memories of that trip are of the ballet in Moscow and St Petersburg, but I was also struck by the sight of the Russian neurosurgeons stuffing their briefcases with leftover food at conference meals. One day we broke from the conference and went to a local art gallery where one of the other visitors was Raisa Gorbachev, wife of the president. Surprisingly, she had only a few security people with her and I was able to sidle up close. Leigh and I had a few days in France together and then I went on to London and to Cambridge where Damien was to graduate from Pembroke College as a Master of Laws with first-class honours.

Back home, I had a rather short-lived career on local radio station 4BC. I hosted a one-hour Brisbane-focused weekly show, playing music and interviewing people. I chose the people I wanted to interview, such as a woman who was a prolific writer of newspaper letters to the editor, and asked them the sort of questions I had always wanted to ask. Among the high-profile interviewees was Shirley Conran, who wrote the how-to book *Superwoman* in which she declared, 'Life's too short to stuff a mushroom.' It was supposed to be a talkback show as well, but I don't think anyone ever phoned in. I had actually made my radio debut at nine, when a friend of my mother's said I had a good voice on the phone and should audition for Radio Ceylon. I got the part of Puck in *Midsummer Night's Dream*. Like most people I was appalled when I heard my voice on the wireless, even at that early age. In the 1970s I had also stood in for ABC's Blair Edmonds when he was on holiday, and then again during my City Hall years when I co-hosted a show with Bill J. Smith.

But a few months after I started with 4BC, trying to be appropriately hyper, the station was bought by someone who wanted it to broadcast country music. With relief on both sides, my radio career came to an end.

During this period I was launched into my non-executive director life, which was to last on and off for many years, in fact to this day. I have sat on a whole clutch of commercial boards, public and private companies, as well as not-for-profit organisations. The boards covered a variety of enterprises, including construction companies like Abigroup and Barclay Mowlem, the media group APN, and companies that provided services such as TriCare which owned and ran aged care facilities, and ABC Learning, which ran childcare centres.

In the 1990s there were almost no women in senior executive roles, unlike today. Chief executives of companies make a natural choice as non-executive board members, for they understand how businesses run. As the numbers of women on boards began to increase, it seemed mainly lawyers and accountants were chosen. These women were always very strong in their knowledge and experience, but I think it's a mistake to suggest that only women with a technical background should participate on boards, and it may lead to a false view among some female lawyers and accountants that they are automatically right for board positions. I've always felt that directors on a company's board should bring something of a world view to the company, an outside perspective; it's always possible to buy technical expertise.

The very first board I had ever been on was that of the Australian Elizabethan Theatre Trust back in 1980, and it gave me the first of many experiences of being the only woman and the only Queenslander. The Trust had been set up in 1954, the year Queen Elizabeth made her first visit to Australia, and its aim was to encourage 'high culture' by establishing national opera, ballet and theatre companies. It was co-founded by Sir Charles Moses, general manager of the ABC, and John Douglas Pringle, editor of the *Sydney Morning Herald*, its first chairman had been H.C. 'Nugget' Coombs, inaugural governor of the Reserve Bank.

I was the only person under 60 and almost the only non-knight. Board members included Sir Charles Moses, Sir David Griffin, formerly Lord Mayor of Sydney, and Sir James Darling, a former headmaster of Geelong Grammar School. It was a stimulating experience, not just for the quality of the men on the board but for their old-fashioned courtliness, much despised nowadays, and for the subjects of our discussions. One meeting, when the discussion continued past the appointed hour for our very good lunch, Chairman Sir Ian Potter stopped and asked, 'Mrs Atkinson, do you feel strong enough to continue?' I was able to say I did.

My first public company board was Caltex, the Australian arm of the international petroleum company, a joint venture between America's Texaco and Chevron, which was the largest oil company retail network in Australia at the time. In a variation of the Old Boy network, chairman and CEO Barry Murphy had been at university with me in Brisbane. I was the first woman on the board, an historic breakthrough. I was also the only Queenslander, which prompted someone to say, in those pre-PC days, 'It's a pity you're not black.'

I was under no illusions in those early years that I was being invited to sit on boards because I was a woman, and one with a high profile, but I hoped a factor was also my role as what had amounted to executive chairman in a very large company – the Brisbane City Council – with experience in budgets and human resources and much besides. I thought it was important that I could bring a view from outside the business.

For many of my new colleagues, having a woman on the board was unsettling. After my first board meeting and before the lunch that followed, I met a company solicitor in the bathroom who told me she had been invited to the lunch to keep mc company. We had actually been discussing at the meeting the great savings this particular young woman had made for the business, and I had assumed that was the reason she was being asked to lunch. Some time later, one of my board colleagues confided to me that they enjoyed having me there: 'We were worried, you know. We thought you'd be very strident.'

I had determined early on in my non-executive director career that I would only accept invitations to sit on boards of companies whose business I understood and in whose management I had confidence. One appointment was to the Australian advisory board of a major international IT equip-ment and services company chaired by a very distinguished businessman. I discovered I didn't really understand what they did and at the first meeting I asked about a hugely complicated on-screen diagram. Afterwards, one of my fellow directors (male, of course) said, 'I'm so glad you asked the question, I've never understood that. I didn't ask because I didn't want to look stupid. It's all right for you!'

I also joined the board of a financial advisory company whose purpose I could never really understand, and so I resigned. If I didn't quite understand the technicalities of petroleum I did know where it came from, what you did with it and the variables in the marketplace.

Young women frequently seek my advice about getting onto boards, and I always ask why they want to and to be clear in their reasoning. They usually see board membership as the peak of power and as the ultimate status symbol in a business career. The board of a company, either listed or unlisted (not-for-profits), has a clearly defined role and the power of individual board members is limited by that role. A board does not run the company but it is responsible for its management, for strategy and direction and ensuring that management puts them in place. The board is there for its shareholders, to look after their investment and to make decisions on their behalf.

I took a break in my career as a board member when I decided to throw my hat into the ring, as they say, for the 1993 federal election. I ran for the seat of Rankin on the southern outskirts of Brisbane. My candidature was announced by the party with a great deal of fanfare, and caused quite a stir, not least because the previous year I had publicly announced that I was finished with politics.

What had not been made public was that soon after I ceased to be Lord Mayor the Liberal Party president Paul Everingham had tried to persuade me to run for the Senate. I had turned down his offer. Leigh was fiercely against my having anything further to do with politics after his years as a political spouse, and restoring my marriage was the priority. I was keen to please.

And indeed things were happening in the family. In February 1992 I went to the Winter Olympics in Albertville as part of the Sydney bid team. I also met my eldest daughter Nicola in Paris. She had been studying for her Master of Environmental Laws at the London School of Economics and announced that she and her boyfriend, Ted Ringrose, were engaged. We had our first family wedding in July that year, in Brisbane. The ceremony was at St Patrick's in Fortitude Valley and the lunchtime reception in the grounds of Old Government House in George Street, then a National Trust property. Nicola's three sisters were bridesmaids and her father made a witty speech in which he said he'd told them to lower their necklines and raise their hemlines and hoped it was a sellers' market. Ted had his brother Bill as best man and Damien as groomsman, which meant his sister Kate might have been left out, so she was a groomslady in a tailored jacket and suit. It was an ideal mother-of-the-bride wedding, because the bridal couple lived in London so planning was simple and straightforward. They arrived home a week before it, Nicola bringing her wedding dress which was in a very pale green.

When I was approached to run for Rankin, I considered the question carefully. My announcement that I was finished with politics had been made with the hope of improving my marriage. But I was starting to realise that I could not deny who I actually was. I had a real yearning for the political life, where I could make a contribution. The suddenness of the Council election loss meant that the political blood had not quite drained from my veins. As well as missing the interaction with people that was part of political life, I was starting to have a slow-burning anger about what was happening in the country, with increasing levels of unemployment, for instance. Politics was the only way I knew to make a contribution, to do my bit.

Besides, the Liberal Party had asked me for help. The endorsed candidate for Rankin was finding that a political campaign was not what he had thought it would be, the seat was winnable with the right candidate, my murmurings about missing politics had been heard and I should have a go. And so I did, although I had some explaining to do about having changed my mind.

The political pundits and many other people besides said I was foolish. They said it before the election, when it was certainly a high-risk gamble, and they said it afterwards when my run was seen to be a failure. It's something I have never regretted. Running for Rankin was one of my most worthwhile experiences.

Rankin was a rather mixed-up electorate. On the southern outskirts of Brisbane, it stretched all the way to the country towns of Beaudesert and Boonah and to the Gold Coast hinterland of Tamborine and Canungra. It contained the state's safest Labor seat of Inala and the adjoining suburbs of Durack and Oxley, some marginal voting areas around them and the dyed-in-the-wool National Party areas in the country beyond. It was held by David Beddall, the Labor Minister for Small Business, Construction and Customs, and it would need a swing of about five per cent to unseat him: a swing to the Liberals was expected and so the seat was considered winnable. However it was also the GST election, when Liberal leader John Hewson, an intelligent and articulate economist, was having trouble explaining the intricacies of a new goods and services tax.

I had never been particularly interested in state and federal levels of government, in spite of being interested in politics. I liked getting things done, and the parliaments of a nation seemed to be places where people did a lot of shouting at each other. It's curious now when I read some of the old cuttings that I'm quoted as having federal ambitions, because I certainly never did. I think when I was asked if I might run for federal office, because it was assumed to be a natural progression, I didn't rule it out on the basis that the future was a long way off.

There were a lot of snide comments about a former Liberal Lord Mayor campaigning in Inala, but Rankin was more than Inala. During the campaign I said, 'Every Australian lives here, poor urban dwellers, large ethnic groups, single mothers, retired people, dairy farmers, people growing beef, carrots and potatoes, suburban business people who have escaped the city to live on acreage. I feel absolutely right in Rankin.'

There was also some disjunction between perception and reality, a sort of reverse snobbery. When I went to Inala the day after I was preselected I was dressed casually, as I would normally be on a weekend. I was criticised for 'dressing down' on purpose. One day in a shopping centre, an elderly chap said to me, 'You really should dress properly when you come here, like you did in City Hall.' I pointed out that I was actually wearing one of my better dresses that day, but then realised that he and most people had only seen me on television in the Lord Mayoral role.

I covered about 17,000 kilometres in that campaign through the summer of 1992–93, driving round in a small Daihatsu Charade that my daughters had nicknamed Harry, through the outer suburbs of Marsden and Browns Plains all the way down to the sparsely populated areas on the Lamington Plateau towards the New South Wales border. I went to old people's homes and public meetings and sat drinking cups of tea in community centres, and became even more convinced about the rightness of Liberal philosophy, of the importance of strengthening the individual. The women I met thought themselves helpless without government support, and had been made to feel so by the Labor emphasis on dependency and acceptance of their low socio-economic status. I said in one interview, 'It's ALP propaganda that I don't fit into Inala. It's putting down the people there. Labor is disgustingly patronising about people in lower socio-economic areas.'

I was enraged by the Labor message that I was somehow 'too good' for Inala, and their encouragement of a victim mentality. One day, over coffee in a community centre, the women were discussing the different brands of cooked chicken they bought. I asked, 'How often would you buy a cooked chook?' and the almost unanimous answer was, 'Every day.' I was surprised: 'But, it's cheaper to buy a raw chicken, and very easy to cook one. You just buy one frozen at the supermarket, let it thaw, whack it in the oven and you've got your cooked chicken.' One lady said, 'It's all right for you. You've got a university degree.' The rest of the women nodded in agreement.

One good thing I did do for Inala was to get Prime Minister Paul Keating there. He came one day to campaign and a Labor stalwart said to me, 'We've never had a Labor prime minister here before. It's such a safe area for them that they take us for granted.'

The election was held on 13 March 1993. Veteran political reporter Wally Brown had described Rankin as a litmus test, saying that if the Liberals won Rankin John Hewson would be Australia's next prime minister. On election day, the Labor Party was to show its real strength. Busloads of trade union-ists arrived at the booths. One of their key messages was that the Liberals would scrap Medicare. My sister-in-law, Mary Lou Gilroy, a doctor in Ipswich who was handing out How to Vote cards for me, said that was just not true. She was told by Labor volunteers, 'That's what we've been told to say.'

When the results came in that night, David Beddall was still the member for Rankin. The *Courier-Mail* on Monday reported 'Rejected twice in little more than two years by voters, Sallyanne Atkinson was clinging yesterday to the slimmest of hopes that about 16,000 uncounted votes might win her the seat of Rankin.'

These were the votes that would come in late from the country areas. But it was not to be. The final results had David Beddall winning with 32,157 votes to my 25,635, and Marian Schwarz, the National Party candidate and a farmer's wife from Beaudesert, on just over 5000. It was this result that fuelled my determina-tion and support for a merger of the Liberal and National parties in future years. It had shown me how silly it was to have two conservative parties competing against each other. Early in the campaign, Doug Anthony, former National Party leader and deputy prime minister and a friend, was guest speaker at a garden party in Beaudesert, a joint fundraiser for Marian Schwarz and me. Everyone had a happy time.

At the election the Liberal Party increased our primary vote by 15 per cent and the Labor Party vote decreased by 3 per cent. However, the National Party vote fell by 18 per cent. I made my views known wherever there was someone to listen, and took part in the debates and discussions that eventually led to the merger of the two parties as the LNP.

Campaigning for the seat of Rankin led to other projects. During the campaign I had a lot of contact with Jan Joyce from Beaudesert, who dealt extensively with graziers' associations. She asked me to take the chairmanship of a new committee, the Drought Funds Co-ordinating Committee, whose role would be to work across a range of organisations, such as Red Cross, Lions, Rotary, Salvation Army, Lifeline and St Vincent de Paul. All of them, and some others too, had been working to help Queenslanders who were suffering from the worst drought on record. But sometimes the charities were falling over each other metaphorically, and co-ordination was needed.

I agreed to chair the committee and found the job was both depressing and uplifting. Conditions in the bush were dreadful, but the spirit and generosity of city people who wanted to help restored my faith in human nature. I did a drive with army captain Kevin Moss through southwest Queensland, up through Chinchilla and Miles to Bollon and St George and back through Goondiwindi. Afterwards, I wrote an article for the *Courier-Mail* to let people know of the dire straits Queensland was in. I wrote:

Today the women of Western Queensland are depressed and fearful, and look forward to a future filled with debt and children leaving the land for city life. They worry fretfully about how they'll ever replace the stock that have died to produce the income to pay the debts and support their families. Country towns are tired, the grass has turned grey as if in despair and fear is everywhere … At least 19 properties in the district [of Bollon] have no one living on them. So there's no work for the townsfolk, the shopkeepers, the numbers have dropped at the schools and the only dentist has left St George, the nearest town.

Convoys of trucks organised by various organisations headed west from Brisbane and the Gold Coast, with food for the farmers and hay for their stock. Sometimes this was less than successful when, for example, the hay had weeds in it. But what was most appreciated was the knowledge that people cared, and in a practical way – schoolgirls went out to help with small children and give their mothers a break.

In September of that year I went with the Sydney Olympic bid team to Monte Carlo. By this time I had been part of three bid teams. Prime Minister Paul Keating was part of the presentation, and a bevy of political and business luminaries joined the team. Dame Joan Sutherland attended, and Brisbane swimmer Kieren Perkins who had recently won gold in Barcelona. One morning, while we were all standing about in the hotel lobby Dame Joan said, 'Sallyanne, do you know Kieren Perkins? Do you think you could ask him for his autograph for my grandson?' I went over to Kieren and said with a grin, 'Joan Sutherland is too shy to ask you for your autograph!'

In November 1993 I was with Leigh at a neurosurgeons conference in Mexico when I got a call from John Fahey, Premier of New South Wales, and an invitation to serve on the organising committee for the Games in 2000. I said yes with great enthusiasm, without realising it would be short-lived. Something unexpected was about to happen.

LEAPING OVER THE PRECIPICE

SOON AFTER MY appointment to Paris was announced, I had a phone call from a woman who said, 'You don't know me, but I wanted to tell you that you have fulfilled every middle-aged woman's fantasy – you've left your husband and run off to Paris.'

Early in 1994 I was offered the role of Senior Trade Commissioner with Austrade, the Australian Trade Commission. This was the federal government's international trade agency but was run as an independent authority, and had recently introduced a policy of recruiting from outside. The appointment meant relocating to Paris for three years.

I did not accept immediately. It was a big move and would mean leaving the children in Australia, even though they were all grown up. I had recently been appointed to the Board of the Sydney Organising Committee for the Olympic Games (SOCOG), which was seen as a huge coup and important because I was the only woman. But, my daughter Eloise gave me some timely advice. 'Listen, Mum, how many women of your age get offered three years in Paris?'

At the age of 51, I didn't have a good answer.

Somehow, Paris seems to be synonymous in people's minds with escape. So many people speak of living in Paris as one big adventure, an endless series of champagne evenings on the Champs-Élysées. Of course, it's not like that. For one thing, the Champs-Élysées was basically a street of fancy car showrooms. And working is still working, even if some of it does involve going out to some of the world's most beautiful restaurants. But secretly, I thought that by going to live in Paris I would get thin and chic and learn the secrets of French style.

After the appointment was announced, a friend said, 'You've done everything in reverse. Usually girls grow up, go to work overseas, come home, get married and settle down. But you grew up, got married, settled down, got unmarried and went to work overseas.'

Which was, of course, true. It meant another transition. I was going through an emotionally difficult time, having just left my marriage for the second time. Contrary to public opinion, the leaver of a marriage can be as upset as the leavee. All the reasons you have left are not far away, in time and in your mind.

I had left our marriage after Christmas, statistically the time when most marriage break-ups happen. I just didn't want to be with Leigh any longer and with the children grown and scattered there didn't seem to be any purpose in putting up with being unhappy. I had tried and it hadn't worked. Of course, any description of a marriage break-up is usually from one person's perspective. To me marriage was about love, respect and support and in ours there just wasn't enough.

Even if you marry young and may grow and develop in parallel, you are still individuals. One of the major differences between Leigh and me was what had served us well in our careers – I was a risk taker and he was not, as befits a neuro-surgeon. For each of us the other was not the person we most enjoyed being with. We were disconnected, and I don't believe we even really liked each other.

I think men and women have different needs and expectations from marriage. When I was young, in my late twenties, I wrote, 'For a man marriage is part of his world, that part that is not his work life. For a woman it is her whole world.' So when I first left Leigh in 1989 and he said, shocked, 'But we've had twenty-five years of a very happy marriage,' he was speaking his truth. When I replied, 'I don't think I was there. That must have been someone else,' I was speaking mine.

Looking back, I can see my mistakes. One of them was trying to be what I was not. At the beginning of our marriage, when I was in my early twenties, I wanted to please Leigh in the way that I had always tried to please my mother. So I tried to be the wife I thought he wanted, but I was not authentic. And Leigh was always a bit confused, I think, about what he wanted – a wife who would run a good home, but also one who was, in his words, a contributor. It was hard to be both very well.

I believe one of our problems right from the start was that we had no time for companionship, the habit of friendship. Leigh was studying every evening for his surgical fellowship and I was pregnant and occupied with that. There had been little scope for discussion about our individual wants and needs in our relationship.

So I left my husband and went to Paris.

There I was, suddenly a single woman in a whole new world. At the time I was quoted in a newspaper as saying, '… it seemed like a great leap over the precipice'. I'd grown up in a large family, I'd had lots of kids, I'd always worked with people and had people around me, and then all of a sudden I was in a rowboat in the middle of the ocean with nobody around. That was just how I felt. When you have people all around you, such as in a big family and a large organisation having time alone seems like a wonderful concept. And I had always cherished time alone. Now it was not a respite, but part of my life.

My appointment in to the new role was a bit of a scramble. I had met Dieter Le Comte, Austrade's Europe manager, at a Sydney Christmas party. In the course of conversation I commented on how unimpressed I had been with Austrade in Paris a few years before. In late January he rang me saying he'd heard my marriage had ended. He asked me if I'd put my money where my mouth is, and apply for the vacant post. I was hesitant, but Paris was my dream city; I had to decide quickly.

Once again, I had to have a security clearance. The man from the agency in Canberra came to Brisbane and asked me a series of questions to establish my fitness to serve my country abroad. One of them was, without a hint of embarrassment, 'Are you, or have you ever been, Mrs Atkinson ... a homosexual?'

I replied, 'Well, no ... but if so, would this be a problem?'

My questioner said, with a perfectly straight face, 'Not if you told us first.'

It's extraordinary to imagine now that being gay would be a cause for blackmail, which was what I had to understand was the concern.

When I took the job I knew I needed to be in Paris in time for Prime Minister Paul Keating's planned visit in June as part of the D-Day celebrations. My departmental briefing was confined to a mere three weeks and involved a lot of travelling about Australia. My title was Senior Trade Commissioner, and when I asked in Canberra who was the junior, I was told in puzzled tones that there wasn't one. This was my introduction to the lack of logic in bureaucracies. I said. 'Well if there's no junior I can't be senior. I'm just the trade commissioner.' Not acceptable: I was told that it was the title that was important.

Before I went to Paris I had not experienced the frustration of working *for* government, the endless rules and regulations, the forms to be filled, the reports to be written and sometimes, I suspected, never read. I went into the role with some strong ideas about what was required based on my knowledge of France and the French, the trade missions and promotions I had led. But I now had to do things the Austrade way. There seemed to be quite a few people telling me what I should do and how, including the ambassador, Dieter Le Comte in Frankfurt, and the people in Canberra. Once when I complained about this, I was told I must have experienced bureaucracy in City Hall. The difference, of course, was as that as Lord Mayor I had been running things.

Being the first female Senior Trade Commissioner in Europe was also interesting. Someone sent me a 1963 minute paper addressed to the director, and that caused me some amusement. It began: *'Even after some deliberation it is difficult to find reasons to support the appointment of women Trade Commissioners.'*

The nine reasons given for 'difficulties' included such gems as: *'A man normally has his household run efficiently by his wife, who also looks after entertaining. A woman trade commissioner would have all this on top of her normal work.'* And *'A spinster lady can, and very often does, turn into something of a battleaxe with the passing years. A man usually mellows.'*

I lived in the Australian Embassy on the Rue Jean Rey almost next door to the Paris Hilton and within waving distance of the Eiffel Tower. The embassy had been designed by Harry Seidler in the 1970s. It was built on the site of the old railway yards from which Jewish families had been shipped to concentration camps in World War II. This had made it hard for the French government to sell the site. There did seem to be a nice irony in the Australian government's appointment of a Jewish architect to design its French headquarters there. The building itself, in the brutalist architectural style and in the shape of a large concrete S, was controversial among Parisians, in the way of the Pompidou Museum. Mr Seidler had been dogmatic about the decor. Told in Canberra that the Austrade apartment was due for a revamp, I said I'd like to change the 'dreary' colours, beige, brown and olive green, to bright greens, pinks and yellows, my favourite decorating colours. I was told that Mr Seidler wouldn't like it, to which I had to reply that Mr Seidler wasn't going to see it, and I got my way. I thought it should reflect the Australian personality.

Living in Paris, even in the embassy rather than the city itself, was an extraordinary experience. I was never to learn the secret of French chic but I did have some interesting conversations in my search for it. A French friend was surprised that I should think that style was something special rather than being taken for granted. Growing up in France, she told me, little girls understood they had a responsibility to look good for the people who would be looking at them. It was not vanity but a social obligation. She also told me that French women stayed slim because morning and afternoon teas were not French habits.

I had to learn to deal with the dreaded *placement* when officially entertaining. In Paris there was a hierarchy of who could be invited with whom to a dinner and great offence would be taken if mistakes were made. The afternoon of one dinner party I had a phone call from the Baron de Rendinger saying he and his wife couldn't come that evening because they had the flu, and all I could think of was: 'What about the *placement*?' The one person who was a definite dinner drawcard and who everyone wanted to sit next to, even though he wasn't the head of his company, was Rugby legend Nick Farr-Jones, who was living and working in Paris. Being a 'rugbyman' outranked all else.

I found all kinds of bureaucratic rules in place for *Canberra sur Seine*. There was tight security, too, though not as tight as it probably is today. Our security guards, like other Australians working in the embassy, had come from all kinds of back-grounds and were usually young graduates keen to work in Paris but unable to do so under French law. For example, we had a Sydney lawyer who was keen to study the wine industry. Damien, coming home late one night and not being able to remember my apartment number, buzzed the guardhouse and asked to be let in. Not surprisingly, the guard asked for some proof that he was who he said he was. Damien proceeded to recite 'Clancy of the Overflow'. He was let in.

As part of my contract I had a car for my own use, which implied I would have to drive it. There were two problems. It was a big car, bigger than I was used to. And it would have to be driven on the wrong side of the road. The first problem I solved, though not without difficulty. The car was due to be changed at some stage, so I said I'd like a smaller one please. This caused consternation because my rank entitled me to the bigger one and what, said Canberra, about my successor? I suggested they put a note on the file, or whatever, saying I had chosen to take a smaller car but that whoever came after was entitled to a larger model.

I decided I would begin my Paris driving around the Arc de Triomphe. That famous monument to victory in the heart of

Paris is in the middle of a great circle with eight great boulevards radiating off it. Vehicles roar up the boulevards towards it, crossing the circle to reach another boulevard, and who has right of way is a mystery. I was told it was the only place where insurance companies automatically decreed that both cars were at fault in an accident. So I gave myself the scary and exhilarating experience early one quiet Sunday morning and found that driving around the Arc was like riding the dodgem cars at the Brisbane Ekka. It became my best party trick for visitors, to really frighten them. I recall one of my children saying, 'That's how Mum always drives!' Paris policemen signal drivers to move faster '*Vite, vite!*' When I came back to Brisbane I kept getting speeding fines.

Negotiating the highways of France was another challenge entirely. I had enrolled in a language course at Pont l'Esprit in Provence and for the first time had to navigate the countryside. The problem was that driving *in* the country meant driving *to* it, and that in France meant down the huge motorway. There were trucks on either side of me so large it was like driving between tall buildings. Just before I got to my destination I had an accident. Tired after so many hours of unfamiliar terrain I turned to take the exit and sideswiped a fast-moving sports car. No one was hurt but it was a very French experience involving excited police and ambulance, and my inadequate language skills. The damage to the embassy car meant I did get the smaller one sooner than I might have.

As trade commissioner I saw my role as promoting Australia as a whole, which meant the way we lived as well as the products we had to sell. Austrade's brief was to help Australian companies sell their products and we helped them by finding particular opportunities and researching and developing markets. Liz Johnston, a journalist friend on the *Australian*, quotes me as calling it 'a sort of Shop Australia promoting the idea that Australia is a good place to do business and a good place to buy from'.

Australia's main exports to France were wool and coal but they were established and didn't need our help. We organised companies to participate in food fairs and leather goods fairs, and we were part of the first Australian label in the French fashion shows. Collette Dinnigan was showing her lovely dresses in the famous Angelina's coffee house on the Rue de Rivoli and we lent her dress racks from the embassy. Australian wine was just becoming known in France and being promoted by young French winegrowers who had done stints in Australia and loved the new ways they had learned. I tried to explain to people in the French industry that we didn't regard Australian wines as in competition with theirs, just different from them. Our climate, our sun, our soil all made our wines unique. We promoted businesses that were starting off and gave them advice about their potential success. A Queensland friend was keen to export opals to France, but the local staff in the Austrade office told me they were considered bad luck.

The French are fairly obsessed with good health and the variety of 'cures' that contribute to it. One's doctor can recommend a week or two at a spa and the state will pay for it. A company that ran a seawater health resort on the coast of Brittany consulted me about bringing their seawater techniques to Australia. I had to explain that Australians were accustomed to getting their seawater for free.

My official title in France was *Ministre des Affaires Commerciales* which gave me diplomatic ranking but also involvement in political issues. The big one was the French nuclear testing in Tahiti and politically there was a stand-off. Trade was affected, according to official figures, with sales of champagne and other luxuries falling in Australia. There didn't seem to be much of an effect at the French end. Although Australian unions had banned the loading of coal to France, it was simply shipped to Belgium or Holland and freighted down. Certainly the French, long reliant on nuclear energy, could not understand our position.

Trying to explain it to a French business associate, I said, 'We might have been happier if you had conducted the tests in France, rather than in Tahiti.' He looked at me in astonishment. 'But, Madame, Tahiti is France!' The French attitude to colonies is quite different from the English. These countries became part of France, even to having representation in the French Parliament.

One thing that did suffer was Brisbane's sister-city relationship with Nice in the south of France. It had been initiated early in my time as Lord Mayor by a group in Nice, a city much given to having sister cities. They had researched Australian cities to find the most suitable match, and that was Brisbane. I, of course, was amenable to anything French. The sister-city concept can be misunderstood and seen simply as an excuse for Council junkets. But properly used sister-city relationships are vehicles for business-to-business opportunities as well as opportunities for young people. For example, a schoolboy football team from the Brisbane suburb of Inala went on an exchange to Nice. For some years we had exchanges with the botanic gardens in Nice, whose conditions were remarkably similar to ours. A young woman wrote to tell me of losing her money and passport and going to the Nice offices and being helped when she said she came from Brisbane.

In protest at the nuclear testing, my successor Jim Soorley publicly tore up the sister city agreement. Actually he tore it up several times for the cameras, leading someone to drily remark that I must have left photocopies. The people in Nice thought this was rather rude but as they had about 20 other sister cities, they could just shrug their civic shoulders.

The other two sister-city agreements I signed as Lord Mayor of Brisbane were with Auckland and Kobe. I was only much later to hear of the background sensitivities. Apparently, way back in Frank Sleeman's time the city of Fukuoka in Japan had approached Brisbane but Frank Sleeman had been a prisoner of the Japanese in the war, and he was having none of it. Years later when Kobe made overtures and was accepted, Fukuoka was affronted. They then became a sister city with Auckland so we ended up being related after all. Auckland had a very personal connection – I had become friends with Mayor Dame Cath Tizard, later to be Governor-General of New Zealand, when we were both members of our respective councils and had met at library conferences.

I was also accredited to the former French colony of Algeria, as well as Morocco, Tunisia, Belgium and Luxembourg. Algeria was considered so dangerous that I wasn't allowed to go there, and as there were horrific stories of barbaric butchery, including of a group of French nuns, I was happy to obey. I did go once, when there was a temporary cessation of hostilities and our ambassador was able to present his credentials, but it was not a happy place. I almost made a great faux pas on my first visit to Belgium; I was to make a speech in Antwerp. I had carefully prepared it in French but was luckily warned in time that 'you'd have rocks thrown at you' in Flemish-speaking Antwerp. English did very well in trilingual Belgium.

In Morocco I experienced the difficulty sometimes experienced in doing business in different cultures. I was speaking with a government official about the potential for selling Australian windmills in that drought-prone country, and he outlined the costs involved, which included some unofficial payments to government officials. I explained that I represented the Australian government and we couldn't possibly do business that way. He just shrugged.

My Olympic connections stood me in good stead, and John Coates gave me the title of *Deleguee Europeene* of SOCOG with nice big business cards in the French style on which I had my name written the French way, as two words, Sally Anne. Austrade organised an Olympic business seminar in Paris and among the speakers was SOCOG president, Gary Pemberton, who was so perfectly coached by our Nathalie Curtis that people kept speaking to him in French later.

I had kept in touch with various IOC friends and among them was the Comte de Beaumont, who also happened to be President of the Cercle D'Union Interalliee, the smartest club in Paris, to which he got me instant membership. The count, at this stage aged 90, had been president of the club for 20 years. He was a very distinguished Frenchman who had represented France in hurdling and clay pigeon shooting in the 1924 Olympics, and had also been the member for Indochina in the French Parliament.

One of my more memorable Paris experiences was a lunch he hosted for me and Pamela Harriman, the newly appointed American ambassador to France, but most famous for having once been married to Randolph Churchill. The count said, 'I hope you will not mind if she is on my right and you are on my left', which of course I didn't. My only disappointment was that I would have had to peer past him to look at her and the equally famous facelift, but I did observe that no matter how good the facelift, old-lady hands are a giveaway. A few years later Pamela Harriman came to the embassy for Australia Day. I noticed she was standing alone and went over to talk to her.

She told me she had been in Australia when she was three and her father had been aide-de-camp to the Governor-General, a fact not known. I said, 'Which Governor-General was that?' But she quickly laughed: 'Oh, you're not going to catch me like that!' I had forgotten that her age was a well-kept secret.

Austrade in Europe was organised so that each post had lead responsibility for a particular sector. Ours in Paris was education, which I was very pleased about. I had good contacts in schools and universities in Australia but I also believed that educating young people from other countries here in Australia was the best way to increase trade and business in the future. Education was an important 'export' even then, but today has become a huge industry. In 1996 there were about 70,000 overseas students in Australia. The figure is now over 660,000.

Something I tried to do was encourage Australian companies to venture outside Paris to the provinces. Chambers of Commerce in all the major French towns were formal organisations, financially backed by government and often with impressive headquarters. They were very happy to help us with seminars on doing business in Australia and buying from Australia, and we organised them in Bordeaux, Marseilles and Lyons, to name a few. Nantes was memorable. Australia's new Deputy Prime Minister Tim Fischer was coming to France and was keen to drive a train. I think he actually requested a TGV, the fast train, and the closest TGV journey was to Nantes, 385 kilometres west of Paris. I rode in the driver's cabin with him to help with translation. It turned out I was not needed – he and the driver could communicate without language and the driver was overwhelmed at Tim's knowledge of signals and interchanges. In Nantes, the local chamber of commerce, also overwhelmed at being visited by such an important politician, had organised a seminar çomplete with a translator for the ministerial speech. But Tim had only uttered about four sentences when the translator burst into tears and rushed from the hall. She couldn't cope with the Australian idiom.

There were other Australian promotions in Cannes, home of the famous film festival but also of trade shows for the music industry, property and IT, all of which required the presence of the Senior Trade Commissioner. They were exciting times, staying at the Ritz-Carlton hotel, where there were always welcome flowers from Xavier Roy, the head of Reed Midem, the company organising the trade fairs. There were lunches and dinners at restaurants on the Corniche, but most of all I enjoyed being able to talk up with pride the best Australia had to offer.

I had other duties. I took a phone call one day from Tony Roche, Pat Rafter's coach. Pat had reached the quarter- or semi-finals in the French Open tennis championships. He would be playing against a Spaniard who would have his family in the players' box, while Pat, so far from home, would have no one. Tony asked if I would go out the next day and watch the match. It wasn't hard to say yes. That night French television identified me as Pat Rafter's mother.

I did miss Brisbane and family, but Paris is a magnet for visitors to Europe and I had friends to stay. I found I could spend more time with them than at home, and the children were able to come at various times, including a magical snowy Christmas when we all went to church together. I went home for Stephanie's twenty-first birthday and then the wedding in Toowoomba of Eloise and Seamus.

I popped over to London for the birth of my first grandchild, Matilda, born to Nicola and Ted. I was fortunate enough to be there for the actual birth. Being present at a birth is a wondrous experience and I was lucky to have several of them. It was particularly wonderful after having given birth five times myself. Childbirth is a miracle indeed, and I've felt privileged every time I've been a part of it. I do sometimes think it is more natural to have older women present – mothers rather than husbands – which now seems to be the modern way.

Not long before I was due to leave France, Eloise and Seamus came from Brisbane with Ruby, who was three months old, breastfed and perfect to travel with. We stayed in bed and breakfasts in provincial France, and went to Prague for a weekend where cooing waitresses in restaurants would carry blonde-haired, blue-eyed Ruby off to the kitchen.

Damien, Genevieve and Stephanie all came to visit. Damien and his English girlfriend came over from London. They experienced firsthand the language problem when they were leaving from the nearby railway station and wanted a meal at the cafe beside it. The issue was solved in a typically French way. No English was spoken but the manager took Damien by the hand and led him around the occupied tables so he could point out what he wanted.

My three-year contract with Austrade was to finish in mid-1997. I had an option to renew for a further year, and it was tempting, but, apart from missing family and friends, I thought three years was a proper length of time to stay away from Brisbane. If I stayed away any longer it would be difficult to go home.

BRISBANE IS NOT PARIS

I ARRIVED BACK in Brisbane in time for my fifty-fifth birthday and the birth of another grandchild, which happened to be two days apart.

Looking back now, 55 seems quite young but at the time it seemed old, particularly to be starting a whole new chapter of my life. I didn't know what that was going to look like, nor where I was going to live. I had plenty of options for temporary accommodation and moved between Eloise and Seamus's house in Whynot Street, West End, my friend Andree's historic home Nyrambla in Ascot, and Bill and Imelda Roche's Gold Coast holiday house. I was a grandmother of no fixed abode. Actually, my first priority was not finding a house but finding a car, because Brisbane is not Paris and public transport did not provide an easy way to get around. Being mobile was a priority, especially with so many of the children and grandchildren living in Brisbane.

My return reinforced some of the lessons I had learned and observations I had made in Paris. Back in my home town, I understood again the importance of family and friends. Though I was very much a single woman, I was lucky to have adult children to give me help and advice, and old friends who were pleased that I was back among them.

I brought back with me a whole new appreciation of what it's like to be a foreigner in a country where you understand some of the language but not all of the nuances. And there are a whole range of small social rules that are never quite formulated but really *do* matter: in France, for example, cutting the cheese the wrong way. I had brought up my children not to put their elbows on the table, but in France that's polite. I was told by a French business colleague that it was an old social rule – that keeping your hands under the table meant you could have one on your sword. To which his friend added, 'Or on your neighbour's knee!'

At a French dinner party no one leaves the table to go to the bathroom. I did, early in my stay in Paris, and remarked to a French friend the next day about the untidy state of my hostess's bathroom. My friend was shocked … by me, rather than my Parisian hostess. At a big formal dinner, there are long queues for 'the facilities' before the meal but no 'comfort stops' during it. I had an embarrassing moment years before on the Olympic trail when I was hosted at a lunch in the magnificent *hôtel particulier* that was the home of the Paris Chamber of Commerce. I asked for milk with my coffee. Then I noticed a waiter slipping out of the front door and returning a few minutes later with a carton of milk in hand. Coffee at lunch should be taken black.

I had learned many things during my three years in France. I had also developed an appreciation for the innate confidence of the French, sometimes described as arrogance. They know who they are as a nation and don't have to keep talking about it. What I *didn't* learn was how French women stay so slim, because everyone I knew seemed to eat whatever she liked, and that was quite a lot. I think I came home not quite the Francophile I had been when I left. Paris, beautiful and exciting city that it is, is a wonderful place to visit but not quite so comfortable to live in. The long summer days do not compensate for the short, dark and cold days of a European winter that seems to go on and on.

In contrast, I was reminded how easy life in Brisbane was and how good it felt to be among familiar surrounds. Still, I had the practical demands of finding somewhere to live and looking for a job. I bought a small and sensible car and looked for a house that was close to the city and small enough for me to manage. Though I was grateful to have places to stay, and family and friends to support me with their hospitality, I was keen to get settled. This would be the first time I would be buying a house on my own.

One of the advantages of being a middle-aged single woman was only having myself to consider. For example, I didn't have to think about such things as living near schools. I particularly wanted to indulge my love of Queenslanders and toyed with the idea of restoring something old and derelict. Luckily, I had just enough insight to realise I lacked the necessary practical skills and patience.

I finally found what I thought was the perfect house in Red Hill, only minutes from the city. Like most things in life, it was not quite perfect. It was situated on busy Waterworks Road, which meant I had to back out into streams of rush-hour traffic. Damien asked the real estate agent, who happened to be a friend of mine, 'Are you trying to kill my mother?' My children have never had much faith in my driving ability.

Built in the 1890s the pretty wooden worker's cottage had been given a second storey underneath. From the street you walked into the kitchen and living room and out on to the obligatory deck, and then went downstairs to the three bedrooms. The views from both levels, across to the hills and valleys towards Mt Coot-tha were spectacular, especially when the purple jacarandas and then the red poincianas were in bloom.

I must say I loved that house as I have loved no other, but after a couple of years its drawbacks began to show. Waterworks Road became busier, and backing out into traffic did become more challenging, for visitors if not for me. I found that those old Queensland builders had never quite understood we did have cold weather. In winter the wind would whistle up through the floorboards and through the walls. And I was burgled twice. Nothing really precious was taken apart from a suitcase with some of my Paris clothes, but someone invading your home is emotionally disturbing. The second time the burglars took only some china eggs that I had collected from various places and had on display, and the spice jars from the kitchen, which was odd enough to be even more disturbing.

Afterwards, I moved into an apartment on the river at South Brisbane, which Leigh and I had once bought as an investment and which I had kept as my share of property when our marriage ended. It had two bedrooms but I did need a third, so I later moved to a three-bedroom apartment next door, where I still live now and intend always to be. I look up and down the river and over to the Expo site and across to the city, and cannot imagine anywhere more perfect.

Re-establishing myself in Brisbane after a three-year absence was a time of real self-assessment. I was concerned about work, about earning a living. I realised I didn't have any formal

qualifications. My only actual training had been as a journalist, but I was rather too old to be getting a job as a reporter.
I was faced with the same dilemma that many young people
face – what do I want to be when I grow up?

My problem was that I was grown up, and still felt uncertain.
What I did have was experience, and a lot of it. I had been at
the head of a large organisation in Brisbane City Council and in
Paris I had been a middle manager as the head of a unit within a
department. I knew about international trade and business and I
had international contacts through my Olympic bid campaigns.
I also had a profile. I realised it was time to capitalise on those
skills. Whenever someone, usually young, complains to me that
they have wasted time doing study they weren't suited for or
working in a job they didn't like, I tell them sharply that nothing
is wasted. Every experience is another layer in life, and prepares
you for the next one.

Before I left Paris I'd been approached by the ABC Television
program *Australian Story*. Now a regular and popular Monday
night feature, it was then in its early days. I was reassured by the
fact that former Brisbane surgeon turned senator John Herron
and his wife, Jan, who were also distinguished by having ten
children, had appeared in an earlier episode. A crew came to
Paris and filmed me in the embassy and at a footpath cafe.

In Brisbane they followed me around for six weeks as I was
house hunting, playing with Ruby, talking to friends, speaking
at a function. It was quite a weird experience because after a
while they became part of daily life, to be taken for granted, at
least by me. It was sometimes intrusive having a camera crew
hovering. Nicola strenuously objected to their turning up in the
park at Milly's third birthday party. Genevieve and Stephanie
did on-camera interviews, and the finished program, which

after all that filming only ran for half an hour, was called 'The Homecoming'. I was asked, mainly by family, why I had ever agreed to it. I think my answer was that it just seemed rude to say no. Perhaps too, my inner PR consultant thought it would be good positioning.

By the time I returned to Brisbane, I was already on the board of the Australian Ballet. Mel Ward, a vice-president of the board had tracked me down when I had visited Melbourne a few months earlier. Mel, now a Victorian, had been at school and university in Brisbane. I had been staying with my friend Jeanne Pratt and her husband Richard, generous benefactors to Australian arts and theatre. Jeanne, who like me had once been a reporter on the Sydney *Telegraph*, has made an enormous contribution in her own right to Australian theatre as the producer of The Production Company, which presents musicals that might not be well-known enough for commercial theatre, and gives famous performers the chance to play roles they might not normally get. Through the Pratt Foundation she has recently endowed a chair in musical theatre production. Mel asked me if I'd be interested in joining the Ballet board and I gave him an instant yes. It was an honorary role but a childhood dream come true. I was to serve on the board for 12 years and loved every minute of it. Directors were encouraged to travel with the company on overseas tours at their own expense and I had wonderful experiences in Shanghai, New York, Paris and London, enjoying the response of audiences and critics and feeling proud to be part of such a world-class company. A country's culture is so much what defines it in the eyes of the rest of the world and our national ballet company showed that we could excel in such a refined art form. There was the Dancers Company, too, the Australian Ballet's second company for training young dancers, which often toured throughout regional Queensland, and I tried to attend when I could.

Soon after my return I was offered non-executive directorships for two ASX listed companies, again through the old connection network and these would be paid positions. Tony Clark, a Queenslander and a Sydney partner at accountancy firm KPMG, had been asked by a colleague to suggest a Queenslander for the board of Abigroup, a major construction company with work up and down the east coast; my name came up and I accepted. Similarly, Sir Leo Hielscher, former Under-Secretary of Treasury in the Queensland government and a great help and support for me in the City Hall days, was retiring from the board of APN News and Media and suggested me as a replacement. APN was Australia's largest regional newspaper company, whose major shareholder was the Irish Rugby star and millionaire businessman Tony O'Reilly, and the CEO was his eldest son, the handsome Cameron, whose first base in the Australian newspaper empire had been provincial Rockhampton, where he cut a swathe with his charm and Irish accent. There was always a percentage of Irishmen on the board with accents that were hard to understand in our telephonic board meetings. I was the only woman and the only Queenslander on both boards but this time I was also the only journalist and felt I could make a real contribution.

As well as commercial companies, I held positions on government boards and not-for-profit organisations. Towards the end of 1997 I was appointed chairman of the Queensland Tourist and Travel Corporation, later sensibly abbreviated to Tourism Queensland. The Minister for Tourism was a rambunctious and effective former bait shop owner from Noosa named Bruce Davidson. It was a great job, not only because I was able to travel throughout Queensland and promote it, but also because I have always believed in the importance of tourism – an industry that has not always been taken seriously.

In 1998, as chairman of the tourism authority I went to Winton for the opening of the Waltzing Matilda Centre which celebrated the story of Banjo Paterson's iconic poem; it is the only museum named after a song. Later, Bruce Collins, the Mayor and chairman of the board, asked me to be on it. I accepted and am still a member. I also joined the board of Binna Burra Mountain Lodge, one of Australia's earliest eco-resorts, and subsequently became chairman. Binna Burra is on the Lamington Plateau, less than two hours' drive from Brisbane, and where I had spent family holidays and later gone for fresh air and rainforest walks.

Promoting Queensland also took me back to France, because we had decided to try again for another Expo, this time in the Gold Coast region. Sir Llew Edwards having been chairman of Expo 88 led the bid to the Bureau of International Expositions in Paris, but we were beaten by the Philippines, who presented a lot of very cute children singing and dancing. Unfortunately, their presentation was not backed by solid financial management and their Expo never happened. By the time this became known, the Queensland government had changed and any Expo enthusiasm was lost. The new government also removed me as chairman of tourism, and from Austa Energy, another government board to which I'd been appointed by Queensland Treasurer Joan Sheldon. This underscored for me the fragility of government appointments.

The 1998 state election had been an odd one, which I rather crassly described in an article in the *Australian* as the 'Up Yours' election. This was what I thought the electorate had been saying to the major parties when they gave 23 per cent of the vote and 11 seats to the One Nation Party. Labor won office from the Coalition and Peter Beattie became premier. While it was a flash in the pan then, 18 years later One Nation leader, Pauline Hanson, was back in office with her own party.

A Coalition government in Canberra meant I was appointed to a raft of national committees: the Citizenship Committee, the National Capital Authority (NCA), and the France Australia Industrial Research Group. The Citizenship Committee was set up to examine the concept of Australian citizenship and what it meant. It was chaired by Sir Ninian Stephen and included Robert Manne and Mark Ella. Our most interesting recommendation was to allow Australians to hold dual citizenship. The NCA is the planning authority for Canberra, which also has its own ACT government looking after domestic issues of health and education. We made decisions for Canberra as the national capital for all Australians. I was also co-chairman of the France Australia Industrial Research Group. This was an organisation set up by a previous federal Labor government to promote joint research projects with two chairs, one French and the other Australian, and we met each year either in Paris or an Australian city.

These were busy years professionally and on the family front as well. Nicola and Ted had been married in Brisbane in 1992, and had produced Matilda in London, Beatrice in Hong Kong, and Eleanor in Brisbane, the event I returned just in time for. Eloise and Seamus, married in Toowoomba in 1995, now had Arthur, a brother to Ruby. In the next decade Eloise and Seamus had

Frank, while Damien and his wife, Marilyn, had Leila, Abraham and Miriam. Genevieve's daughters to her first husband, Jamie, were Georgia and Maggie, and she had Bridget with her second husband, Tim. Stephanie and Bruce would produce two boys, Gabriel and Sebastian.

These years saw my disengagement from the Catholic Church with the annulment of my marriage. I first heard about this in a letter from the Church. Leigh and I had divorced, but the letter pointed out that Leigh wanted to marry again (he had in fact been married a few years earlier, in the Anglican Church) but would be unable to do so as our divorce was not recognised by the Catholic Church: we were considered still to be married. I certainly understood that it was the law of the Catholic Church that marriage is indissoluble. I knew that, strictly speaking, a divorced person cannot take part in the rites of the Church. But the Church has managed to be flexible in so much else, and in fact has not always insisted that someone whose marriage has been annulled must be married in the Catholic Church before taking communion.

There are about 20 conditions for declaring a marriage invalid, including non-consummation (which was a nonsense after 30 years and five children), alcoholism, a determination not to have children and 'my mother made me do it'. I once read that in Spain in previous centuries mothers wrote and kept letters ordering daughters into their impending marriages, thus providing grounds for annulment. The grounds chosen in our case were incapacity to make a proper decision about marriage, which I did think odd given that Leigh had been a registrar at the Mater Hospital, and the priest who married us had been one of his schoolteachers who knew him well. Certainly Leigh and I had been young – 21 and 25 – but we had both been university students with responsible careers, and had both been in full possession of our wits.

The process was pretty dreadful. The decision was made by a tribunal in Sydney, but I was never allowed to appear before it in person. I was interviewed about our personal lives by a nun in the Church offices in Brisbane. I had been asked to provide three witnesses. I chose a Catholic friend, Julien Beirne, and and anglican one, Margaret Blocksidge, and my sister Louella. Julien said she found it a very degrading experience.

When I was told of the decision to grant the annulment on the grounds specified, I said I was going to appeal, and I did. The appeal was to be heard in Sydney, too. Again, I was told I could not appear or speak for myself. I felt that I was being denied natural justice and not given a fair hearing; I really did want to have a proper discussion on the validity of our marriage. I was deeply concerned about the legitimacy of my children in the eyes of the Church, which would be an obvious consequence of their parents not being married.

My appeal was not upheld, and I received a letter telling me so. It also informed me that if I wished to get married again in the Catholic Church I could show the priest the letter, which just confirmed for me that no one was listening or understood my very real distress. When I went into the Catholic office headquarters in Brisbane to discuss the decision, I was told I was not allowed to see the documents giving the reasons for the annulment, they were confidential. This seemed to me unbelievably mediaeval. I contemplated appealing to Rome, as one of the Kennedy wives had done in the US, but decided that would take too much time, energy and money. In the end, my marriage was annulled, which meant that in the eyes of the Church it had never existed.

The experience left me feeling deserted and betrayed. I had embraced the Church willingly, had gone to mass each Sunday and made sure my five children did, too. In my public life, I had stood up as a Catholic. Yet in spite of my connections, not one priest contacted me later to offer any support. I had made my feelings about the annulment very clear, even to the then archbishop, but he didn't want to talk about it and suggested I speak to his canon law expert. I said, 'Your Grace, I'm not concerned about the legal side, but the spiritual.' (In fact, one priest did express sympathy and antipathy to the annulment process but this was because his own mother had experienced the process herself.)

I had joined the Catholic Church with my brain and mind as well as my faith – and now my faith had been destroyed. I stopped going to mass.

The Constitutional Convention, or ConCon, was a special event held in Canberra in 1998. I was a delegate for the Australian Republican Movement (ARM), led and largely funded by Malcolm Turnbull in his pre-political days. Michael Lavarch, former federal Attorney-General and current Dean of Law at the Queensland University of Technology, told me that our mutual friend Quentin Bryce had suggested that I might be interested in the Republican cause.

And I was, to the surprise of some, including myself. While I had always been fascinated by the royal family – my sister Louella and I had played at being princesses and I knew the story of every British monarch from the Middle Ages onwards – it seemed to me that that had been then and there, and Australia was here and now. I thought that Australia should be an independent, stand-alone nation and we had a chance to become one in a seamless, tidy manner; so many republics had been born out of turmoil and bloodshed. I was also influenced by the nonsense of explaining to our French clients that the Australian Embassy in Paris would be closed on the holiday for the Queen's birthday, when that queen was English and in London.

I only went to one ARM meeting, upstairs in a hall in Paddington. Halfway through I muttered out loud, 'God, this is boring. It's just like a Liberal Party branch meeting.' The man sitting next to me turned to me with a surprised look and said: 'Yes, and it's just like a Labor Party branch meeting!'

At the Canberra convention we were joined by members from Australians for Constitutional Monarchy and other groups, including one led by Clem Jones who wanted a president elected by the people at large. We felt this was impractical and in the months before the convention, former NSW Premier Neville Wran came to Brisbane and we met Clem in the office of Glyn Davis, then head of the premier's office and later to be Vice-Chancellor of Griffith and Melbourne universities. Despite Neville's charm and impeccable ALP credentials, Clem was intransigent.

Also at the convention were a group of people from around the country chosen by the government, and I must say that it was the people gathered in Old Parliament House that made the meetings memorable. The state premiers were there, as well as media personality Steve Vizard, trucking magnate Lindsay Fox, the first Indigenous member of Parliament Neville Bonner and local government folk including the Mayor of Longreach Joan Moloney and Councillor Paul Tully from Ipswich. Archbishops Pell and Hollingworth and academic Greg Craven, now Vice-Chancellor of the Australian Catholic University, all attended:

154 people in all. The speeches waxed on over two weeks, some fiery and passionate, all thoughtful. Towards the end I had dinner one night with former Labor minister Barry Jones whom I had got to know in Paris. During the meal Barry was lamenting the fact that no one had yet made some point he considered terribly important. I said, 'Well, I can get a speaking spot before we finish, so if you write me a speech I'll give it.' I had the lovely experience of delivering a speech to the chamber with the chairman in the Speaker's chair nodding in agreement with his own words. No one, of course, was any the wiser.

The Constitutional Convention came up with its final recommendation, and the Australian people cast their vote on a referendum almost two years later in November 1999. Referenda have historically failed, and this one did too. The final vote was 54 to 45. If the question put had been a simple one – 'Should Australia be a republic?' – the outcome may have been different. But the questions were not simple and as even republicans couldn't agree on the best way of choosing a president, it was not surprising that the electorate felt it shouldn't have to.

FINDING SOMETHING USEFUL TO DO

FOR MANY PEOPLE, the year 2000 brought the excitement of the new century, with fireworks in every major city and Australia being among the first countries on earth to see the sun rise on the new millennium. For me it was to be a decade of diversity – the Sydney Olympics, representing Queensland in South East Asia and the most challenging time in my business career.

It was also the time I became a bit of a property tycoon. I had discovered and fallen in love with Port Douglas in Far North Queensland in the 1970s when it was a raffish Somerset Maugham kind of place where people dropped out from Sydney and Melbourne. Since then it had become decidedly upmarket. I invested in a villa on the golf course, which didn't quite have the raffish charm I liked but did have wonderful views to the hills. A few years later I also bought a house in Buderim, a village on the hill behind Mooloolaba on the Sunshine Coast. This was to be my principal place of residence and my plan was to live there and pop down to Brisbane two hours away for various meetings and activities. Over time the Brisbane activities got busier and

Buderim became the place the family would gather for holidays, although I did enjoy having a house and garden to potter in.

I had a couple of relationships during this time with very nice men, but sadly they were not to last. One was Bruce Green, Mayor of Warwick, whose 2000 election loss resonated with my own. Relationships in later life are tricky because there is all the baggage of the lives that have been lived. I do know of very happy couples who have met in what are called 'the twilight years', yet few of us older singles are properly single because we have existing relationships with family that need to be considered. I'm ever-optimistic, although I do have gentlemen friends who tell me I can be scary and a little bit bossy. It's hard to believe!

The 2000 Sydney Olympic Games became the culmination of my Olympic involvement. John Coates, Australian Olympic chief, had asked me if I would be Deputy Mayor of the Athletes' Village for the 2000 Games. My instant retort was, 'Why deputy? I've been a real mayor!' Graham Richardson was appointed as mayor and it was indeed a great choice. I don't think I or anyone else could have dealt with the demands and complaints at the daily team managers' meetings with Graham's firm humour.

Living in an apartment within the Athletes' Village was a rather different kind of Olympic experience. The village itself was part of an estate of very nice houses that had been developed by the private sector and were sold off after the Games. I lived next door to the team from the Central African Republic, which included four athletes and twelve officials. There was a huge communal dining room for the village where every kind of food was served by young Australians of every origin. I loved the fact that behind the counter would be young people who looked Asian, Arab or African yet they all spoke in broad Australian accents. It seemed to me the best thing about Australia.

As Deputy Mayor I had a golf buggy to get about in and a smart navy uniform to wear, which made me look like a camp commandant from a war movie. I was overseeing protocol and every day in the lead-up to the opening we had a ceremony where we raised the flag of each country in front of its team and various dignitaries. A local Sydney school would sing the anthem of that nation. These were usually very moving ceremonies, none more so than that of new nation East Timor. I had been told that because they didn't yet have a flag that a ceremony wouldn't be possible. I insisted because of the hopeful young athletes, and the fact that Nobel Peace prize winner José Ramos-Horta, who would become President, had visited the village. A ceremony took place. Later, at the official opening ceremony the East Timor team marched under the Olympic flag to resounding cheers.

A flag was to cause another protocol problem. An athlete from one of the African nations was killed in a road accident and his teammates wanted to fly their flag at half-mast. I was told this would have to be cleared with the International Olympic Committee in Lausanne, but we allowed it without permission.

Perhaps the most exciting guest to the village was Nelson Mandela, who came in a tracksuit to visit his team. As he arrived he said to me, 'Can I put my arm around you, so I can lean on you without looking as though I am?' Wherever Mandela went young people pressed close to touch him, though the adulation was strongest in the South African camp.

The new decade brought changes back home in Brisbane as well. Whenever I saw Premier Peter Beattie around town, as you tended to do in Brisbane, he would say, 'We should find you something useful to do.' Peter and I went back a few years, to his days as secretary of the ALP in the early 1980s and then member for Brisbane Central. In spite of our political differences, we had always got on well. At the funeral for former Labor Prime Minister Frank Forde, whose daughter was a friend of mine, I found myself seated in front of Peter in the church. At the point in the mass where you say to your neighbours, 'Peace be with you,' I turned to the pew behind me and there was Peter Beattie and ALP president Denis Murphy. As I said, 'Peace be with you,' one or the other replied, 'I'll have that in writing!'

Even so, it did come as a surprise when one day in early 2000 I had a phone call out of the blue from Beattie's deputy, Jim Elder, asking me if I would be a trade commissioner for Queensland in South East Asia. The role, for which I would be paid for two-and-a-half days a week, was essentially to help Queensland companies do business in South East Asia by making contacts and opening doors for them. I would report back to the government on regional conditions and economic potential in the countries there. The state government was planning a trade presence in the United States, the Middle East and Asia.

Labor Minister for Tourism, Bob Gibbs, was to leave parliament and go to Los Angeles as the full-time Queensland government representative, while former National Party Premier Mike Ahern and myself were to work part-time, based in Brisbane. I certainly didn't want to move overseas again. My countries of focus were Indonesia, Thailand, the Philippines, Singapore, Malaysia and Brunei. Mike looked after India, Africa and the Middle East. Former Labor Deputy Premier Tom Burns was our man for China, where he had been part of Australia's first-ever delegation with Gough Whitlam in the 1970s.

After my appointment there was a lot of media controversy, outrage from our side of politics, and great cynicism that it was all a plot to get rid of Bob Gibbs. The criticism included a rather vitriolic editorial in Brisbane's *Courier-Mail* in which the writer accused the premier of 'subsidising' and 'showing generosity' to Mike and me in our paid positions.

The paper published my spirited 15-paragraph defence in which I wrote:

> ... *the premier knows that there are some societies more hierarchical and less informal than our own, where age and experience and a position in public life make a great difference to building business relationships ... in economic development terms the government has recognised that there are some trade areas of great potential which are sensitive and difficult and is despatching them on a part-time fixed-term basis to experienced people with demonstrated skills in business and diplomacy.*

I had always held the view that Australia's practical trade connections were with South East Asia and Queensland's most of all. As Lord Mayor I had often talked about Brisbane being the fastest-growing city in the Asia Pacific, which was the fastest-growing region of the world. One of my selling points to the French was that Australia should be France's gateway into Asia.

In my role as 'Special Representative' we took trade missions in mining and agriculture to Indonesia and the Philippines, and signed trade agreements in Thailand and Singapore. One of my most interesting and unnerving experiences was just after the tsunami in March 2005, representing Queensland at the Medan Summit on Reconstruction in Indonesia. I spoke at the conference to offer Queensland's support and outline our capabilities and then visited refugee camps in Aceh. I witnessed the very real devastation and human tragedy which had ensued. I observed the way this played out differently in men's and women's lives – the women were occupied, albeit with difficulty, in caring for children, cooking and washing. The men had nothing to do but hang about all day.

I got to travel extensively throughout South East Asia and it brought back childhood memories of Ceylon. Experiences were varied, from visiting Indonesian presidents in great luxury to watching cattle being slaughtered at 2 am in 'wet' markets, where there was no refrigeration and meat was sold straight from the kill. With other trade issues there were difficulties mainly as a result of Australia's very firm health and quarantine regulations. With the Philippines we had the problem of our banning their bananas for fear of importing disease. No matter how much we protested it was a quarantine issue, the Filipinos saw it as a trade restriction. In Thailand it was the same with cooked chicken.

The mutual tropicality of Queensland and South East Asia offered all kinds of synergies for research in plants and tropical medicine. Our experience in a hot climate was also useful. Fresh milk was much in demand in our South East Asian markets, and we were encouraged to export dairy cattle to provide it. But our customers wanted picture-book cows, the black-and-whites they knew from Europe. We had great trouble explaining that these breeds were not at all keen to travel to tropical climes, and the more appropriate breeds like Zebu and Brahman, while not so milk-giving, would do better.

In late 2000 I also took on the chairmanship of a company that was soon to be listed, and it would play a major role in my life for many years. ABC Learning was a company that owned and operated childcare centres and as a mother and grandmother I felt I was experienced in that, and understood the demand for it in this age of working mothers. I spent time in discussion with the management and its advisors. I could not then foresee the consequences that would reverberate through the next decade.

This was the first time I had been chairman of a listed company and this was a very different kind of business from the other companies I had known, with a very different kind of chief executive. ABC Learning, at one stage the world's largest provider of early childhood education, the darling of the financial world and the media, will always be a case study in the uncertain world of corporate boards and companies and a parable for our time.

It would turn out to be a tragedy on many levels. It was a tragedy because a lot of people, parents who had invested in it and creditors who had done business with it, lost their money when it collapsed. I lost a lot too: the shares I had bought because I believe the chairman of the board should have the confidence to invest in the company they represent, and my home at Buderim when I had to find the money to pay off the margin call when the share price plummeted. Port Douglas had to go, too. I was lucky in a sense because money was not especially important to me and I just felt grateful that I was able to borrow from the bank so that I could keep the shares. This proved to be a good moral decision but a poor financial one – the shares ultimately disappeared but the loan didn't.

More important than the money was the very real concern for the people directly affected – thousands of children without childcare and staff without jobs. Fortunately, the federal government put up $22 million to make sure that didn't happen in the short term and subsequently many of the ABC centres were bought by other childcare operators, some who formed companies not dissimilar to ABC.

It was also sad because ABC was originally a very good company, founded on proper ideals with good management. Because the idea of a listed company running childcare for profit was new it caught the imagination and attention of the media – as did its founder Eddy Groves, whose life was not only a great rags-to-riches story but who was charismatic as well. He was the original seller of ice-creams to Eskimos. I never had a problem with the concept of private childcare. We had private schools and private hospitals and they certainly didn't plan to run at a loss. And governments, while understanding the need for childcare and being prepared to subsidise it, have not wanted to run childcare centres.

The ABC story had been a fascinating one. In 1988 Eddy and Le Neve Groves, a young couple in their twenties – he an entrepreneurial milkman, she a trained teacher – had opened a childcare centre in Ashgrove, Brisbane. By early 2001, with 44 centres, ABC Learning was floated as a public company. Early childhood education had changed since my children were small. In the late 1970s when my youngest was in kindergarten I was one of only two working mothers. Now, stay-at-home mothers were the exception rather than the rule. The Groveses recognised that professional parents wanted to ensure their children had high-quality childcare and that first centre at Ashgrove had people travelling from all over Brisbane to take their children there. Standards were high, not only in the quality of the care and education but in the buildings, their fitout and maintenance.

ABC began to expand and by the end of the 2002 financial

year there were 94 centres, and childcare places had increased from 3956 to 7626. By 2003 the number of centres had risen to 187 and by 2004 there were 327. Much of this expansion was through other centre owners approaching ABC to take them over. Such was its reputation that developers were asking ABC to put centres in new areas. The company went into the business of corporate childcare with companies such as Westpac, the Commonwealth Bank, Optus and Chisholm TAFE, providing childcare for their employees. As a working mother I used to think how wonderful it would have been to have work and childcare synchronised so that you had just one daily destination and could pop in to see your child during the day. The company provided for the Department of Defence with 35 centres over their areas of operations. To provide the proper staff for all these centres two training colleges were set up, one in Brisbane and one in Cairns.

All through these early years there was rampant euphoria in the financial markets. Brokers were constantly recommending ABC as a buy. Banks were continually wanting to lend the company money. At its height ABC Learning had more than 2000 centres in Australia, New Zealand, Britain and the US. The move to the US did make the financial sector nervous, given the history of Australian companies in America, but I still think it was right, because women there were also becoming mothers later and continuing their careers, and governments there also provided financial support.

Through these years ABC had the backing of major financial institutions, such as the Commonwealth Bank, Morgan Stanley and the Singapore government's investment arm, Temasek, which had invested $400 million as late as 2007. But this greater spread was a management challenge, in spite of reassurances from management to the board and even though we had great executives in the US. I don't believe problems were caused by the move overseas, but by the resultant complexity of the operations and the opportunities for extra layers of involvement. By the time things started to go wrong towards the end of 2007, ABC was a web of intertwined companies and relationships. It was becoming impossible to get a very clear picture of internal operations.

When the subprime mortgage crisis in the US began closing in and led to the tightening of global credit markets, ABC Learning owed more than $1 billion to the banks. Our revenues were falling, partly affected by the rising Australian dollar. Everything fell in a heap at the end of February 2008 – the share price had slipped from around $8 to about $4 in January and then crashed to a little over $1. In the early years it had been as high as $14. I stood down as chairman in May and the company went into voluntary administration later that year.

Over the next seven years I spent many hours being questioned by the Australian Securities and Investments Commission (ASIC) and more hours in the witness box of various courts, as did my fellow directors. I spent even more hours in discussions with lawyers. The legal fees, which totalled $50 million, were covered by insurance, which is a lot of money to come out of the Australian economy.

There were obviously problems with the internal financial management of the company, providing a very salutary lesson for non-executive directors. You can ask all the questions you like, but they're useless if you're not given straightforward answers. I had heard rumours that one senior executive was moonlighting at another job but when I asked him about it he looked me in the eye and flatly denied it. I found out later that the rumour was true.

ABC had begun as a simple business, albeit one with a lot of branches, but the company had always been clear in its goals and missions. In my report to the AGM of 2002 I said:

> *Our main focus, and that of all who are involved in ABC at what-*
> *ever level, will always be the care and wellbeing of our children. We*
> *are constantly aware of our responsibilities to the families who put*
> *their trust in us and to the children upon whose development the*
> *future of this country depends.*

Eddy and Le Neve were joint CEOs, he in charge of finance and property and she – with a PhD in early childhood education – in charge of education. They both sat at the table in board meetings. It wasn't until 2005 when I was on a plane with Eddy to discuss the US acquisitions that he told me he and Le Neve had been separated for some years. I was stunned. Soon after I had taken on the chairmanship, back in 2000, I had had them to dinner with their two daughters and hadn't been aware that this was not the happy family it seemed. When I asked Eddy on the plane, 'Why didn't you tell me this at the beginning?', he replied, 'You wouldn't have taken it on.' But of course I would have; I just wouldn't have been describing it as a close family business.

ABC Learning taught me some tough lessons, very expensive ones in terms of time and money but also about trust and direct dealing. I often wished I had learned them earlier when I could have put them to good use.

One day in 2005 I took a call from Julie Bishop, then Minister for Ageing. She told me she was setting up a committee of experts to advise her on dementia, which was becoming a national health priority for the government, she wanted someone high-profile to chair the committee and asked whether I would do it. I laughed and said, 'You're obviously looking for someone in the demographic!'

This was one of many committees I have chaired where I haven't known much beforehand about the subject. I think it's valuable to have an outsider with an objective point of view oversee a group of experts who know what they're talking about but have widely differing views. The chairman – and I never allowed myself to be called a chairwoman – needs to be interested and intelligent and strong enough to keep the group focused and on track.

But I did learn a lot and I was to learn more when I became chairman of the advisory board of the Queensland Brain Institute nearly a decade later. The Clem Jones Centre for Ageing Dementia Research, so called because Clem's estate gave money for its foundation, is Australia's first and so far only facility focused entirely on research into the prevention and treatment of dementia.

Dementia is a disease that causes impairment of brain function and is most common in older people. Because the number of older people in Australia is rising, so is the number of cases of dementia which has even been called an epidemic for our times. At the moment there are about 300,000 people living with dementia. By 2050 this is expected to rise to one million. It's one of those diseases that everyone is terrified of getting, and a 'good brain' is no protection. Most of the people I know with dementia are very clever people. The neuroscientists say this is just coincidence. They also say that exercise is a better preventative than playing bridge and doing crosswords.

The people on the taskforce did know a lot about dementia. They were geriatricians and other doctors, nurses and hospital administrators, and the CEO of Alzheimer's Australia. Alzheimers disease is the most common form of dementia, though only one form. Our remit was in the area of the investigation of care and treatment, rather than scientific research into causes. It was the kind of work being done by one of our members, Henry Brodaty, Professor of Psychogeriatrics at the University of New South Wales.

After the government changed in 2007 and my local member of Parliament Kevin Rudd became prime minister, I continued as chairman. This time I had a co-chair, Sue Pieters-Hawke, daughter of former Prime Minister Bob Hawke, whose mother Hazel was suffering from dementia.

This was to be a difficult decade in many ways. It was true that I too was not getting any younger. When I turned 65 I found it unexpectedly discomfiting. It was unexpected because I had never felt uncomfortable about the idea of getting older, in spite of all the outward and visible signs like a thickening waist and greying hair. I had liked turning 30 because I felt I was properly grown up. Turning 40, 50, even 60, were important milestones, assurances that my life was continuing as a series of transitions. This is especially true in the lives of women, and the changes are dramatic, starting with getting breasts and periods, becoming pregnant and giving birth, and going through menopause. Problems with these natural changes are often concerned with body image.

But somehow turning 65 was different. I gave a speech at a seminar on Positive Ageing at the Bardon Professional Centre and said rather crossly that there was nothing positive about it. I think my discomfort came from the feeling that I no longer had anything to aim for or work towards. This is not to say there was no pleasure in life, but ever since I was little I had always anticipated the next stage – the next year of school and exams to be sat before you get there, university, a job, marriage and babies, the family growing and studying, marrying and succeeding, and me progressing through different roles. There had always been the next hill to climb, and some of the hills had been big ones. At 65 I couldn't see what the next stage would bring. In our society there is no longer a role for a Wise Woman, the village elder, the old grandmother dressed in black and dispensing advice. Grandparents are now helpers and babysitters, and it is we who accept the advice of younger people on keeping up with technology and social media.

I found the transition to getting old the most difficult of all, because of the loss of hope: not hope as the opposite of despair, but hope in the sense of something ahead, something to aim for. There had always been something ahead for me, some new challenge, and now there wasn't. It seemed there was only a downward slide to look forward to.

Depression is a strange and mysterious thing, hard to define, except in a clinical sense. It's almost impossible to describe to someone who has never suffered from it, and it is also difficult to remember what it feels like when you no longer have it. There are certainly degrees of it. Some months after my first child was born I thought I was going nuts. I took myself off to a psychiatrist I knew through the Mater, who assured me I wasn't. He said that having a baby so soon after marriage, living in a flat with a husband who was working long hours and having to deal with a small baby meant that feeling stressed was quite natural.

This immediately made me feel better. Nowadays I might be diagnosed with post-natal anxiety, but this did not seem to be a known condition then.

The several times in my adult life I have been severely depressed I have sought help. I was never concerned about any stigma attached to seeing a psychiatrist. I once wrote a column, back in the days when people didn't talk about such things, pointing out that psychiatry was a practical tool: after all, if you have a toothache you go to a dentist. But perhaps that's the most debilitating thing about depression, it's not like toothache and not simply fixed. It's different from grief, because you know what's causing that.

When I have been depressed I haven't been able to work out why. I remember walking down a street in Paris one Sunday morning and feeling absolutely miserable and thinking, 'Here I am in the city of my dreams, with a beautiful apartment and a very satisfying job – why do I feel so dreadful?' My therapist (American, not French) was able to point out that being away from family and friends was leaving me emotionally bereft, which of course I could work out for myself, although it did help to have someone else articulate it. Other times I have just felt like a large black blanket was enveloping me, and luckily six months of medication always helped. But I do empathise with people who are continuously and continually depressed.

I am now in my seventies and it's been some years since I was depressed, and I'm thankful for that. I cannot give myself reasons why this is so, just as I could find no reasons for my last bout of depression a while ago. Perhaps there are biochemical changes that happen with age. Or perhaps I have a better acceptance of life.

I think there's a differentiation between depression and grief although both are terrible and debilitating and are sometimes linked. In 2007 our family knew deep sorrow when we had to come to terms with the tragedy of the death of Miriam, Damien and Marilyn's little girl. She was 11 months old and had been born with a congenital heart defect. Her short life had been a series of operations and procedures, and it ended in Melbourne where she had been flown with Marilyn six weeks earlier in the hope of a heart transplant.

I don't think there is any grief that comes even close to that of losing a child. For the grandparents, for the siblings, for the extended family there is sorrow and sadness. Their grief is for the parents as well as for the child. Miriam's funeral was very beautiful and in the same church where Damien and Marilyn had been married. The empty coffin had been brought to Currumbin where we had all gathered for Christmas. My grandchildren, Miriam's siblings and cousins, spent time painting it pink with flowers and hearts. So when we gathered for the funeral mass in early January the children had a share in and an understanding of her death and dying. Damien gave a very brave and beautiful eulogy.

The death of a child seems so illogical that it gives a sense of unreality to the life of those who are bereft. I realised that the Catholic faith was of enormous comfort to some in the family and the friends surrounding them, but for others there was a real questioning and a wondering why God had allowed this to happen. And of course, as with all the other significant questions about life and living, for most of us there is no answer. I was unutterably sad, not just for Miriam but for her parents, and I too was asking the big and difficult questions. My sadness had left me floundering, if not actually on the meaning of life generally, then more specifically on my own future and purpose.

In another of life's twists, I would soon see there was much to look forward to.

A BEND IN THE RIVER

WHEN I WAS chosen as the University of Queensland's Alumnus of the Year in 2014 I was inordinately thrilled. My public life had brought me my share of honours. The Australian Government had made me an Officer of the Order of Australia and the French a Chevalier, or knight, in their National Order of Merit (*Ordre Nationale du Mérite*) and the Queensland government had declared me to be a Great. I'd been honoured by other organisations, such as Rotary and Lions but this was special because it was chosen by the Friends of the Alumni Association, my peers.

In the past I had been awarded honorary doctorates from three universities – the University of Queensland (UQ), Griffith University and the Australian Catholic University (ACU) – I was Dr Dr Dr Atkinson. I feel quite strongly that the honorific should only be used in a university context and think it's a bit odd for honorary doctors to use that title in the world outside the university; you never know what the person is a doctor of, whether this is a professional appellation or recognition of a higher postgraduate degree. There are people who disapprove of honorary doctorates, and I must say whenever I've received one I've felt I should apologise to the PhD graduates, I appreciate that they have spent many years of their lives working towards their honours.

Still, honorary doctorates are a recognition by universities that learning is not just a matter of studying for a degree; they recognise non-academic contributions. While my tertiary career was brief, my involvement with universities has been lengthy. I chaired the ACU Foundation soon after I came back from Paris, and then ran a drive to raise funds for a joint chair in midwifery with ACU and the Mater Hospital. My involvement with Griffith goes back to its beginnings in the bush at the original Nathan campus when it was established as an environmental university. The first vice-chancellor, John Willett, had a little office in the ABC Radio building in Toowong, where I would sometimes work. At UQ my wheel has turned full circle, through honorary lectures in politics and journalism to student projects when I was in Opposition, to becoming President of Women's College and working with the Queensland Brain Institute.

Over the years I have been involved in a host of community organisations. Sometimes I inherited them. In the 1970s Sir Reg Groom, the last conservative Lord Mayor, handed me both the trusteeship of the Queensland Womens Amateur Sports Council and a directorship on the Australian Elizabethan Theatre Trust.

I have had what could be called a bit of a portfolio career, a collection of different companies and voluntary organisations, always concerning something for which I've had a passion. I've been chairman in Queensland of Greening Australia, an organisation committed to the conservation of Australia's native vegetation, and when I stepped down from that role I became its patron. The Crawford Fund is a national body promoting agricultural research in developing countries and its benefits to Australians. It has been chaired by former MPs on both sides of politics, including Tim Fischer, Neil Andrew and John Kerin. I spent seven years as chair of the Queensland committee and was full of admiration for those who gave their professional expertise to further the work in Cambodia and the Philippines.

I'm patron of the University of the Third Age for the education of older people, and of Friends of Newstead House, Brisbane's oldest house. Tony O'Reilly, Irish Rugby hero and iconic businessman asked me to join the Board of the Australian Ireland Fund he had founded and I spent about 15 years helping raise funds for 'peace and goodwill' in Ireland. Some years ago, when Ireland was at the height of its EU-driven prosperity, my daughter Stephanie came with me to one of the very glamorous lunches the Fund held each year on the lawn of Lady Mary Fairfax's house by Sydney Harbour. After Tony O'Reilly had given one of his usual rousing speeches about the work of the Fund in Ireland and our contribution to it, Stephanie leaned over to him and asked: 'Is there a committee in Ireland raising money for Australia?' The question was perfectly timed. Many people were starting to think that charity should begin at home. In recent years the Australian Ireland Fund has extended its reach to help support Indigenous communities in Australia.

One of my most interesting involvements was with the Brisbane Writers Festival (BWF) for which I was chair for four years from 2001. The BWF had evolved from Warana Writers Week which was part of the Warana Festival, a Brisbane street festival of the early 1960s. Warana is an Aboriginal word meaning 'blue skies' and was adopted after a public competition run by the *Courier-Mail*. There is a lovely story, untold until now, that two cadet reporters had been sorting out the entries on a big table in an office and had gone home or to the pub, leaving them overnight. The next morning, to their horror, they came back to find that a cleaner had swept all the paper into the rubbish bins. Just one piece had fallen under the table and it bore the name 'Warana'.

Writers' festivals have taken many forms since Australia's first, in Adelaide in 1960. Sometimes they are free and informal, as ours was when I took over. The events were in and around the old State Library on South Bank and when that was closed for renovations for three years it moved to the green lawns by the river in front of the theatres. There were marquees and people wandered in and out to listen to authors speak. Now it is more structured with formal ticketing, and held in the new State Library, which is somewhat grand and daunting.

Actually, I think writers' festivals should be called readers' festivals. What they are really about is letting writers and readers get involved with each other. When I chaired various sessions, I always found that the most common questions were about the process of writing.

When I became chairman we were heavily in debt, which people were resigned to: there seemed to be an attitude that this is how it was in the arts. I promised then Arts Minister Matt Foley that we would turn that around and we did, thanks largely to treasurers Angus Blackwood and Karen Mitchell, good financial managers who encouraged sponsorship.

I'm still involved with Queensland Leaders, an unusual organisation that brings new and developing companies into contact with a range of established businesses to give them support and advice, and which is now national. It's very inspiring to hear the stories of young companies from their executives. Basic to all business success, however important the product and the marketing of it, is good financial management.

In recent years I have chaired two commercial companies. Barton Deakin Pty Ltd is a national government relations and lobbying company that is unabashedly conservative. Its establishment coincided with the coming to power of Liberal state governments across Australia. In a fine piece of symmetrical political history, its founders were the people I had worked with on the *Australian Liberal* back in the 1970s, Peter Collins and Grahame Morris. Peter is a former New South Wales Opposition leader and Attorney-General; Grahame had been at Liberal Party headquarters in Canberra and was former Prime Minister John Howard's chief-of-staff. They headed up Barton Deakin in Sydney and Canberra as I did for Brisbane in 2013, in time for an incoming LNP government under Campbell Newman. Campbell's demise as premier in 2015 meant that I was no longer required.

Lobbying, which is what government relations outfits are presumed to do, has a bad name with very little attention given to its real value and activity. Barton Deakin in Queensland didn't do much lobbying in the real sense of the word, which involves pushing government towards a particular outcome. I thought our real role was helping companies do business with government (we knew the politicians and their policies) and helping government understand the issues surrounding particular business sectors. Ministers are often too busy to absorb some of the finer points of the issues they are dealing with and it is useful as well as efficient to have them explained by someone they trust, who understands the political viewpoint.

Another company I'm involved with, Fidelis Investment Group, is going strong. It's a specialist property fund manager that offers opportunities to investors, a small company with a group of people who know a lot about property investment and management. My job as chairman is to run meetings, set directions and monitor governance, and the deputy chairman is my old friend and campaign manager, real estate-guru Rod Samut.

I also kept myself busy with a role as the Honorary Consul to Brazil in Queensland. Why Brazil you might ask? It happened almost accidentally. I was in Canberra at a conference for the Crawford Fund and struck up a conversation with the Ambassador for Brazil, Fernando de Mello Barreto. We got talking about my hero, Arthur Phillip, who had spent some years in Brazil before he became Australia's first governor, which was news to the Ambassador. The First Fleet had stopped in Rio de Janeiro in 1787 on its way to New South Wales, so Australia and Brazil have strong historical connections. All this the ambassador included in the opening of his speech about ethanol, to the interest and admiration of the assembled scientists.

Later he told me that the Brazilian government had decided to appoint its first honorary consuls in the Australian states, and asked whether I knew anyone in Queensland who spoke Portuguese and did business in Brazil. I did not. A few days later he rang to ask whether I'd like the job, to which I had to reply that I neither spoke Portuguese nor had business in Brazil. We decided that I should do the job until someone else was found. This turned into a seven-year stint, far beyond the four mandated by the Brazilian government.

The role of an honorary consul is just that, honorary. It was a satisfying post in many ways, not the least of which is spending time with all the other consuls representing their countries. Queensland is the only Australian state with a sister-state relationship in Brazil and an office in Minas Gerais, whose mining interests match our own.

Brisbane's West End was where Australia's first samba school was established by Tarcisio Teatini-Climaco in 1987. I learned the samba there, not well, and in 2010 took myself off to Brazil as part of Tarcisio's team for Carnivale in Rio de Janeiro. I actually got to ride on a float, which was unintended but there was a sudden space and someone hauled me up on it. I'd like to have been able to say I was feather-clad, but I was dressed as a lion. After all that excitement I went to Minas Gerais, São Paolo and had a couple of days in Brasília, that monument of a city, Brazil's answer to Canberra, although it is still to acquire the lived-in feel of our capital.

I had been learning Brazilian Portuguese at the University of Queensland evening classes, but that visit totally destroyed any smidgen of confidence I'd gained. The spoken Portuguese seems to bear no resemblance to the written and I couldn't understand a word of what anyone was saying. When any Brazilian rang me at home and, quite naturally, wanted to speak Portuguese, I would say '*Nao falo bem Portuguese ...*' ('I don't speak Portuguese very well').

My interest in Brazil and my interest in Arthur Phillip had begun almost simultaneously. Like every Australian child I knew that Arthur Phillip had sailed from England to establish a convict colony in Sydney, a fact that we celebrated every Australia Day on 26 January as the birth of modern Australia. But I knew nothing else of Governor Phillip at the time.

While I was working in my Paris office one day I heard that as part of the Embassy library's closure they were throwing out books. I rushed down and one of the books I rescued was one of the few biographies of Arthur Phillip, *Admiral Arthur Phillip:*

Founder of New South Wales, 1738–1814 written in 1937 by George Mackaness. I found that Phillip, to outward appearances an ordinary man, had done some quite extraordinary things in the course of a fascinating life. He was extraordinary for having brought 11 small ships and more than 1000 reluctant passengers 15,000 nautical miles to settle in an unknown land. But what was most extraordinary was that he has never been properly honoured. I started to read all I could about him, which wasn't very much.

When a dear young Australian friend from Paris, Nic Martyr, was posted with her husband and children to Rio de Janeiro I took the opportunity to visit them, and Arthur Phillip. I had the moving experience of retracing Arthur's steps through the square in front of the Paço Imperial, and walking up the stairs – now underneath a freeway – that he would have climbed from the harbour so like the one he was to later find in Port Jackson.

Since then, the life of Arthur Phillip has been a thread through many of my travels including visits to London, Lisbon (where he joined the Portuguese navy), Paris and Toulon (where he spied on the French for Britain). I wanted to write his biography, and intended to. The book was finally written by Sydney judge Michael Pembroke, *Arthur Phillip: Sailor, Mercenary, Governor, Spy*. I was pleased that it had been done, and better researched and written than I could have managed, and that Arthur was finally being properly recognised. I was also pleased and proud to be in Westminster Abbey in 2014, on the bicentenary of his death, when a plaque in his honour was unveiled by the Duke of Edinburgh, and in Bath (where he died) where there is a beautiful sculpture dedicated to the former Australian governor. Arthur and I will always be friends and I will continue to promote his name. In many ways he reminds me of my father, in character and attitude.

The G20, that grand gathering of leaders from all over the world or at least the 20 leading countries was held in Brisbane in November 2014 and I had a small but interesting involvement. Brazil was one of those countries and President Dilma Rousseff was one of our guests. As honorary consul I had no formal role but informally I would discover the intricacies of international protocol. Some months before the G20 event the Brazilian delegation had expressed that they were not happy with the hotel they had been allocated. The Royal on the Park was not in the first line of our hotels but it was a very good hotel, and in fact where I had launched my Mayoral campaign. But final accommodation decisions had been made. In the week before the opening, Brazilian officials were still not happy with the President's suite in spite of the fact that the Sultan of Brunei, who owns the hotel, had spent his own money doing it up. They wanted some Aboriginal art on the walls. By this late stage I had no idea where I could find any so I had the brainwave of offering some of my own. I propped a couple of paintings on the sofa in my living room, photographed them and emailed the pictures. Back came the reply: 'We like those but we also like the paintings behind them. And the sculpture you have there.'

We packed up everything from my apartment walls and they graced the walls of the Presidential Suite for the weekend of the G20 summit.

I met Dilma Rousseff only briefly when she arrived, and saw her again the next morning when she chaired a meeting of the BRIC nations (Brazil, India, Russia and China), all considered newly advanced nations. I couldn't actually go into the meeting, but I was able to get a good look at Russian president Putin.

I have never quite lost my girl-reporter enthusiasm from the *Telegraph* days.

The G20 was the biggest thing ever to happen to Brisbane, with 4000 delegates and 2500 media. There were policemen for security on every street corner. American President Obama went to the University of Queensland and the security was such that people had to wait for hours before he arrived.

In 2009 Brisbane Lord Mayor Campbell Newman told me he was setting up a board to run the Museum of Brisbane and wanted me to chair it. The museum had been on the ground floor of City Hall, which was being renovated, and both the museum and the Council Chambers had been relocated to a building in Ann Street, officially named the Roy Harvey House but always known as The Roy.

Campbell had just discovered that the next major exhibition of the museum, then part of a Council department, was to display the history of gay and lesbian Brisbane. I had to contain my mirth at his rage, and readily accepted his invitation to chair an autonomous board to control the museum. As it transpired, *Prejudice and Pride* was a great success and there were none of the political consequences that he feared. Interestingly, in 2016 Council passed a motion supporting gay marriage.

Back in City Hall, though now located on the top floor, the museum showcases wonderful exhibitions with a good balance of history and art. Our mission is about being 'all that is Brisbane', which can be achieved in many ways. Arguably our most successful exhibition in terms of numbers has been *Costumes from the Golden Age of Hollywood*, which might seem to have nothing to do with Brisbane, but was a collection of movie star costumes from the 1930s and 1940s that had been collected over a 24-year period by a Brisbane lawyer and kept in his garden shed. (Who knows what other treasures might be lurking in Brisbane backyards?) I particularly enjoyed this show because every film star from my childhood was represented, and all the great movies. Most exciting for me was Esther Williams' swimsuit. Dad, keen to encourage Louella and me in our sporting endeavours, had taken us to every Esther Williams movie. She would have been in the Olympics except for World War II, and she became the on-screen pioneer of synchronised swimming. We asked people to sponsor a costume for the exhibition and I chose the swimsuit she wore in *Million Dollar Mermaid*.

Among the many exhibitions have been those of Brisbane artists like William Bustard who not only painted but did the stained-glass windows in several Brisbane churches, and Stephen Nothling whose show called *The Last Street in Highgate Hill* was an evocative collection of paintings around one neighbourhood. We have had a collection of jewellery-as-art by local jewellers and we asked six young artists to be inspired by the writings of David Malouf, arguably our most famous author. The result was a wonderful show, and David himself wrote the program note and gave public talks. Timed to coincide with his eightieth birthday, and as someone who grew up in Brisbane all those years ago, he could give audiences great insights into life back then. For example, he talked about the Queensland primary school readers which contained excerpts from classic books and gave schoolchildren examples of fine writing. I too remember the books well from my first years at Southport. His point was that Queensland children in those days had great literary opportunities, despite our reputation as a cultural backwater.

Every city should have its own museum, to display and explore its character and establish its identity. My favourite exhibition so far has been a three-year display on the Brisbane River, which like the river itself wound around the museum space and was constantly being changed.

And so it has been with my life, twists and turns and sometimes meeting the unexpected around the next bend. I can see how important it was to face my challenges head on and overcome adversity, even when I was faced with choices that I had not necessarily planned or hoped for. In adapting to life's ebb and flow I made many new and wonderful discoveries. After all, who wants to float along in a straight line where the scenery never changes? I'll keep navigating my way around through each turn.

EPILOGUE

THE FIRST TIME a man stood up for me on a tram I knew I was grown up. I was 22 and pregnant; I was very pleased. The other day a young man leaped to his feet when I got on a bus. I was not very pleased, but I thanked him for his good manners and gratefully took the seat. It struck me that I am now of an age that I once would have thought of as properly old.

Life can be like a game of Snakes and Ladders – you can be up a ladder one minute and down a snake the next. My own life has been one of unexpected lessons. Through the highs and lows I have found resilience and have learned much. Some of these lessons came early, from my wonderful grandmother who taught me that when your knickers fall down in Martin Place you simply step out of them, your head held high, and stride on. I still adhere to one of her maxims, 'Never stand when you can sit, never sit when you can lie, and never pass a lavatory without going.'

I have learned that success and leadership, two topics that I'm often asked to speak about, aren't always what they seem.

Success can be defined by money, though not by me. It can be defined by achieving a goal, making a scientific discovery or painting a great picture, although you need to find the goal in the first place.

To me, true success should be about personal satisfaction and to me this means having the love of family, the affection of friends and the respect of people who matter. My greatest personal success is having five children who each make a contribution to their world, who are all nice people and the ones I most like to spend time with. I've also thought of the extraordinary accident of birth, that my five children are each so different from one another. We are each conceived in an instant, our conception a coming together of genes, and if that conception happened a second later or a second earlier we would each be a different person.

I've heard leadership defined as getting people to do things they don't want to do. I think it's about a whole lot of indefinable qualities, not just about being the captain of the team or the leader of the Party. It can be about setting a good example in an ordinary life. At Women's College, one of our mantras is 'Ready to Lead', which means we want our young women to be very good at whatever they do in whatever life they lead.

In the leadership of organisations, teams and political parties I believe there are several specific attributes that a leader should possess. Being able to take risks, make decision and nurture followers are the top three. Implicit in the first two, taking risks and making decisions, is the willingness to fail and then being able to take responsibility for that failure.

I've learned some lessons about our political culture. Politics is about approval, or at least getting elected is. And so is staying there. But it's somewhat disconcerting when the approval isn't of the things that really matter and is often about how things are portrayed. It's a dilemma for politicians when perception gets confused with reality. In politics the perception is reality.

I believe politicians fall into three groups: the true believers, the technocrats and the people persons. True believers are so ideologically committed that they cannot believe anything good can come out of the other side. When they go into politics they see their role as furthering the cause. In the words of Graham Richardson, doing 'whatever it takes'. Technocrats are managers who want to be in politics to make things happen and to ensure things are properly run. People persons are usually extroverts who get their energy from other people. Most politicians are combinations of at least two of these personality types; I think I'm a combination of the second and third.

I grew up wanting to be useful and going into politics was a way of doing that. The former Mayor of New York, Ed Koch, was once quoted as saying, 'I'm an ordinary man doing an extraordinary job.' I knew what he meant. I am indeed an ordinary person, and I have been lucky to have been able to have an extraordinary journey.

I've always had a theory that nearly all male politicians are eldest or only sons: I haven't done a study of women yet. But eldest children are conditioned to seek approval. The first baby's first tooth is a major event for the parents, the first step a cause for applause, the first day at school an emotional happening. In my own case, growing up as the eldest child I became used to applause and looked for it. Without it I was vulnerable.

Looking back over the various stages of my life I have had some recurring voices in my head – those of my mother and my father, my ex-husband, two schoolteachers and my first editor, Erica Parker. Things they have said and views they have expressed, in both positive and negative ways, have influenced me greatly. I realise that subconsciously I have been seeking their approval. I think now I must be old enough to let those voices go.

Today, as I sit on my balcony overlooking the Brisbane River and across to the city's Botanic Gardens I think how much the city has changed and how its life, like mine, has been a series of transitions and transformations. The Botanic Gardens were once the vegetable gardens for the officers when Brisbane was settled as a penal colony in 1824. When I first came to university in Brisbane in 1960 the south bank of the river below me was a collection of wharves and rickety old buildings. Over time it has been miraculously transformed into the site for Expo 88 and is now the South Bank Parklands and the cultural centre of the city. The Brisbane skyline I look out over is now dotted with buildings 30 storeys high; once they would have been no higher than three storeys.

As I contemplate these great changes I appreciate the importance of place, and how certain places have left their mark on me. Like everyone, I have been shaped by place, by where I have belonged. Colombo, Belfast, Sydney and the Gold Coast were all different parts of my childhood – moving between them showed me a great variety of possibilities and helped me adapt to change. As an adult I lived in and was shaped by Edinburgh and Paris.

But central to my life is Brisbane. Back when I was a 36-year-old suburban wife and mother I wanted to be the alderman for Indooroopilly. I said in my first electioneering pamphlet, 'Brisbane is a unique city. Nowhere else has our winding river, our flowering trees, our distinctive architecture, our subtropical lifestyle.'

This city, like all others, has changed in the years since then, and so have I. But essentially we're still the same and it is my city, my place. I wonder what the future will bring for us both and look forward to exploring the next twist in the river, the next chapter of my story.

ACKNOWLEDGEMENTS

I ALWAYS KNEW that writing a memoir was going to be difficult. It's the ultimate exercise in the examined life and then having that life exposed. All lives in one way or another set examples and give directions to those who come after, and all are a product of their time. I didn't want this to be a book only about me, although by definition that is what a memoir is. Rather, I wanted it to be a book about my life, lived as it has been in different times – growing up on the Gold Coast before it became a tourist destination, being a working mother before anyone had even thought of maternity leave, taking on roles that I was told were 'no job for a woman'. Nor was this to be a political book, though it is a book about politics. I wanted to show how politics can be lived, from the inside, and to give people some understanding of the workings of government. And I wanted to write about cities, where most Australians live. My city is Brisbane, but all cities have similar issues.

Writing a memoir involves a lot of remembering and sometimes I have remembered too late things which I had forgotten about and so are not in the book. I hope anyone who feels neglected will forgive me.

I have a lot of people to thank. First of all my children, for being such wonderful people and also for trusting me – they never asked to know what I was writing. And thanks to my sisters, who have not checked up on my family memories.

Many friends have given me support, especially in moments of panic: Marina Hamilton Craig, Susan Johnson, Margot Anthony, Robert Allan, Dan Wood and Carmen Findlay.

Rachel Dixon, who doubles as my personal trainer and personal assistant, gets a special thank you for typing the manuscript and offering comments and feedback, and laughing a lot.

I am absolutely blessed to have UQP as my publishers because they have been such good friends through the process. Madonna Duffy went beyond her role as Publisher, from persuading me to write in the first place to visiting me often at home to give me encouragement and support. The two Jacquelines, Kent and Blanchard, did more than I assume editors do, and listened to my moans of despair when I thought I could not go on. Jacquie K was the objective observer from Sydney and Jacq B followed on with Brisbane scrutiny and a lot of hand-holding. I had no idea the process of publication was so complex and I am filled with admiration for all those who go through it regularly and by choice.

By one of those coincidences with which my life seems to be filled, I started this book on the veranda of the North Gregory Hotel in Winton and I am finishing it on the veranda of the North Gregory at the Outback Film Festival. So thank you also to the NGH, for being part of my childhood and my life thereafter.

INDEX

INDEX